CALIFORNIA STUDIES IN THE HISTORY OF ART
Walter Horn, General Editor
Advisory Board: H. W. Janson, Bates Lowry, Wolfgang Stechow

The Drawings of Edouard Manet

THE DRAWINGS OF
EDOUARD MANET

Alain de Leiris

UNIVERSITY OF CALIFORNIA PRESS : BERKELEY AND LOS ANGELES : 1969

University of California Press
Berkeley and Los Angeles, California
University of California Press, Ltd.
London, England

THE DRAWINGS OF EDOUARD MANET
is a volume in the
California Studies in the History of Art
sponsored in part by the Samuel H. Kress Foundation

TO
MARY

PREFACE

MANET's drawings number approximately six to seven hundred. The higher figure makes allowances for lost drawings or for sheets which may have remained in private hands, undisclosed to the public. The known drawings listed in our catalogue are both large and small works, some elaborate compositions and a great number of thumbnail sketches. Their total number does not represent a very considerable fund for an artist of Manet's stature. Moreover, relatively few of the extant drawings have been published, and these are in most cases the same chosen few. These limitations of number and availability have not been favorable to an objective evaluation, but they do not explain entirely why Manet's drawings have received relatively little attention. The critics who have approached Manet's oeuvre with sympathy and insight have considered the drawings to be minor complements of Manet's paintings. This reservation has left the impression that Manet, if he is indeed a draftsman at all, is a very unobtrusive, unortho-

dox, or erratic one, and that his artistic personality cannot be precisely grasped in the summary form of most of his drawings.

The following study and catalogue have been motivated by our conviction that Manet's drawings deserve to be better known. We have attempted to do justice to the drawings' intrinsic artistic value and originality. We have also considered Manet's drawings as the sources of certain technical innovations which have been significant for later developments in French art. For example, the vivid posters of Toulouse-Lautrec, and the deceptively simple book illustrations of Matisse are the heirs of Manet's forthright and witty drawings.

The following text focuses on Manet's drawings almost exclusively. We shall consider, in turn, the classification of the drawings according to their respective function, the artist's choice of media, and the evolutionary sequence of stylistic patterns. In conclusion, the drawings are evaluated in the context of their native French tradition.

ACKNOWLEDGMENTS

MY THANKS are extended first to Miss Agnes Mongan, Assistant Director of the Fogg Art Museum in Cambridge, and to Professor Frederick Deknatel of Harvard University. They encouraged me to undertake this study and have been generous with their help and counsels ever since.

I am indebted also to the many curators of public and private collections, and to the individual collectors who have made available to me Manet drawings from their holdings.

I wish to extend my special thanks to Monsieur Maurice Sérullaz and to Madame Jacqueline Bouchot-Saupique, Conservateurs au Cabinet des Dessins of the Louvre, and to Monsieur Jean Adhémar, Conservateur au Cabinet des Estampes of the Bibli-

othèque Nationale, Paris, for allowing me to visit their respective departments so freely, and for making available to me for study their entire holdings of drawings and prints by Edouard Manet. I am indebted to Monsieur Sérullaz also for allowing me to illustrate extensively the early drawings in the Louvre collection, and to Dr. E. Haverkamp Begemann and Dr. H. R. Hoetink, Curators of the Museum Boymans-van-Beuningen, for making available to me illustrations of the outstanding group of drawings in the Museum's collection.

I also remember with fondness the welcome which Madame Ernest Rouart extended to me in Paris, permitting me to study at leisure and to photograph the many fine drawings in her collection.

ix

CONTENTS

LIST OF ILLUSTRATIONS

Unless otherwise indicated, the works illustrated in this book and listed below are by Edouard Manet. The numbers following the titles in parentheses refer to our Catalogue numbers.

ILLUSTRATIONS IN THE TEXT

xiii

ILLUSTRATIONS FOLLOWING THE CATALOGUE

xxi

FIGURE 1 *(Cat. No. 212)*.

Chapter I

MANET
AS A
DRAFTSMAN

" . . . ce dessin qui semble étreindre et
définir d'une seule coulée toute une figure."
Paul Jamot[1]

MANET is not a draftsman in the accepted, historical meaning of the term, for two principal reasons. In the first place, the lines of demarcation which distinguish drawings, paintings, and pastels are particularly difficult to define in Manet's oeuvre. Secondly, Manet does not exploit drawings for some of the practical ends commonly served by the drawings of artists universally acclaimed as draftsmen. No one will deny the title of draftsman to Rembrandt, Raphael, Géricault, and Ingres. Painters as different as Degas and Matisse belong to this category. An important part of their artistic production consists of drawings which differ from their paintings not only in technique but in the particular roles the artist has reserved for them.

An important category of drawings by artists recognized as draftsmen consists of studies or related groups of studies which were intended to serve in the elaboration of a painting. Each drawing in such a series (apart from its intrinsic artistic worth) reveals in an imperfect or incomplete state certain aspects of the final composition. To the extent that such a drawing is employed by the artist as a tool to guide an idea to its final and most lucid statement, it is not an end in itself, nor is it an idea in its final form. "Imperfection," in this context, contributes to the universal appeal of the "study" drawing. To view a series of them is to follow the direction and formation of the artist's idea and to become aware of the several technical inventions which it has called for at various stages of its development. A viewer almost literally enters the artist's mind, divines its

---

[1] "La Poésie de Manet," *L'Amour de l'Art* (May 1932), p. 151.

habitual functioning, overcomes obstacles *with* the artist himself.

The visual evidence of a tentative effort and of a progression in preparatory drawings by draftsmen of all ages is commonly found in initial sketches or first ideas for a composition, in drawings representing subsequent elaborations, and in intermediary drawings of details later incorporated into the final work itself—be it a finished drawing, a print, or a painting. The drawings of Delacroix include examples of all these types. They illustrate a gradual process of enrichment of an idea which has been vigorously but roughly stated in the initial sketch of a long and complex series. Degas's drawing studies are the instrument of a keen analysis of formal balance, movement, and expression, which is carried on with visible intensity and quasi-scientific precision. Matisse and Ingres, each with quite different expressive results, seek in their preparatory drawings the perfect marriage of observation and abstraction.

The rarity of study sheets among Manet's works is conspicuous. He has left us very few drawings which give evidence of an arduous search, or of the hesitancies and frustrations which he surely must have experienced. This fact tempts one to assume that he may have destroyed drawings which showed traces of struggle too plainly. But a more satisfactory explanation suggests itself after closer scrutiny of all the extant drawings.

On the evidence of the time required for the completion of a painting, and the repeated sittings which he demanded of his models, we know that Manet was not free from the frustrations, the uncertainties, and even the occasional failures which every serious artist is bound to experience in his search for perfection. Now and then we are aware of weaknesses in drawings which have not quite the ease or boldness we have come to expect from Manet, but seldom do we meet one which seems to be a tentative or partial solution to a larger and more complex problem. The majority of the drawings would appear to have been executed effortlessly and decisively. Each is a complete and final response to a deliberately limited set of challenges.

Certain facts, which will be elaborated upon in the following text, support this general observation. We notice for instance—especially from 1870 on—series of drawings which do not illustrate a progression or elaboration of a theme or image, but which are variants on a single motif (figs. 56, 57). Each drawing in such a series is based on an original sheet (usually a sketch in pencil) on which the image appears in its definitive form. The other items in the series are merely faithful repetitions of this initial image in different media (pencil, ink wash, or watercolor). Their graphic form faithfully retains all the idiosyncrasies of the basic silhouette and pattern of the first sketch.

We also have the evidence of a personal technical procedure, particularly apparent in the master's early drawings after Italian Renaissance frescoes, which is symptomatic of Manet's desire to arrive at a conclusive form in each new drawing, be it the slightest pencil notation. In these instances (figs. 2, 29, 31 and many others) we notice two distinct steps in the execution of the drawing. First, a faint pencil line with which Manet records very freely and impressionistically the major outlines of his model or pictorial source; and second, a definitive drawing over the first, in a bolder and more accented line. This second and final linear pattern is not an elaboration of the first, but, more precisely, a selective tracing of it.

FIGURE 2 *(Cat. No. 35)*.

FIGURE 3 *(Cat. No. 188)*.

We conclude that it is primarily with respect to the traditional category of "study" drawings, that Manet's oeuvre differs most from that of draftsmen of the past and of his own time. These artists have, of course, produced drawings which are ends in themselves and have not necessarily required preliminary studies. Ingres's pencil portraits are of this type. Manet consistently sought this finality of form in a self-contained image in every drawing, whether a portrait, a drawing to be transposed into an etching, a study after an old master's painting, or a direct sketch of a city crowd or of a landscape.

Manet's drawings and his methods as a draftsman cannot be defined solely on the basis of their departure from a traditional norm—although this is important. We should attempt in this introduction to define their more outstanding qualities irrespective of category, function, or technique. We shall do so here in admittedly broad and somewhat subjective terms, since our analysis of specific drawings will be the subject of the following chapters.

After glancing at, and even studying at length, any number of the drawings, one retains a lasting impression of their *luminosity* —a particular brightness which results from the positive interaction of a flowing but firm open line with the areas of the white sheet itself. Shading of form, which is always used sparingly, is never opaque or impervious to light. Whether it is obtained with loose line hatchings or transparent washes it enhances the play of light on the planes and its free flow between the lines.

The form of the drawings also has a *synthetic* quality. By this we mean that a number of distinct sensations having to do with volumes in space, with the dramatic oddity of a silhouette, and with the independent and sometimes eccentric patterns of light, are condensed and revealed synchronously in the abbreviated form of any single drawing (fig. 3).

An artist who draws directly from his model, as Manet often did, is engaged in a dual activity: observation and critical interpretation of the data observed. These two operations are, of course, never separate, but the nature of the final abstraction—the style of the image itself—reveals an individual interaction of the two activities. A Manet drawing (and his works in other media) gives the viewer an intense illusion that no time elapsed between the original visual experience of the model and its critical transposition into an autonomous pattern on the paper. This accounts for the immediacy of one's own response to it, and one's grasp of all of the drawing's graphic components si-

4

multaneously—what may be called the shock effect of the drawing. The less complex and inherently dramatic the subject matter, and the more economical the line, the more immediate the visual shock. The term "object-image" might be proposed to characterize the drawings in which this coincidence of the summary form with a keenly observed likeness to the model is most vivid. It would apply more specifically to the later drawings, from 1875 on, in which an object is singled out and its image dominates the entire page (figs. 4, 377).

A review of the literature on the subject of Manet's drawings reveals a frequently recurring criticism. This interpretation of Manet's style would have Manet the painter exclude Manet the draftsman. According to this view, Manet is "uncomfortable in the world of line" (pure line), and at his best in "light and dark boldly indicated" reproducing "color sensations."[2] The currency of this opinion explains in part the relatively limited space given to the drawings by the authors of monographs on Manet. A sustained analysis of the drawings may reveal that Manet was as sensitive to purely linear values as he was to "color sensations."

[2] This view is expressed in J. Rewald, *Edouard Manet: Pastels* (Oxford: Bruno Cassirer, 1947), from which the passages cited are taken (pp. 38 and 39). Among the few authors who have recognized Manet's ease "in the world of line" are E. Bazire in *Manet* (Paris: A. Quantin, 1884), p. 10; and Paul Jamot, the most sensitive commentator on Manet's style—see his article, "La Poésie de Manet," *L'Amour de l'Art* (May 1932), p. 151.

FIGURE 4 *(Cat. No. 577)*.

Chapter II

CLASSES
OF DRAWINGS

I

THE DRAWINGS of Manet can be grouped in distinct categories on the basis of the particular role which the artist assigned to them. These factual considerations will be our main concern in this chapter (the stylistic aspects of the drawings will be investigated more specifically in chap. IV). For our present purpose it will not be necessary to distinguish between drawings of different media. The majority of the watercolors can be considered to be drawings. However, the watercolors conceived and executed as paintings, such as *Desboutin* (fig. 53), and *Courses à Longchamp* (fig. 233), remain outside the scope of a study devoted to drawings. All are included in the catalogue.

II

Perhaps the most important category in scope and quality consists of drawings done during the artist's formative years of the 1850's from drawings, paintings, frescoes, and sculpture by Italian masters. These drawings number approximately one hundred and thirty. The majority were done during Manet's early trips to European museums, and are records of his curiosity for the works of Renaissance and baroque masters.

With one important exception mentioned below, the dates and itineraries of Manet's early travels cannot be precisely established, since consistent and documented information from reliable contemporary sources is not available. We can only deduce from the mass of confusing and partly contradictory statements on the subject that Manet made two or three such trips: one in 1853, and one or two between 1856 and 1858. He probably visited Florence, Perugia, Rome, Venice, Basel, Vienna, Munich, Dresden, The Hague, Amsterdam, Antwerp, and Brussels. The number of extant drawings based on Florentine frescoes would indicate that his most extended stay was in Florence; and although he may have worked in Flor-

6

ence on an earlier trip (1853 and/or 1856), we now have proof that he studied the frescoes by Andrea del Sarto in the cloister of the church of the Annunziata in Florence in November 1857.[1]

Of the one hundred and thirty "drawing copies" known to us, one hundred and ten belonged to the Pellerin collection and were acquired by the Louvre in 1954.[2] They are copies of frescoes, of sculpture, and, in a few instances, of drawings of the fifteenth and sixteenth centuries. The precise pictorial or sculptural source of sixty drawings in this group are mentioned in our catalogue. This represents a large enough proportion of the total to make possible an evaluation of Manet's predilection for certain phases and aspects of Italian Renaissance art. Our cata-

logue will show that he was particularly impressed by the monumental works of Fra Angelico, Ghirlandaio, Luca della Robbia, Fra Bartolomeo, and Andrea del Sarto.[3]

Each drawing in this group transposes certain familiar features of the model's style, but does so without academic preoccupations for precise documentary recording. Indeed, it would be impossible to reconstruct the originals accurately from Manet's sketches of them. His interest lies elsewhere; he sees his models primarily as solutions to problems of form.

A few examples will show the variety of expressive formal idioms which he interpreted with a great economy of means in his own personal graphic style. In the drawings (e.g., fig. 65) derived from Fra Angelico's

[1] Precise references to Manet's early trips are to be found in the following: Antonin Proust, *Edouard Manet, souvenirs*, A. Barthélemy, ed. (Paris: H. Laurens, 1913), p. 31; E. Bazire, *Manet* (Paris: A. Quantin, 1884), pp. 10 ff.; P. Jamot, G. Wildenstein, and M. L. Bataille, *Manet*, 2 vols. (Paris: Les Beaux-Arts, 1932), p. 74 (hereafter cited in the notes and text as "Jamot"); P. Colin, *Edouard Manet* (Paris: Floury, 1932), p. 20; A. Tabarant, *Manet et ses oeuvres* (Paris: Gallimard, 1947), pp. 18 and 22; H. Perruchot, *La Vie de Manet* (Paris: Hachette, 1959). A perusal of these references soon proves to be discouraging since no common pattern of agreement emerges. Proust mentions Antwerp, Amsterdam, Brussels, Haarlem, Dresden, and Basel, among others, as cities visited by Manet; Bazire names Kassel, Dresden, Prague, Vienna, Munich, Florence, Rome, and Venice. Bazire claims that a trip to Germany came first, while Colin states that Manet's first trip took him to Florence and Rome, and most other authors include Italy on the itinerary of both trips. Equally confusing and uncertain are the dates given for these trips. Tabarant places the date of the first trip in 1852 while most other sources place it in 1853. (Colin, with undocumented precision, states that it took place in the fall of the year. Perruchot also places the first trip in the fall of 1853, and states that Manet spent two months in Florence at that time. It appears [there is no foot-

note to refer to] that Perruchot based this statement on the contents of a manuscript diary of Manet's travel companion, Emile Ollivier, to which he had access [see Perruchot, p. 335].) There is general agreement on the year of the second trip—1856. I am indebted to Mr. Lamberto Vitali for bringing to my attention a letter in his possession. It is written in French by Manet, and it requests of the President of the Academy of Florence permission to work for thirty days in the cloister of the Annunziata. The letter is dated "Florence 19 Nov. 1857." On the same letter appears a statement granting Manet's request: "19 Novembre 1857 conceduto per trenta giorni." Thus we have proof that Manet was in Florence in November 1857. It is most probable that on this occasion Manet stayed in Florence at least until the middle of December and that the drawings derived from Andrea del Sarto's frescoes were made at that time. It is still a possibility that Manet was also in Italy in 1856 as his biographers state. However, the majority of the drawing copies may well have been done in the fall of 1857.

[2] Sale at the Galerie Charpentier, June 1954, Maître Etienne Ader, auctioneer.

[3] References to specific sources (fresco, sculpture, or drawing) of each drawing—whenever such sources have been ascertained—will be found in the catalogue.

Mystical Crucifixion fresco in San Marco, Manet has responded to the serene strength of the figures in the original, obviously impressed by the clarity and simplicity of their contours. The figures in the drawings reflect the particular restfulness and the monumentality, without ponderousness, which are distinguishing marks of the fresco models. A drawing after Perugino (fig. 74) interprets the slightly mannered elegance and the ballet-like stance of the original figure with flowing and delicate lines. In contrast, drawings based on Ghirlandaio's *Visitation* and *Birth of the Virgin* (figs. 30, 31) stress the anecdotic or ornamental detail, and are true to the straightforward representation of the human scene found in the frescoes. But a quickened rhythm is introduced; the patterns have a decidedly modern touch, an air of playfulness resulting from the varied tempo of the pencil lines. Nevertheless, the point of departure of Manet's graphic inventions in this case seems to be the crisp decorative details of the originals, which we associate with Florentine quattrocento styles. With equal gusto, Manet evokes the breadth and sturdiness of Roman Renaissance models. Selecting a figure from Raphael's *Incendio* fresco (fig. 89), he transposes its noble proportions and statuesque impersonality. Drawing copies after Andrea del Sarto's fresco cycle in the Annunziata are especially numerous. We shall discuss later the apparent affinities of Manet's style with Sarto's, but we may already notice in passing (figs. 5, 99) Manet's interpretation of Sarto's stately groups in broad sweeping silhouettes strengthened by equally broad masses of light and shadow, and the particular insistence on the rhythmical contrapposto of the poses.

Most of Manet's early drawing copies are derived from Italian frescoes; but we do find occasional examples based on sculpture. One among the latter (fig. 169) holds a surprise for us. It may first appear to have been done in the studio from a professional model, but its original source is a Roman statuette in the Louvre—a replica of a Hellenistic original.[4] This drawing is added proof of the importance of the classical tradition in Manet's artistic formation.

---

[4] The model for this drawing (fig. 169) is a statuette in the Louvre (*Chrysippos*, inventory no. 80, Salle des Caryatides), a Roman replica of a Greek portrait of the stoic philosopher Chrysippos by the sculptor Euboulides (see *The Sculpture of the Hellenistic Age* by Margaret Bieber [New York: Columbia University Press, 1955], p. 69). The statuette (fig. 170), in Manet's time, was fitted with a head of Aristotle (now a cast from a head of Chrysippos in the British Museum has been substituted for it), and this accounts for the different character of the head in Manet's drawing from that of the statuette in its present restored state. But the pose of the body, the character and folds of the drapery, the gesture of the right hand with "constricted fingers to indicate numbers" (see Bieber, p. 69 and figs. 238–242), and the block seat on which the philosopher is seated, all correspond exactly to the drawing by Manet and make the identification positive. Manet made an unexpected use of this drawing or of its model in his painting of *Le Vieux musicien*, 1862. It is generally conceded that the type of subject matter and certain aspects of the composition, such as the foliage of the tree on the left and the dark standing silhouette of a figure in the opposite corner, are derived from Velasquez's *Los Borrachos*—but the seated Chrysippos was certainly the model on which Manet based the pose of the central seated figure of the *Vieux musicien*. We recognize the square block serving as a seat, the position of the feet and hands—only very slightly changed to make the holding of the bow and of the violin explicit—and the disposition of the drapery over the shoulder and legs found in the classical statuette, and in the early drawing copy of it by Manet. For a fuller study of this drawing see A. de Leiris, "Manet, Guéroult and Chrysippos," *The Art Bulletin*, XLVI (Sept. 1964), 401.

8

FIGURE 5 (*Cat. No. 34*).

FIGURE 6 (*see Cat. No. 34*).

The physical characteristics of most of these early drawing "copies" are fairly constant. The majority of them are quite large drawings which fill sheets 10 x 7 inches. These dimensions are in accord with the monumental scale of the fresco models. The media are pencil, sanguine, or black crayon. Brush work is very rarely introduced. When the brush is used, it adds color washes to a drawing already completed in one of the media above, but is not employed for direct graphic notation (fig. 180). The drawings are usually not elaborated beyond an intelligible statement of the essential lines of the model. When, as in most cases, only a section of the original is transcribed, the drawing is nevertheless self-contained. Single figures or groups of figures are selected, but very seldom is a detail such as a limb, a head, or a segment of drapery studied independently.

The latter characteristic suggests that Manet was not engaged in a systematic study of the works he had chosen as models. Drawings which record the entire composition of a fresco are exceptions (fig. 110). It seems more likely that these "copies" were means to a purely artistic end. They reveal Manet's intention to develop and perfect a personal vocabulary in the drawing technique. This function is served, for instance,

9

in a series of drawings, all of which are based on one particular figure or group of figures found in the original source (figs. 2, 5, 103, 104, 105, 107). Each drawing develops a distinct linear pattern which is not merely an elaboration of other drawings from the same series. Thus the original fresco is an inexhaustible source from which the artist derives a series of autonomous graphic variations. The dominant expressive content of the original is echoed in each drawing but the individual "copy" exploits the new technique—drawing—and its specific vocabulary of line to its own artistic end of form and expression.

III

A second category includes drawings which are derived from paintings by Manet himself and by other artists. Unlike the early copies, these drawings served a practical purpose of reproduction. They were used by Manet as models for lithographs and etchings. These drawings are intermediate steps in the elaboration of a print and, as such, submit to a predetermined technical program. They are nevertheless original in form, even when they transcribe a painting with fidelity.

Occasionally, even a tracing, which is by definition a passive mechanical step for transfer, has intrinsic artistic interest and should be included in this category. We reproduce two examples of such tracings, *L'Enfant à l'épée* (fig. 7) and *Le Chanteur espagnol* (fig. 205). Each represents a step in a series of transfers of an image first realized in a painting, retaining only major contours from the original, and greatly simplifying them. By this means, the image transferred to the stone or the plate can be elaborated once more, quite freely, in the print media. Tracings also make possible the reversal of the original image on the plate or on the stone, so that the final step of printing, reversing the composition again, will make it conform to the painting.

These tracings could not have been made directly from the original paintings but were either derived from a drawing or watercolor done in the dimensions of the intended etching or lithograph, as is the case with Le *Chanteur espagnol* (figs. 203 and 205), or, in what we have reason to believe is the majority of cases, from a photograph of the original painting. This second procedure eliminates the cramping experience of reproducing, in reduced dimensions, a preexisting, larger composition. In one of a few

FIGURE 7
(Cat. No. 156).

documented instances, we find Manet making use of a photograph for this purpose and, paradoxically, producing a most original and brilliant drawing in the process, thus transcending the mechanical limitations of such a step. This drawing, *Jeanne* or *Printemps* (fig. 423), was derived from the painting of the same subject (fig. 424) of 1881. The drawing is a tracing of a photograph of the painting. This photograph appears on the verso of the drawing which was probably executed from its image seen in transparency against a source of light such as a window.[5] In spite of the tracing procedure involved, the drawing is an original artistic statement in its own right. The only "mechanical" version of the original painting is the photograph. Manet himself must have appreciated the intrinsic value of the drawing since it was published in the *Gazette des Beaux-Arts* in 1882.[6]

A few drawings by Manet served as guides for the transcription of old masters' paintings in the etching medium. Three etchings were done after paintings by Velasquez or his followers in the Louvre, *Les Petits cavaliers*, *L'Infante*, and *Philippe IV*, at a time when the taste for things Spanish prevailed in Paris. In preparation for these etchings Manet executed sketches (Cat. No. 142 and figs. 197, 199). The *Philippe IV* drawing (fig. 197) reproduces the original painting (fig. 198) with precision but without fussiness. It was probably made after the painting itself or after a good reproduction of it. The drawing was traced, face up, on the plate. As a result the etching reproduces the painting in reverse. This is not in keeping with the degree of fidelity to the original design maintained in all other particulars of the drawing; but as we pointed out with reference to the drawing *Printemps*, the execution of a design in reverse on the plate would have made the transcription of each detail awkward. Manet may have preferred to retain a relative freedom of interpretation and accepted the drawbacks of a print reversing the original composition. As an intermediary step in the completion of the etching, the drawing transcribes the main outlines of the image, thus making a tracing of it on the plate a relatively simple matter. But the drawing is executed in an original linear style, and, unlike the etching drawn from it, leaves out the coloristic and chiaroscuro qualities of the Louvre painting.

Manet transcribed many of his own paintings in the media of etching and lithography. For this purpose, tracings were practical steps, but more elaborate or more self-sufficient versions in the media of watercolor and line drawings were also required. Among these are found extremes of painterly and graphic interpretations, but no sharp line of demarcation can be drawn between the two types.

The watercolor *Le Chanteur espagnol* (fig. 203), at one extreme, is pure painting. Its form closely resembles the original work in oil (fig. 202). No intermediate drawing between this watercolor and the etching (fig. 204) (Guérin, no. 16) is extant.[7] But

---

[5] The etching (M. Guérin, *L'Oeuvre gravé de Manet* [Paris: Floury, 1944], no. 66; hereafter cited in the notes and text as "Guérin") is closely allied in style to the pen drawing, but since it is smaller in size, one may well assume that Manet again made use of a photograph of the painting for the purpose of reduction in size and transfer to the plate.

[6] *Gazette des Beaux-Arts* (June 1882), p. 545.

[7] The possibility that such a drawing exists or once existed is not to be rejected with complete finality, but in view of the character of the etching, it is doubtful. Manet did make use of the tracing already mentioned to transfer the image to the plate.

FIGURE 9 *(see Cat. No. 181)*.

FIGURE 8 *(Cat. No. 181)*.

in this instance, the sketchy and linear form of the first state of the etching suggests that Manet may have directly transcribed the watercolor into the etching medium.

The watercolor *Victorine Meurend en costume d'espada* (fig. 8) takes greater liberties with its model painting (fig. 9). It is a sketch in the wash technique, rather than a painted replica. The reversal of the original composition is proof that it is the direct source of the etching (figs. 10, 11). Every detail of the drawing corresponds so exactly to the painting that it is tempting to assume

that at this early date, 1863, Manet employed a photographic reproduction for the transfer. The watercolor does not simulate the density of the forms or the depth of color of the oil. It is constructed with loosely connected brush strokes which are imitated by the new technique in the first state of the etching (fig. 10). Only the second state (fig. 11) reintroduces a pictorial complexity resembling that of the painting, and for this purpose exploits to the full the coloristic qualities of the etching medium. A similar relationship between a watercolor and a cor-

FIGURE 10 *(see Cat. No. 181)*.

FIGURE 11 *(see Cat. No. 181)*.

responding painting and etching can be observed in other watercolors of the same period such as *Buveur d'absinthe* (fig. 201),[8] *Olympia* (fig. 228), and *Lola de Valence* (figs. 214, 216).

Many extant drawings are related to the painting *Olympia* (fig. 229). The majority were done prior to the painting, but at least

one watercolor (fig. 228) was executed subsequently, and probably did serve as a guide for one of the two *Olympia* etchings (first plate, fig. 226; second plate, fig. 227). The watercolor is much closer in many respects to the second plate or etching (fig. 227) and to the original painting than to the first plate (fig. 226).

---

[8] See A. Tabarant, *Manet et ses oeuvres*, p. 30: the author mentions this watercolor as preceding the painting, giving no reason for such a chronology. It seems that the synthetic, simplified version

of the motif which this drawing represents is better explained once one assumes that Manet relied on the more elaborate version of the painting already executed at the time.

Only the figures appear on the first plate and its format has been elongated to fit them. In the watercolor, Manet included the painting's composition as a whole and gave it its original format. In the second plate etching, the whole composition appears again but the general proportions are changed so that the figures appear smaller and the total field more squarish. These observations show that the watercolor did not introduce radical in-novations. Its function was to establish a simplified graphic image as a base to develop the etching.[9]

The drawing *Printemps* (fig. 423), which is also intermediary between a painting (fig. 424) and an etching (fig. 425), is an exception in one important respect. The etching relies primarily on the drawing for its form, and does not transpose in black and white the painting's color values.

IV

MANET occasionally made etchings and lithographs from drawings which were not preceded by paintings of the same subjects. The prints developed from these drawings were shown and sold to a restricted and dis-criminating public. Neither drawings nor prints were to be viewed by visitors and popular critics of the salons, as were Manet's paintings. In these circumstances the artist felt at liberty to indulge in freer and bolder experiments, and to draw his subject matter from many sources, as his fancy dictated.

In this category of drawings we discover candid and spontaneous works produced in a light-hearted vein. Some are casual sketches; others—these are some of the exceptions to the rule proposed in chapter I—are more carefully planned and studied with the end product, the etching or lithograph, in mind. Large or small, spontaneous or deliberate, these drawings introduce us to Manet's more personal thoughts and passing fancies. We know Manet cared for the most incidental among these drawings, since he translated many a sketch of this type into an etching or lithograph.

Manet enjoyed losing himself in an anony-mous crowd, observing, yet unobserved. In such circumstances he would quickly jot down on paper his impression of a figure or two, or of a whole segment of the crowd. In an uninhibited sketch he would catch his subjects unaware. Places of amusement, the circus, the theater, the café, were his favorite haunts on such occasions.

Le Montreur d'ours (fig. 246), a sepia drawing (and the corresponding etching [Guérin, no. 41]), portrays a circus act in-volving a tamer and his bear. It records the clumsy and humorous pantomime of the pro-tagonists, with broad spreading strokes of the brush. The color emphasis of these black shapes isolates the performers from the crowd, which is barely hinted at as it ap-pears beyond the arena. Manet reveals him-self a dispassionate observer. Unlike Goya, whose drawings this sketch brings to mind, Manet's curiosity and interest are purely visual. His response to the spectacle, like that of a caricaturist, is immediate, and his re-cording of it primarily descriptive. The com-position of *Les Saltimbanques* (fig. 12) is

---

[9] A. Tabarant, *Manet et ses oeuvres*, pp. 77 and 78. Here Tabarant once again ascribes to this watercolor the role of first sketch for the painting, as he did with the watercolor drawing of the *Buveur d'absinthe* (see n. 8). The observations

which we made there would hold weight here also to support the assumption that the watercolor was based on the painting and was not a preparatory sketch for it.

FIGURE 12 *(Cat. No. 217).*

more elaborate, both in composition and technique. It is tempting to presume that Manet once intended to produce an etching or lithograph from it. No such print exists, however.

Manet often turned his attention from the performance and the actors to the spectators.

However deliberate his selection of a particular group of figures among the crowd may have been, the resulting drawings always give the impression of a casual choice. *Au Paradis* (fig. 370), an autographic drawing transferred to a stone,[10] was published in a series of illustrations called "Croquis pari-

---

[10] An autographic drawing is a drawing done in lithographic pencil or ink on paper. Such a drawing can then be transferred to a stone by running both paper and stone through a lithographic press. The impression on the stone (now in reverse) can then be printed as would a drawing done directly on the stone, one major difference being that the autographic drawing, once printed, reappears in its original composition (no longer reversed), while a drawing done directly on the stone will, of necessity, be reversed in the process of printing.

siens" in the *Revue de la Semaine*[11]—a fit destination for this unpretentious and candid bit of Parisian life. The youths, who are shown intently watching a stage performance, are behaving like true *titis*—those alert and gay Parisian urchins. Their lively postures and their mischievous expressions are interpreted by dashing brush strokes and synthetic massing of lights and darks. However rapid its execution, and summary its form, this drawing on stone could only have been done in the studio from pencil sketches made on the scene. *Au Paradis* (fig. 283), a pencil drawing, is an outstanding example of this type. It represents spectators at a moment of relaxation rather than alertness; but the figure types and some of the gestures are very similar in both versions.

Manet and the artists of his generation introduced a new category of subject matter: the café. It takes its place in history as the heir to tavern scenes and family repasts. The café is of course the favorite meeting place of artists who enjoy the anonymity and conviviality of its atmosphere. Manet chose on one occasion to interpret this "professional" function of the public café. It is the subject matter of a large pen drawing, *Au Café* (fig. 250), and of autographic prints derived from it (Guérin, nos. 80 and 81). Manet's drawing reconstructs in tableau form a typical gathering of friends and habitués in familiar surroundings. Every prominent object included—the hanging hat and coat, the gas lamp, the costume of the waiter—adds a

specific realistic accent to the casual and convivial atmosphere of the scene; and these accents are cumulative in effect because of their relative separateness within the composition. The bright image as a whole expresses joie de vivre and abandon to the well-being of the moment.

Manet's lively interest in contemporary political events is shown by a number of works. Two of these are paintings—one a naval battle, *Le Combat du Kearsage et de l'Alabama* (1864), and the other, *L'Exécution de l'Empereur Maximilien* (1867). Prints are traditional media of propaganda, and there is little doubt that Manet recognized their effectiveness for dramatizing topical political subjects.

Two lithographs of 1871 record episodes of the outbreak of the Commune in Paris: *Guerre civile* (Guérin, no. 75) and *La Barricade* (Guérin, no. 76). Both are factual interpretations of tragic scenes.[12] The lithograph *La Barricade* reproduces the composition of a wash drawing (fig. 287). The grouping and the poses of the firing squad were borrowed from the earlier composition of the painting *L'Exécution de Maximilien* (see fig. 285, a tracing which was used for the composition of *La Barricade*). The visual facts (building, firing squad, sunlight) and the mechanical action of the soldiers are interpreted objectively. Nevertheless, the drawing is exceptional among Manet's works based on tragic subject matter, because its form appeals with special force to the

---

[11] See Guérin, no. 82.

[12] For a thorough documentation of the series of paintings entitled *L'Exécution de Maximilien*, see Nils G. Sandblad, *Manet, Three Studies in Artistic Conception* (Lund: The New Society of Letters at Lund, 1954), pp. 109 ff. This author suggests that Manet's "cultivation of the motif," his thorough documentation, results in a heightening of the drama (pp. 145–146): "Does not the

drama remain in this calm, restful composition?" (he is referring to the Manheim version). He concludes that "the drama has not been forgotten; it has merely been raised above the purely temporal character of the event." In our interpretation of this painting, the drama is inherent in the topical subject matter which Manet has objectively interpreted, and not in the form which is rigid and cool.

16

FIGURE 13 *(Cat. No. 453)*.

viewer's emotions. It not only narrates an event but creates an atmosphere of confined space and brutal sunlight. As a result, the action has the immediacy of an actual drama, even with the absence of obvious staging. The color nuances and the cursive strokes envelop and link the groups of executioners and victims, and both groups are blended into their background as impersonally as they might have appeared to a casual witness of the actual event. However, the tragic content of the scene seems subdued when the drawing is compared to one of Goya's major historical paintings, *Tres de mayo*, which represents a paroxysm of actions and emotions.

Genre subjects are ideally suited to the small scale of drawings and prints. They may also have appealed to Manet because they have no inherent pretension to higher moral or aesthetic significance. Manet es-

tablished his own hierarchy of subject matter, but he did not conform rigidly to traditional norms in this matter. The compositions of his "history" paintings and of his "academies" (*L'Exécution de Maximilien*; *Olympia*) are formal and monumental. But so is the ambitious work *Bar aux Folies Bergère*, whose subject matter is in the genre category. Manet intuitively chose for each work a format in keeping with the degree of complexity and formality of its composition. We can distinguish large genre paintings, whose subject matter offer a primarily aesthetic challenge to the artist, and genre works in small scale—paintings, prints, drawings—whose descriptive and illustrative functions called for a small format. *L'Enfant au chien* (fig. 206), *Marchande de cierges* (fig. 207), and *La Convalescente* (fig. 13) belong to this category, both in their drawing and etching forms (corresponding etchings: Guérin, nos. 17, 19, 65). These images are calm and composed, although they are not devoid of sentiment. Their tone of human warmth and familiarity is in keeping with the intimacy of this subject matter. Greater stress is placed on effects of natural illumination and textures. The poses and expressions of the figures—the praying woman, the boy embracing his dog, the woman at rest—are interpreted sympathetically but make no overt appeal to the viewer's sentiments. *La Convalescente*, for instance, is a very touching and discreet image of womanhood and old age. This awareness of human values is often too rigidly denied to Manet. This may be because the sentiment is so tactfully controlled when it does appear in individual works.

Manet could look back to historical precedents in the realm of genre painting. In many instances the examples which he followed are easily recognized. *L'Enfant au chien* calls to mind similar groups of urchins or dwarfs and animals painted by Velasquez or Murillo. But Manet limits his subject matter to one or two protagonists. The attitudes of boy and dog are playful and casual and psychologically convincing. The subject is sentimental, but not its interpretation. There is no doubt, however, that Manet deliberately exploited the inherent picturesqueness of such a genre scene for

its appeal to a public familiar with seventeenth-century popular genre. Other works of Manet's early period claim the attention of the salon crowd by similar means.

The motif of the reclining female nude has a long and glorious history in Western art. Manet's *Olympia* claims its rightful place in this distinguished history. But among Manet's drawings of reclining females the *Odalisque* (fig. 222) strikes an unusual romantic note. It is the source of an etching of the same title (Guérin, no. 64). Its exoticism resembles that of Delacroix's and even of Ingres's odalisques; explicitly picturesque in form, it is sensual in mood. Unlike the model Victorine Meurend in the *Olympia*, the reclining Oriental girl is relaxed. The profiles of her body are rhythmically coordinated in a series of slow, continuous curves. The swastika pattern of the arms is clearly inspired by similar artistic devices in the paintings of Delacroix. The pose recalls that of the Assyrian king in Delacroix's *The Death of Sardanapalus* (Louvre). Needless to say, the Byronic *beau geste* eloquence is absent from Manet's *Odalisque*. The drawing strikes a note of intimacy and seems true to life, an effect which the deliberate artifice of form does not dispel.

Manet interpreted another academic theme, the bather or bathers, in a number of works, including drawings.[13] He drew upon a variety of artistic sources for the

---

[13] Manet seems to have drawn his inspiration for compositions on this theme from Venetian, Flemish, Dutch, and French precedents. The first painting in this group, *La Nymphe surprise* (Jamot, no. 55, fig. 64) of 1861–1862, is a direct descendant of the Bathshebas, Suzannas, Dianas of the past. The second, *Baigneuses en Seine* (Jamot, no. 264, fig. 63) of 1874, is a close relative of Courbet's *La Source* and *Baigneuses* in its more direct and bold realism, free from dependence on mythology and biblical history (a wash drawing of

the painting's composition is listed by A. Tabarant, *Manet et ses oeuvres*, no. 66; the quality and exact function of the drawing as a preparatory sketch or drawing derived from the painting cannot be determined from the thumbnail-size illustration in Tabarant's book). In 1878 Manet gives the theme a final interpretation in a series of pastel studies. *Femme dans un tub* (Jamot, no. 424, fig. 237) is a representative example of the series, which was inspired by Degas's pastels of intimate scenes of women at their toilette.

compositions of this type. A large drawing representing a seated nude figure, *La Toilette (1)* (fig. 218), recalls precedents among the works of Rembrandt. The concept of the group of woman and servant, and the enveloping chiaroscuro which Manet develops in the corresponding etching (fig. 221), suggest such a source. But it is clear that there are no elements directly borrowed from a specific etching or painting by the Dutch master. Once again, in the medium of etching, Manet has gone beyond the more objective and direct study of the model which the drawing represents.[14] He has enveloped the whole composition—perhaps with the Rembrandt precedent in mind—in a deep but light-pierced gloom. It is interesting to compare with the preceding example another drawn version of the same subject, *La Toilette (2)* (fig. 44), of which no corresponding etching exists. It may well have been an earlier idea for the theme, superseded by its companion drawing. The interpretation of the subject matter differs in the two drawings, and the change of emphasis from one to the other may reflect Manet's desire to approach more closely traditional precedents of mythological or biblical genre scenes. The etching comes closest to this goal.

V

Manet's contribution to book illustration is very limited in scope. The drawings produced with this specific end in view do not differ radically in style or technique from other types. Most of them were reproduced almost exactly as they were done in their original and final form. The physical qualities of the image originally drawn with pencil, brush, or pen appear intact in the reproduction on the printed page. Therefore, we shall not find in these works the uniform stamp of a special "style of illustration" which usually marks the works of professional illustrators. Manet's production in this vein is as varied as the sources which inspired it.

Manet always reserved the liberty to give a personal interpretation to the text chosen for illustration. This being the case, we would normally expect few if any works of illustration from him, since tradition usually requires a relatively close collaboration of the illustrator with the writer or the editor of the book, and the acceptance by the artist of a certain number of directives and limitations applying to the technique to be used and, to a lesser degree, to the interpretation of the text. Manet resented such impositions on his freedom. He expressed his views on the subject in a letter to Mallarmé, who had asked him to illustrate his translation of poems by Poe: "A few things which you indicated to me appeared impossible of execution, among others the woman seen in her bed through a window. You poets are *terrible*, and it is often impossible to understand

---

[14] The possibility of there having been an earlier drawn version is strong, since certain contours in this drawing appear to be a typically selective condensation of the more complex and less precise ones of the hypothetical sketch.

your fantasies. . . ."[15] Only remorse and a feeling of duty to accommodate a friend prevailed upon him to accept the task proposed to him by the poet. It appears that on those few occasions when Manet accepted the task of illustration, his collaboration had been sought by friends, and therefore a bond of sympathy already linked the author of the book and the painter. The writers Champfleury, Charles Cros, Mallarmé, whose works Manet illustrated, were all his close friends. Only under such conditions could Manet hope to have the understanding of the author in spite of his own unorthodox approach to the task.

Manet was fond of vignettes and tailpieces. Their modest size and their decorative function in relation to the printed page make them the ideal vehicle for pictorial understatement. Manet had planned to adorn

his etched portrait of Baudelaire (Guérin, no. 38), published in 1869,[16] with an allegorical motif referring to the author's *Fleurs du mal*. A pen and sanguine sketch (fig. 244), which appears on the margin of a proof of the second state of the etching (third plate) but was never incorporated into the etching, is a typical example of these escutcheon-shaped inventions dear to Manet.

The vignettes which Manet made for Mallarmé's *Après-midi d'un faune* in 1876 (figs. 14, 349) were originally pen drawings on wood blocks which were subsequently engraved.[17] This is again one of the rare instances of Manet drawings done from imagination. In most instances Manet preferred to make use, directly or indirectly, of sketches done from nature.[18] The adaptability displayed in these spirited pen draw-

---

[15] Letter quoted by A. Tabarant, *Manet et ses oeuvres*, pp. 417–418. Tabarant tentatively dates this letter August 1881. Written from Versailles, it follows an earlier letter from Manet to Mallarmé, also from Versailles, which is dated July 30, 1881. The August letter actually expresses Manet's desire to take on the task of illustrating Mallarmé's translations of Poe, a task which he had previously declined to undertake (see the letter of July 30, 1881, quoted in n. 18 below). The following are additional excerpts, translated from the French, from the August 1881 letter: "Versailles—My dear friend, I am full of remorse and am afraid that you might be a little angry with me, because, as I reflect on it, it is selfish of me not to have accepted in spite of everything the work which you proposed to me. . . . If it is possible to renew this affair on my return to Paris, I shall try to do honor to the poet and to the translator, and I shall have you there to give me momentum. . . ." The Mallarmé translation of Poe's poems was finally published without Manet's illustrations in 1888 (*Les Poèmes d'Edgar Poe* [Bruxelles: Edmond Deman, 1888]).

[16] In Charles Asselineau, *Charles Baudelaire, sa vie et son oeuvre* (Paris: Lemerre, 1869), facing

page 99.

[17] Guérin, no. 93; Stéphane Mallarmé, *L'Après-midi d'un faune* (Paris: Alphonse Derenne, 1876). Although not drawings strictly speaking, these wood engravings were probably cut by a professional from pen drawings executed by Manet on the blocks, and therefore they are for all intents and purposes pen drawings by Manet. As such they are included in the catalogue.

[18] This preference is indicated by Manet's reliance on direct studies from nature whenever the text to be illustrated would allow it, and by Manet's letter of July 30, 1881, to Mallarmé (quoted by A. Tabarant, *Manet et ses oeuvres*, p. 417). The letter, written while Manet was sick in Versailles, expresses the artist's reluctance to undertake the task of illustrating Mallarmé's translations of Poe's poems; as indicated above, it also states his desire to rely on direct studies from nature: "Versailles, July 30, 1881—My dear Captain, You know how much I like to embark with you on any endeavor; but today it is beyond my strength. I do not feel capable of doing well what you ask of me. I have no model and especially no imagination. I would do nothing worthwhile. So excuse me. I am not too happy about my health. . . ."

ings illustrates that attribute of which Rosenthal speaks when he ascribes to Manet "an intelligence capable of applying itself to the most diverse intentions."[19]

If imagination and intelligence serve Manet well in the field of illustration, they are present also as creative tools when he describes in poetic terms the more familiar aspects and objects of his environment, as in a quick sketch of a cat, of a snail, or of a hat. The nymphs and faun of the two vignettes illustrating *Après-midi d'un faune*[20] are drawn with the same spontaneity and

FIGURE 14 *(Cat. No. 458).*

sketchiness which we invariably find in Manet's most casual studies from nature. This does not preclude in either kind of drawing a critical process of adaptation and selection, as the illustrations for *Après-midi d'un faune* show. They capture accurately the spirit of Mallarmé's fable with a flickering movement of lines briskly drawn. The images evoke light, air, animal being, and a feverish movement imparted to both the natural setting and the mythological figures

inhabiting it. In form as well as content Manet has been faithful to the intentions of the author as only a sympathetic and imaginative reader could be.

Manet also produced eight etchings as illustrations for a poem by his friend Charles Cros entitled *Le Fleuve* (Guérin, no. 63).[21] There are no extant preparatory drawings for these, but there are a number of drawing sketches related to the etchings. These illustrations are close in form and content to those produced for *Après-midi d'un faune*. However, in keeping with the epic form of the poem, Manet's illustrations are more descriptive and their lightness relieves the monotony of the profuse text. They consist of a few lines and dashes drawn directly on the plate but leaving much of it untouched. One etching of the series, *Le Flot marin* (Guérin, no. 63g) which we reproduce here (fig. 326), will show how close to pure drawing these illustrations are. It might have been drawn with pen on paper, so free are the lines and graphic accents. Some of the sketches done at the seashore were probably the basis for these etchings. In this form of book illustration, in which the tersest sketch is reproduced in its original form, Manet was an innovator. The artist's handwriting and initial intention are thus preserved. Since Manet's time many illustrators have worked in this shorthand manner—Matisse, Picasso, Derain, among others.

In 1868, the publication of Manet's lithograph *Le Rendez-vous des chats* (fig. 49) was a pioneering step in launching the poster as an art form. It prefigured the accomplishments of Chéret, Lautrec, and Bonnard in the later decades of the century. Manet had

---

[19] Léon Rosenthal, *Manet aquafortiste et lithographe* (Paris: Le Goupy, 1925), p. 103.

[20] There are four illustrations in all for this poem, the two illustrated here (figs. 14, 349),

and the small inserts, a spot and tailpiece.

[21] Charles Cros, *Le Fleuve* (Paris: Librairie de L'Eau-forte, 1874).

21

illustrated the book entitled *Les Chats*,[22] written by his friend Champfleury, with an etching, *Le Chat et les fleurs* (Guérin, no. 53)—a technically elaborate and exotic image. The lithograph *Le Rendez-vous des chats* was planned as a poster to advertise the book. The genesis of this image is of particular interest since the final lithograph is the most stylized work of Manet. First came the direct sketches of animals in action, their characteristic poses caught in silhouetted form. Three of these drawings appear on a single sheet (fig. 245). The sketch at the upper left of this sheet represents a cat in a contorted posture, cleaning himself. Manet repeated this motif without change in a small pencil and wash drawing (illustrated in Guérin, under no. 74), contrasting it on the same page with another cat differing in pose and much more stylized in form. This drawing appears to be the first stage of a composition representing cats in an outdoor setting. A large drawing (fig. 50) presents the final synthesis. Its form is caricatural, and the pattern is dense. The two cats are now the protagonists in a ritual dance. The black cat is reminiscent of the animal in *Olympia*. The caricatural element and picturesque subject matter (the moonlight setting and the ghostly actors: cats and chimney pots) produce a

haunting mixture of the strange and the familiar.

Manet began work on illustrations of Mallarmé's poems in 1875. In that year he designed the vignettes for *L'Après-midi d'un faune* and also illustrations for Mallarmé's translation of Edgar Allan Poe's *The Raven*[23] in the autographic technique (see note 10). The effects obtained with this technique and with a Chinese ink wash are nearly identical, and Manet made extensive use of both in his drawings of the period.

The choice of text to be illustrated—works of Poe—might appear strange in view of the contrast between Manet's temperament and style and those of Poe.[24] But it is easily understood when we realize that it was Manet's friend Mallarmé who prevailed upon him to undertake the task and that the challenge of the contrast may have been an added incentive for Manet. An example from this series, the drawing *A la Fenêtre* (fig. 343), representing the flight of the bird into the room, illustrates the following passage of the poem:

Au large je poussai le volet, quand,
avec maints enjouement et agitation d'ailes,
entra un majestueux corbeau des saints jours
de jadis. . . .

[22] Champfleury, *Les Chats* (Paris: Rothschild, 1869). The second edition of the book, published in 1870, is the one in which the etching and the poster by Manet were reproduced.

[23] Edgar Allan Poe, *Le Corbeau*, translated by S. Mallarmé (Paris: Richard Lesclide, 1875).

[24] L. Rosenthal, *Manet aquafortiste et lithographe*, p. 97. The author stresses the factor of friendship between Manet and Mallarmé to explain this undertaking of Manet. Manet's friendship with Mallarmé was cemented by the publication of the latter's article on Manet which appeared in *Renaissance* (April 12, 1875). A letter from Mallarmé to Verlaine, dated 1885, gives

further proof of the friendly character of the collaboration with Manet: "for ten years, I have seen Manet daily and his absence today appears unbelievable to me . . ." (quoted from the catalogue of the retrospective centennial exhibition, Musée de l'Orangerie, 1932, p. 50). The illustrations confirm the interest which Manet displayed for the poem. It is clear, however, that the artist has not steeped his images in the mood of obsession and dream which is built up by Poe in his poem. It is difficult to accept Rosenthal's interpretation of these illustrations as pictorial equivalents of the poem's calculated crescendo of terror. This author may even be overstressing the element of "terror" in the poem itself.

Manet's interpretation is factual. So are the poem's lines quoted out of context (the verses [prose in Mallarmé's translation] assume their familiar resonance only with the accompanying hypnotic repetition of the last word "jadis" ["yore" in the original] and corresponding rhymes). Another illustration, *Le Corbeau sur le buste* (fig. 15), also interprets narrative passages faithfully, but does not convey the vague foreboding mood of their poetic context:

. . . se percha sur un buste de Pallas,
juste au dessus de la porte de ma chambre . . .

. . . je roulai soudain un siège à coussins
en face de l'oiseau, et du buste, et de la
porte; et m'enfonçant dans le velours . . .

. . . cela et plus encore, je m'assis pour
le deviner, ma tête reposant à l'aise sur
la housse de velours des coussins que
dévorait la lumière de la lampe . . .

Manet allows the text to supplement the illustrations in this respect. He thinks of text and illustrations as complementary and distinct entities both in content and form. The draftsman retains the integrity of his own vision without betraying that of the poet. One drawing in this series exhibits certain qualities which set it apart from the others: *Le Corbeau* (fig. 342).[25] It was intended as a design for a poster announcing Mallarmé's translation, and evokes Poe's litany: "this grim, ungainly, ghastly, gaunt, and ominous bird of yore . . ." (in Mallarmé's translation: "*ce sombre, disgracieux, sinistre, maigre et augural oiseau de jadis . . .*"). Rosenthal speaks of this ebony bird (Manet's) as an "emblem of impenetrable and hostile fate."[26] It is a truthful rendering of the bird's species as well; but the vigor and rigidity of the

FIGURE 15 *(Cat. No. 446).*

black pattern creates a symbol of dread. The image, with the black, ragged edges of the ink spot on the white page, intrinsically bears this burden of suggestion, requiring no explicit illustrative comment.

In 1881 Manet collaborated once more with Mallarmé who had asked him to illus-

---

[25] See also the autographic version, Guérin, no. 84.

[26] L. Rosenthal, *Manet aquafortiste et lithographe*, p. 101.

trate his translation of other poems by Poe.[27] He undertook this last work rather reluctantly and primarily in order not to disappoint Mallarmé, as their exchange of letters shows (see notes 15 and 18). Manet was beginning to suffer from the illness which was to take his life two years later. The illustrations were never published. Only a few drawings are extant, which represent Manet's first attempts. They do not form a consistent series such as *Le Corbeau*, nor have they the latter's singularity of purpose. Three of these drawings are preparatory drafts for the illustration of Poe's poem *Annabel Lee*. Two represent a young woman standing against the background of the sea (fig. 429) and do not differ essentially one from the other. The third represents the same figure reclining on the ground against a similar background (fig. 430).

One is struck at once by the gap which exists between the content of the text and its intended illustrations. Manet seems to be farther here than he was in the *Raven* drawings from the mood and spirit of the poem. The expressionless model, a mature and elegant young woman, bears little resemblance to the creature evoked by Poe: " . . . I was a child and she was a child. . . ." But Manet had admitted to Mallarmé his lassitude, his reluctance, and lack of inspiration. Complying at last with his friend's request, he derived the illustration from a painting of the same model (Jamot, no. 321), adding a seascape background which would correspond to the setting described by Poe in *Annabel Lee*. As an illustration, it would have fallen far short of adequacy. As an independent sketch, however, it possesses the charm, not always devoid of a certain "chic"

or facility, which typifies some of Manet's portraits of woman models.

Manet also intended to illustrate *The City by the Sea*. He has left us two very similar drawings, one of which is reproduced here (fig. 431). In its bareness, this drawing bypasses the narrative or descriptive aspects of the poem. It is rather a "title image," similar to the poster form of *Le Corbeau*. A human skull and expanses of sky and sea are statically juxtaposed on the page. The only suggestion of drama is the circling movement of the waves engulfing the city. No other attempt is made in this terse graphic image to transpose the imagery of the poem. How revealing a contrast of two temperaments!

Manet's illustrations of Poe's poem *The Sleeper* are more successful. Two modest drawings of the same subject are extant. One is a pencil drawing *La Dormeuse* (fig. 16). The second is a wash drawing (fig. 17), which was probably meant to be the basis for final reproduction. The subject of both versions is a sleeping woman under bed covers with her head on a pillow. The changes introduced in the wash drawing are subtle ones and in the direction of greater concision. The hair mass is the most intense spot in the whole composition; the cast shadow on the side of the face is omitted, and so is the "curtain canopy" mentioned in the poem. The head, centrally placed, dominates the composition. The solid blacks convey the cold, moonlight illumination of the scene, and something of its "solemn silentness." The pallor of the face stands out against the ghostly shadows. The form of the drawing as a whole transmits the symbolic content of the verses—a longing for the experience to last:

---

[27] *Les Poèmes d'Edgar Poe*, translated by S.

Mallarmé (Bruxelles: Edmond Deman, 1888).

FIGURE 16 *(Cat. No. 596)*.

FIGURE 17 *(Cat. No. 597)*.

. . . je prie Dieu qu'elle gise à jamais
sans que s'ouvre son oeil, pendant qu'iront
les fantômes aux plis obscurs. . . .

Manet's illustrations are reserved statements which do not limit the reader's interpretation of the text, but respect its content. The artist speaks quietly, unobtrusively, for fear of betraying some essential quality of the poem. For these understatements Manet adopts the most succinct and technically simple form of drawing.

VI

Manet did a number of portrait drawings which he planned to develop into prints. Occasionally, his choice of a particular drawing medium appears to reflect a concern for the problems of reproduction in a different technique, such as etching or lithography; but in most cases no such concern is apparent, and the media are quite varied: pen, pencil, wash, or sanguine crayon.

The early drawing of the head of his father *Auguste Manet* (fig. 196), is related to Manet's double portrait of his parents of 1860 (fig. 21) and to etchings (Guérin, no. 5 and no. 10) which were derived from it.[28] The drawing is a more intimate interpretation of the model, and the painted version a more formal and less fugitive one. The etchings closely follow the painting's composition, but also adapt the tonal subtleties of the drawing, and retain its psychological depth.[29]

A drawing labeled "Buste d'homme" (fig. 18) owned by the Bibliothèque Nationale, Paris,[30] can be identified as a portrait of Edgar Allan Poe. It resembles closely the etching *Edgar Allan Poe* (Guérin, no. 55), and it is likely that both drawing and etching

---

[28] Aside from similarities in pose and expression, painting and drawing are distinct interpretations of the model. The illumination of body in the painting is simplified, the form more concisely rendered, and contrasts accentuated; and the glance is no longer directed at the observer.

[29] Two red chalk drawings of the bust of Auguste Manet are mentioned by Jamot but it is likely that the second refers to a preparatory drawing for the double portrait of Manet's parents and bears no direct relationship to these etchings. See Jamot, no. 37, for this description of the two drawings: "(1) 17 x 14 cm. (in the collection of Mme. E. Rouart). (2) 32 x 25 cm. (in the collection of Mme. E. Rouart)." Having had access to the Manet drawings of the Rouart collection, the author is aware of the existence of two drawings in it which are related to the painted portrait of Manet's parents: the first (fig. 196) is,

to my knowledge, the only one ever to have been reproduced; and the other (fig. 20) represents not only a bust of Manet's father but of his mother as well. The fact that the medium of the latter is red chalk also, and that the dimensions are close to the ones given by Jamot for the second drawing listed by him, 30 x 23.5 cm. (the slightly smaller size, 2 cm. each way, may be the result of subsequent cutting or inaccurate measurements), suggests that the second drawing, mentioned by Jamot and listed in catalogues of exhibits whenever the first drawing is being exhibited, is in reality the drawing of the two figures.

[30] Now in the Cabinet des Estampes of the Bibliothèque Nationale in Paris. It is given this anonymous title in Robert Rey's monograph, *Edouard Manet, choix de soixante-quatre dessins* (Paris: Braun, 1932), which reproduces it.

were derived from a common photographic source mentioned by Guérin.[31] Guérin suggests that the etching may have been intended as an illustration for a translation of Poe's tales by Baudelaire.[32] But these were published for the first time in 1856 and

Manet's friendship with Baudelaire appears to date from 1859 onward (this date is based on Antonin Proust's recollections). Although an earlier association cannot be discounted with finality, the problem of the intended role of the etching remains to be solved. Further documents would have to be found to confirm Guérin's conclusions.

Manet left a number of drawings which are portraits of friends and contemporary artists. Most of these studies were originally destined to be reproduced in some other medium for publication. A few actually were. The features of the poet Banville, a close friend of Manet's, appear in two drawings which were preparatory sketches for a frontispiece illustration of the poet's work *Les Ballades*.[33] One of these is a pencil drawing representing the figure of the poet, seated, without background (fig. 334).[34]

In a second drawing, which combines lead pencil, wash and pen (fig. 335), Manet transposed the original pencil portrait into a more complex compositional study, merely by the addition of sundry objects (symbolic references to the subjects of the poet's ballads), without changing in any essential way the general style or the model's pose. Manet could not complete the related etching (fig. 336) to his satisfaction in time for publica-

[31] Guérin, under no. 55: "Manet avait sans doute eu connaissance du daguerréotype pris à Providence en 1848 représentant Edgar Poe. Ce daguerréotype est reproduit sur les couvertures des deux volumes de Marie Bonaparte sur Poe publiés en 1932 par les Editions Denoël et Steele." See also the daguerreotype facing the title page in *The Works of Edgar Allan Poe* (New York: Walter J. Black, 1927).

[32] Guérin, under no. 55: "Il est probable que cette eau-forte fut exécutée en vue d'illustrer les *Histoires extraordinaires* d'Edgar Poe traduites par Baudelaire et publiées pour la première fois chez Michel Lévy, en 1856."

[33] Guérin, under no. 60. Guérin quotes the following letter from Manet to Banville: "Cher Monsieur, j'ai envie de faire pour le livre des *Ballades* l'assembleur de rimes Banville à sa table, écrivant et fumant une cigarette. Dans la fumée qui s'en ira en spirales, j'indiquerai par de petites figures, les principales pièces du livre. Si cela vous va, j'irai faire un croquis chez vous à votre heure et le jour que vous voudrez."

[34] Guérin, under no. 60: "Le croquis a été fait; il se trouve dans la collection Ernest Rouart et a été reproduit dans *Manet raconté par lui-même*, par E. Moreau-Nélaton, T. II, fig. 183."

tion.[35] It remained in a tentative stage (Guérin, no. 61), with unresolved problems of technique—combining etching and aquatint—and Léon Rosenthal chose to omit it from his study of Manet's graphic works;[36] but the two drawings are in no way failures. Seen in chronological sequence, the first (fig. 334) is made directly from the model; the second (fig. 335) is a conceptual and composite image which combines allegory with a likeness of the poet. This sequence reveals a logical adaption of the portrait to its ultimate role as an illustration. The elaboration of the image is an additive rather than organic process.

The evidence of the drawings so far considered suggests that the mechanical process of transcribing a pure drawing into one of the print media was tedious, clumsy, and never fully satisfactory to Manet. Not only did he attempt to overcome this obstacle by occasional use of photography, but in some cases (e.g., the woodcuts of *Après-midi d'un faune* [fig. 14]) the technique and medium of reproduction was handled so as not to alter the form of the initial drawing. The process (woodcut) was an elaborate one nevertheless. In one instance, in the portrait of the engraver Félix Bracquemond of 1865 (fig. 19), Manet overcame this difficulty. He experimented with a mechanical reproduction process invented by Bracquemond.

It is described by the contemporary engraver Lalanne in his *Traité de la gravure*: "After having cleaned a plate thoroughly . . . one makes a drawing on it with pen and ordinary ink. . . . Once the drawing is done

FIGURE 19 *(Cat. No. 214)*.

and thoroughly dry . . . the plate is varnished and blackened with smoke . . . then the plate is placed in water. After a quarter of an hour, one rubs it slightly with a flannel cloth; the softened ink takes off with it the varnish which covers it and lets a very sharp drawing appear which is then etched."[37] The only limitation which such a technique placed on the artist was the necessity of avoiding too intricate and complex a play of lines, or too much variation in their thickness. Manet submitted to it and produced a uniformly accented drawing which gives full value to the energetic lines of the pen.

Manet also had complete freedom from problems of reproduction when he made the

[35] See letter quoted by Guérin, under no. 61.

[36] L. Rosenthal, *Manet aquafortiste et lithographe*, p. 76, n. 2: " . . . je m'excuse de passer sous silence *Le Rêve du marin* (M-N, 42 et 67), où l'on peut reconnaître une esquisse du portrait de Théo-

dore de Banville, parce qu'il m'apparaît comme une erreur regrettable de l'artiste."

[37] Quoted by L. Rosenthal, *Manet aquafortiste et lithographe*, p. 74.

drawing portraits of his contemporaries, Gustave Courbet and Claude Monet. These works were done in an ink wash technique and were then reproduced by a photographic process known as *gillotage*, named after its inventor, Firmin Gillot.[38] The *Gustave Courbet* drawing (fig. 392) was reproduced at the head of a treatise on Courbet by d'Ideville.[39] It was derived from a photograph, but its graphic intensity and the accent given to the personality of the sitter are not to be found in the photographic source.[40] The *Claude Monet* drawing (fig. 393) is an ink wash drawing with touches of watercolor, but was reproduced in black and white by the Gillot process at the head of the catalogue of the Monet exhibition held at La Vie Moderne in June 1880. Unlike the *Gustave Courbet*, this study was done from life, but it has a similar boldness and economy. As spot illustrations, these two portraits are admirably suited for their purpose.

The foregoing review of drawings which served as guides or models for etchings and lithographs, but were not derived from paintings, underlines Manet's reluctance to elaborate upon, or alter in any way, the original drawn study—whether inspired by a literary work, the features of a friend, or the familiar spectacle of street, café, or theater life. The essentials of the sketch were preserved in its final printed form; they include qualities of calligraphic ease, economy, casual wit, and effortlessness.

VII

As stated earlier, the element of experimentation, normally much in evidence in any preparatory drawing, is not prominent in Manet's drawings. With the exceptions of a few early compositions discussed below, this is true of Manet's compositional drawings as well: they are "studies" only in so far as each drawing in a series represents a solution to a common compositional problem. But when viewed independently, each individual drawing gives very few hints of the hesitations and changes of mind which are normally intrinsic parts of a true "study" drawing.

Compositional drawings are few. One explanation might be that only a few have been preserved. However, since many sketches of details, individual figures, or groups are extant, it is unlikely that a number of the more elaborate compositional drawings would have been lost or destroyed. A more probable reason is that Manet made extensive use of thumbnail sketches of single motifs in his compositions but, in most cases, worked out the composite arrangement of these motifs directly in the medium and in the larger scale of the final version in oils or pastels. Each painting would undergo a number of erasures and new starts until the artist could feel satisfied at last with one particular

---

[38] The process of *gillotage* is described in a fine study of the drawing *Courbet*, by Barbara A. Holleman, in "Portrait de Courbet," *Les Amis de Gustave Courbet*, Bulletin no. 28 (Paris-Ornans, 1961).

[39] Henri d'Ideville, *Gustave Courbet, notes et documents sur sa vie et son oeuvre* (Paris: Heymann et Pérois, 1878).

[40] Tabarant lists some of the fake "Courbet" drawings which he has encountered. A. Tabarant, *Manet et ses oeuvres*, pp. 338–339.

stage of its progress.[41] This procedure did away in large measure with the need of drawings as compositional studies.

A consideration of drawings in this category should follow a chronological order since their frequency and the role assigned to them are affected by the artist's changing approach to the problem of composition.

The red chalk drawing in the Rouart collection, *Monsieur et Madame Auguste Manet* (fig. 20), is a preparatory sketch for Ma-

net's portrait of his parents (fig. 21). Manet told his friend Antonin Proust that he had chosen a very casual pose for this portrait, representing his parents in a familiar setting and natural relationship.[42] Much of the charm and modernity of the painting is in its psychological truth. In this respect it is a close relative of Degas' double portraits of the same period. The composition follows High Renaissance precedents, with its pyramidal emphasis, the plainness of the back-

---

[41] Jamot, p. 47, mentions that the engraver Belot posed 60 times for the *Le Bon bock*, and quotes Berthe Morisot's letter relating the series of new starts which parts of the portrait of Eva Gonzales

underwent.

[42] "Quant à mon père et à ma mère, je les ai campés tout bêtement, tels que je les vois . . ."; quoted in A. Proust, *Edouard Manet, souvenirs.*

FIGURE 20 *(Cat. No. 150).*

FIGURE 21 *(see Cat. No. 150).*

ground, and the frontality of the poses.[43] Manet had already established in the sketch the general configuration of the forms. This seems to have been its basic function. None of the component elements is radically reshuffled in the painting. The sketch represents a solution to the problem of composition rather than an experimental stage of development. Once Manet recorded a line, such as the contour of the head of Mme. Manet, its inflections and the shapes which it circumscribed became final. Its nearly exact transcription in the painting makes this clear. Much is left out of the drawing that is later incorporated in the painting, but nowhere do we find a hesitant or tentative line. This double portrait study is of special historical interest. It reveals, early in Manet's career, a limitation of the artist's creative act—yet also, paradoxically, a strength: the simultaneity and inflexible relationship of visual impression and graphic transcription.

Le Christ insulté par les soldats (fig. 46) is an exception to this general procedure. A study for the painting of 1864 (Jamot, no. 113), its unusual quality is that it reveals a search for compositional balance by trial and error. The fact that the final form was not fully visualized by the artist at the drawing stage may account for a similar weakness in the painting, no matter what the other qualities of the latter may be. The component parts of the ultimate composition "fail to coalesce."[44] Manet was clearly inspired by the interpretation of similar themes in Titian's *Christ Crowned with Thorns* (Louvre), and Van Dyck's *Christ Scourged* (Berlin).[45] His painting departs from these two models primarily in the "studio" or "still-life" quality of its principal components. It lacks human drama, and the group of figures is poorly staged if judged by traditional standards. The drawing (fig. 46) gives a clue to the cause. The only form in it with precise graphic consistency is the central figure of Christ. All other elements are merely suggested. The second compositional stage was the painting itself, in which Manet established the final group of figures by juxtaposing other independently studied models to the figure of Christ. The dichotomy of the drawing's composition is a rare occurrence. The only other drawing in which it appears is *La Toilette (1)* (fig. 218). Here also the principal figure is fully defined, but the setting in which she is placed seems to be a second thought, and the form of the servant behind the seated nude is in an embryonic stage. The figure and setting are more fully integrated in the etching (fig. 221) because the tonal contrast with the luminous figure is emphasized, thus throwing the figure into plastic relief.

The subject matter of these works is tradi-

---

[43] There is a formal coherence in the composition which can be ascribed to Manet's early dependence on Renaissance types of composition. This is evident in the *Déjeuner sur l'herbe* and in the *Olympia* as well. This reliance on past models does not deny the refreshingly novel form of portraiture which the artist initiates here. G. H. Hamilton perceptively points out this originality of the portrait in *Manet and His Critics* (New Haven: Yale University Press, 1954), p. 24, but perhaps overlooks the structural unity of the form, which is ultimately derived from traditional composi-

tional precedents, and the convincing psychological relationship of the two elders, when he speaks of "the curiously awkward composition in which the two figures are neither coherently related, formally or psychologically, nor isolated as separate elements."

[44] *Ibid.*, p. 66.

[45] On the composite character of this painting and its specific pictorial sources, see A. de Leiris, "Manet's *Christ Scourged* and the Problem of His Religious Painting," *The Art Bulletin*, XLI (June 1959), 198.

FIGURE 22 *(Cat. No. 171)*.

tional. It is not surprising to find that Manet relied to a great extent on historical precedents for a solution to their composition. The painting *La Musique aux Tuileries* (fig. 23) is more original in concept, although not entirely without artistic precedents.[46] The title indicates a specific locale (the Tuileries Gardens) and reason for the gathering. Manet chose to stress anonymity of setting, placing his personages—many of them portraits—in the midst of a uniform garden setting. Nothing in the painting suggests music. An elegant crowd has gathered in idle gregarious groups. The composition deliberately emphasizes the dominant accent on anonymity by exploiting repetitive effects. The

preparatory wash drawing for this composition (fig. 22), probably executed on the scene, established the main structure of the painting in its final form. Manet juxtaposed a number of independent motifs but visualized simultaneously the grid pattern and formal contrasts of the overall design. The development of the painting from the drawing simply consisted in increasing the variety of motifs of the initial wash sketch (tree trunks, figures, top hats, metal chairs, and so on), some of which were already fully defined in the drawing. The drawing functioned both as a general compositional guide, and as a source of independent factual studies. Its formulation of the theme was essen-

---

[46] N. G. Sandblad, *Manet, Three Studies in Artistic Conception*, pp. 17 ff.

tially complete at this preliminary stage.

From 1870 on, Manet seldom felt the need to elaborate a preliminary composition in drawing form. When he did so, the drawing was reproduced, practically unchanged in design and detail, in the medium of oils. The drawing *Intérieur à Arcachon* (fig. 51) of 1871 is a characteristic example. The corresponding painting (Jamot, no. 193) reproduces it faithfully in all essentials. Manet's solution to composition became increasingly bound to the act of seeing or experiencing a motif or a scene directly. This led him to elaborate a design while at work on the paint-

ing itself. However, Manet did not abandon drawings as a means of recording aspects of his daily environment.

In 1878 Manet painted five versions of street scenes observed from the balcony of his studio which faced on Rue Mosnier (now Rue de Berne). Many sketches of single motifs were transcribed in these paintings: *L'Homme aux béquilles* (Cat. No. 505), *Une Victoria* (fig. 365), *Fiacre et bec-de-gaz* (fig. 364), *Fiacre* (fig. 367). A more comprehensive drawing, *La Rue Mosnier au bec-de-gaz* (fig. 24), is a broader vista, recording a variety of street activities and

FIGURE 23 *(see Cat. No. 171)*.

FIGURE 24 *(Cat. No. 502).*

sights: carriages, street sweepers, a palisaded empty lot, and a street lamp. However, its composition does not correspond exactly to any one painting of the series. Its component elements are more loosely distributed. Manet deliberately sacrificed unity, which the term "vista" implies, and accentuated contrasts of motifs observed singly. This method is a reversal of compositional techniques which he had followed (but none too faithfully) up to this time. The sacrifice of fluency of design allowed him to make the most of the variety of separate observations in the total context. The line of demarcation usually drawn between a compositional drawing and a sketch disappeared.

Chanteuse de café-concert (fig. 377) illustrates the last stage in the evolution of drawings in this category. Its basic formal structure and its choice of motifs were not transcribed precisely in any one painting of the period (*ca.* 1878). Nevertheless, it has a profound stylistic resemblance to many works with similar subject matter, such as the paintings *Chanteuse de café-concert, La Serveuse de bock, Un Bar aux Folies Bergère* (Jamot, nos. 302, 335, and 467, respectively), which were done between 1876 and 1881. The drawing's basic arabesque consists of the broad contour of a standing figure, overlapped by a silhouetted head in the lower field of the page, and juxtaposed to the speckled pattern which fills the voids. The paintings listed above are essentially composed on the same scheme. The simplicity of this common denominator makes possible interchangeability of parts (the three basic patterns described) in any one work. The drawing was probably made from life, and we may conclude that by this time Manet could execute a sketch from nature or a studio painting with equal spontaneity, confidently relying on the inherent virtues of a few basic compositional devices of his own creation.

34

VIII

Manet has left us numerous thumbnail sketches. Their historical importance should be emphasized, since they often played an essential role in the elaboration of paintings. The painting *Sur la Plage de Boulogne*, of 1869 (fig. 254),[47] will illustrate this point. It is one of a number of paintings whose compositions are based almost exclusively on sketches of this type.[48] These paintings have certain features in common: their subject is a panoramic view of a group of figures engaged in a common activity; they were painted in the studio and based upon on-the-scene drawing studies of individual figures or details.

Every motif in the painting *Sur la Plage de Boulogne* corresponds to a pencil notation in Manet's Boulogne sketchbook, now in the Louvre (figs. 251 through 259). Composed of separate groups, each equally emphasized and lacking a single focus, the painting produces a speckled, somewhat disjointed effect. However, this quality does justice to the panoramic point of view of the scene, portraying the homogeneous expanse of sand and sea dotted with the sharp accents of lively details.

A comparison of any one figure or group in the painting with the corresponding sketch—the seated woman holding a folded umbrella, with a small child by her side (fig. 251)—reveals that Manet preserved with exceptional fidelity the form of the original drawing. The painted version of this motif does not elaborate upon the brief graphic note, as might be expected. We may conclude that sketches of this type were not merely reference sources, but played a determinant role in the painting's composition.

IX

One of the virtues of Manet's slightest sketch is its whimsicality. Manet's biographers have often spoken of the artist's reserved nature, but also of his gregariousness and ready wit. His drawings manifest this pointed sense of humor. Manet's creativity was playful in its essence. Unless one recognizes the place of lighthearted sympathy in Manet's art, one is apt to dismiss many of the drawings as entertaining, charming, but incidental works.

---

[47] The genesis of the painting *Sur la Plage de Boulogne* and the role of its related sketches in the Boulogne sketchbook are discussed more extensively in A. de Leiris, "Manet: *Sur la Plage de Boulogne*," *Gazette des Beaux-Arts*, LVII (January 1961), 53.

[48] Other examples of paintings related in type to *Sur la Plage de Boulogne* are the two versions of *Le Départ du bateau de Folkestone* (Jamot, no. 162, fig. 330; and no. 163, fig. 313) for which there exist numerous sketches of personages in the Pellerin collection in the Louvre, figs. 260 ff.; *La Musique aux Tuileries* (Jamot, no. 36, fig. 352) which we have already compared to details of a preparatory sketch; *La Partie de croquet à*

Paris (Jamot, no. 232, fig. 328); *La Partie de croquet à Boulogne* (Jamot, no. 197, fig. 355) (numerous sketches used in the composition of the last two paintings are also to be found in the Pellerin collection; for example: figs. 290, 291, 296, 298, 365, 367). These paintings have in common their reliance on brief drawing notes introduced in correspondingly sketchy form in the painting, the reduction of overall action to a minimum, and an emphasis on the individual pose and character of each figure or group. As will be seen in our illustrations, on many of these sketches Manet made color notations. These color references further indicate Manet's intention to use the sketches as direct sources for his paintings.

This applies to the vignette drawings, which were made for their own sakes and were seen only by the artist's closest friends during his lifetime. The vignettes have a limited iconographical range. They were produced as routinely as the artist's own signature, and appear as unpremeditated in form. These distinctive traits suggest the term "signature-motifs" for their classification. Manet adapted many of them in the medium of watercolor which "illuminated" his personal letters to friends during the periods of his enforced confinement.[49]

The subject matter of these vignettes illustrates Manet's predilection for a number of familiar objects and patterns. The choice of motifs is varied and the objects which engaged Manet's curiosity do not bear any obvious resemblance one to another. Nevertheless, the images which Manet derived from them have design qualities in common which explain the attraction their models had for him.

Distinct patterns recur, enabling us to single out broad classes or families of objects. Each of these classes provides it own kind of visual delight to the artist, and we list them here tentatively, not intending to make of such groupings hard and fast categories, but submitting to their inherent playful unorthodoxy.

Among the objects which attracted Manet for their intrinsic brilliant and festive patterns or for their uncommon shapes and colors are women's stockinged or gartered legs emerging from ample, bell-like skirts and petticoats—depicted without a trace of vulgarity but with humor, they become symbols of feminine charm (figs. 26, 415, 417); flags in crossed pattern (fig. 419); flowers of all species—rose, daisy, morning glory, and so on—usually depicted singly on a leafy stem (figs. 387, 388, 405, 406); Chinese lanterns, gay, fragile, popular, in carnivalesque color (fig. 420). This random list illustrates the playful freedom of the artist. Manet himself realized that such genial interest in the charming surface of things may have appeared to some observers as not serious enough. In a letter, addressed to an unidentified woman friend, and illuminated with the vivacious patterns of feminine legs gaily attired in rainbow hues (figs. 415, 417), he writes: "folie si vous voulez chère Madame, mais dame follie [sic] celle-là, et qui me permet de passer agréablement mon temps. . . ." To Manet, the madness which consists in drawing such trifles is a noble madness—"dame follie"—and its excuse is the pleasure the artist finds in indulging in it.

Out of these odd but familiar objects Manet produces images of heraldic simplicity consisting of frank contrasts of primary colors contained within descriptive silhouettes. In spite of the accent on festive colors, the form is essentially graphic.

Other motifs were chosen for their singularity. The Pekinese dog Tama, which belonged to Manet's friend Duret, was the subject of humorous vignettes (figs. 346, 347, 348).[50] So were a number of portrait heads of women acquaintances. Among these are hatless models treated with graphic and caricatural emphasis on the features (figs. 382, 383, 384, 385). In *Tama*, Manet revealed the nervous nature of the animal's species;

---

[49] A selection of such letters has been published in facsimile in J. Guiffrey, *Edouard Manet: Letters with Aquarelles* (New York: Pantheon Books, 1944).

[50] These are pencil sketches but all their uncanny truth to life is retained in the corresponding autographic drawings transferred to the trial stone. See *Le Corbeau* (Guérin, no. 84).

FIGURE 25 *(Cat. No. 549)*.

FIGURE 26 *(Cat. No. 585)*

similarly in the portrait heads, he accentuated common traits of his coquettish subjects: their facial mobility and their flighty thoughts.

In a different vein, Manet conveyed the intrinsic charm of contemporary feminine fashions in profile heads clad in hats, frills, and ribbons (figs. 409, 418, 422). The features of the model are incidental in this context. The dot of an eye, the curve of a nose, the silhouette of a lost profile, the shape of a collar, or the texture of a veil are merely graphic elaborations of a single pattern—the "object-image" which Manet created from them. Related to these decorative profiles are watercolors representing a single feminine model standing or seated. The same profile pattern often recurs in two or more versions (figs. 412, 413, 414). This pattern preserves in each successive image the self-conscious grace of the figure's stance and gesture. These semi-caricatural silhouettes are devoid of satire. The forms themselves are playful.

Other "families" of objects deserve mention here: objects or living things whose principal external attributes are curvilinear outlines and/or changeable surface texture. Included in this definition are cats (figs. 57, 405, 406) and a variety of fruit represented singly (a plum, a peach, and the like), usually drawn as a frontispiece on a letter (fig. 400). Finally we might distinguish animals and plants whose invariable natural structure fascinated Manet: the snail, with its contrasting rigid spiral shell and elastic body (fig. 25); the lemon, with its star-like cross-section (fig. 408); the oyster or the almond whose external and internal textures are juxtaposed (fig. 399); or the shrimp's bristling, transparent coil (figs. 407, 408).

Such tentative iconographic classifications do not exhaust the fund of objects

FIGURE 27 *(Cat. No. 487)*.

FIGURE 28 *(Cat. No. 488)*.

which inspired these lively vignettes. Many appear in Manet's letters (figs. 407, 408) with or without accompanying text.

In most instances such sketches were either studies from life or replicas of these. Rarely did Manet rely purely on imagination or recollection. His own statements clarify his procedure for us. In one of his illustrated letters (fig. 410) he declared: "Ce qu'on fait de chic ne vaut rien. Si au moins j'avais le modèle devant moi. . . ." He reveals his reluctance to rely purely on memory for his work and his lack of faith in the results of such a creative procedure. This statement is accompanied by drawings of two female heads which betray the weakness that Manet admits is in them. While charming, they lack the accent of truth which every sketch based on direct observation possesses, whether such a sketch be a first or subsequent version of the same subject.

Many of the vignettes in watercolor or ink wash are replicas of thumbnail sketches which Manet made from life on the pages of his pocket sketchbooks.[51] (The distinction made here between vignettes and thumbnail sketches cannot be a hard-and-fast one. We use the term "vignette" to describe a drawing, in any graphic technique, which is deliberately and decoratively composed on the page; whereas "thumbnail" sketches describes the more informal direct sketches.) Two examples among many will suffice. To

---

[51] A quotation from A. Proust, *Edouard Manet, souvenirs*, p. 29, reveals this habit of Manet: "Nous décampions, courant aux boulevards extérieurs. Là, il dessinait sur son carnet un rien, un profil, un chapeau, en un mot une impression fugitive, et quand le lendemain un camarade lui disait en feuilletant son carnet: 'tu devrais finir cela,' il se tordait de rire: 'tu me prends,' disait-il, 'pour un peintre d'histoire.'"

the three snails illustrating a letter (fig. 404) correspond two drawings (figs. 25, 402, 403); to the wash drawing representing a group of spectators at a concert, viewed from the back (fig. 27), corresponds a pencil drawing (fig. 28). There are numerous instances of this parallelism. For example, the motif of a specific woman's head may be found in two or more versions, exclusive of paintings.

The last word on these drawings should be Manet's: "There is only one true way: to do in a single motion what one sees. When it is successful, it is successful. When it is not, one starts afresh. All else is nonsense."[52]

---

[52] A. Proust, *Edouard Manet, souvenirs*, p. 30. It is difficult to convey in a translation the lapidary quality and conviction carried by Manet's original statement in French as reported by Proust: "Il n'y a qu'une chose vraie. Faire du premier coup ce qu'on voit. Quand ça y est, ça y est. Et quand ça n'y est pas on recommence. Tout le reste est de la blague."

Chapter III

MEDIA AND TECHNIQUES

MANET availed himself of a variety of drawing media: lead pencil; red crayon (*sanguine*); black crayon (*crayon noir* or *pierre noire*); pen and ink; brush and ink (ink wash); and watercolor.

Fond of clarity and directness of statement, Manet avoided elaborate or unusual uses of these traditional media, and, in a majority of his drawings, the techniques employed are easily identified. A particular choice of media corresponds to each new departure of Manet's style. The particular sequence of these changes is in itself instructive.

His most versatile medium was lead pencil. He never abandoned it completely in favor of other media, but adapted it to a variety of drawing types, from the large figures derived from Renaissance compositions (fig. 65) to the cursive sketches from life of a much later date (figs. 25 and 27). The range will be more fully illustrated in the stylistic analysis.

Manet chose pen and ink for pure calligraphic effects similar to but sharper than those obtained with a lead pencil line. We find few instances of the use of this medium in early drawings, but Manet employed it more and more frequently as time went on. His late pen and ink drawings are among his most expressive. In an early drawing, *La Découverte de Moïse* (fig. 41), pen and ink are combined with an ink wash which provides mellowing tonal nuances and contrasts. In this example the pen line serves much the same function as the lead pencil line in copies after old masters. It singles out major contours from a faint and more tentative pencil sketch which underlies it, and gives to the latter its definitive form with little elaboration. The technique of pen and ink was also used by Manet for illustrations, in which case the drawings were the models for prints (lithographs or etchings).

Manet produced a number of large drawings in crayon (*sanguine* or *crayon noir*, with a preference for the former), and occasionally in charcoal. The crayons, red crayon in particular, were among the favorite drawing media in the seventeenth and eighteenth centuries in the West. Many nineteenth-century painters and sculptors continued to favor them. Drawings by Millet, Courbet, Degas, Renoir, Maillol, and Redon testify to their lasting appeal throughout the century. Crayons and charcoal were the major drawing tools of any young artist in academic training, and Manet familiarized himself with these media during his stay in Couture's studio. During his formative years of the 1850's, and after taking his leave of Couture's studio in 1856, Manet produced many outstanding drawings in crayon. In a drawing after Raphael, *Porteuse d'eau* (fig. 89), Manet adapted the crayon line to the voluminous forms of the original. The drawing *La Sainte Famille* (fig. 110), based on a fresco by Andrea del Sarto, takes full advantage of the medium's flexibility, particularly in rendering the chiaroscuro of the original. Here Manet demonstrates the red crayon's adaptability to the rendering of tonal nuances and general mellowness of pictorial effect. In the drawings of the 1860's the crayon plays a more purely graphic role. In *La Toilette (1)* (fig. 218), the subtle changes in the quality of the line, its thicks and thins, suggest the resiliency of the model's body, and do this effectively with a minimum of tonal modeling of the forms. In *Olympia* (fig. 228) the variations in color and line are further curtailed, but the body and weight of the crayon line gives sturdiness to the pure silhouette.

By 1865 Manet almost totally abandoned the use of soft crayons—the drawing *La Convalescente* (fig. 13), which we have dated around 1875 on other stylistic evidence, is a major exception. Manet's contacts with Impressionism, and his own experiments in that direction, freed him from his earlier dependence on Renaissance and baroque sources for themes and compositional devices. He drew his subject matter more exclusively from his own physical environment—his studio, streets and interiors, familiar landscapes—and the style of these images became increasingly personal. This change was reflected in his choice of media. He abandoned the soft, tonal lines of the red and black crayons, preferring the less sensuous and more purely graphic pencil and pen lines. The brush strokes in his watercolors unite color and line more completely.

Manet made extensive use of the brush as a drawing tool, with both ink and watercolor as media. But not all his watercolors can be considered with the drawings as essentially graphic or calligraphic in concept and execution. In some instances the brush strokes and washes are secondary enrichments to a drawing whose structure is basically linear, as in *Victorine Meurend en costume d'espada* (fig. 8). In other examples the brush work is the primary constituent, as in *Le Corbeau* (fig. 340) and *Lampions* (fig. 420). Drawings of the first type are generally found among early works, while drawings of the later years conform to the second type. There are of course exceptions to this chronological pattern. For instance, *Musique aux Tuileries* (fig. 22), characteristic of the second type, is a work of the early 1860's. However, in the later years of his career, Manet never went back to the combination of media in which the brush work adds only enlivening touches to a drawing at a relatively late stage of its development.

This change of function of the brush strokes in later drawings can be explained in part by the different aims pursued by Manet at that time. *Lola de Valence* of 1862 (fig. 214) and *Printemps* of 1881 (fig. 423) are both based on paintings (figs. 215 and 424). Both show the use of a combination of media. In *Lola*, Manet first drew the figure in pencil, reconstructing the original as exactly as possible, and then went over the drawing

41

with color accents which gave it some of the pictorial charm of the original painting. In *Printemps* there was only a slight attempt to suggest the actual color effect of the original. Instead, both media, pen and wash, were used simultaneously with an eye to their intrinsic graphic value and to that of the drawing as a whole.

The increasingly calligraphic quality of Manet's brush technique is manifest in a special category of drawings dating from 1875 on. They resemble vignettes in their format and sprightly aspect. They are brief spots done in brush and ink or watercolor. The majority of them are repeats, in the brush technique—with ink or watercolor—of original pencil sketches. *Audience et chef d'orchestre* (fig. 28) illustrates this type of drawing in which the technique reaches its ultimate conciseness. Indeed, Manet's entire stylistic development reveals that he consistently strived for abridgement of form.

Chapter IV

THE HISTORY
OF MANET'S STYLE
REVEALED IN DRAWINGS

I. THE VISUAL

ANY STYLE manifests two distinct aspects. The first, constancy, can be detected in certain physical features or visible signs, and concerns the style's innermost structure and nature. The second is an aptitude to undergo a development, analogous to a biological development, which registers the deepening comprehension and control of the artist himself, and the indirect semi-accidental impacts of his environment upon his sensibility. This inclusive definition suggests that the history of a style must take into account external as well as internal causes, changing as well as constant factors, and therefore does not postulate an autonomous "life of the forms." The artist is seen in the context of his time; his drawing in the context of his oeuvre; and style in the context of both internal, "biological" demands and the pressures of external circumstances, including temporal and technical factors.

What we hoped might be gained by an analysis of style in Manet's case is a perspective against which the originality of individual drawings may be precisely evaluated as facets of a versatile graphic production, and a deeper understanding of Manet's artistic sensibility. A stylistic framework also provides a chronological perspective when other evidence is lacking, such as relation of drawings to works in other media, whose dates are known, or to familiar circumstances in Manet's life.

Stylistic development will be established on the basis of groups of drawings, arranged in chronological sequence, each of which represents a distinct step. However, the dates can only provide convenient landmarks for these steps; they do not establish an inflexible chronological pattern.

We shall follow our study of Manet's style from the early studio academies and museum copies to the late, highly personal "object-images" of the last years, with an attempt to sum up what constitute the permanent characteristics of the artist's style—qualities which are so basic that they are in evidence in all of Manet's drawings, irrespective of their relative dates.

A major consideration in any stylistic analysis is the problem of influences of the work of other artists, past or contemporary. Many such sources have already been pointed out with reference to Manet's paintings. They affected the choice of subject matter, the composition, and stylistic aspects of a number of works by Manet.[1] Thus a so-called "Spanish period" between the late 1850's and 1865 and the dominant Japanese influence on the paintings of the late 1860's are generally accepted facts.[2] Granted the validity, limited as it is, of these broad generalizations, we should recognize the diversity of Manet's sources and realize that the lessons he draws from them vary also with each period. The names of Velasquez, of Titian, of Hals and of Goya appear consistently in studies of Manet's sources. More rarely mentioned, but no less significant, are the names of Chardin, Watteau, Courbet, Rubens, and Géricault, among others, whose works were at one time or another sources of his inspiration.

Except for watercolors which are derived from paintings, such as *Le Chanteur espagnol* (fig. 203), Manet's drawings are not so deeply affected by artistic sources as are his paintings. The economy of means allows him more freedom in this respect.

Our study will recognize the trends of style attributable to prevalent external influences whenever these appear, and however sporadically, in the drawings. But we shall stress the internal changes: Manet's developing grasp of visual facts, and his acuity in transposing these facts into "object-images."

II. 1852–1858 THE MASTERS

This period in Manet's career was influenced by years of study in the studio of Couture and by his travels to the museums of Europe. A brief glance at the drawings which Manet produced at this time tells us that he was not under the tutelage of any one master, but sought contacts with many. His studio master Couture, whose art falls within the academic tradition stemming from David and Ingres, may well have encouraged him in this direction. But, whereas Couture derived certain technical and compositional formulas from tradition—primarily from Venetian sources—and held to an anachronistic Renaissance idealism watered down by eclecticism, Manet approached these sources in a more independent spirit. His drawings, based on the works of masters of the past, sharpened his own perception, so that he was ready to turn to contemporary subjects

---

[1] The following is a list of references in which these influences on Manet's paintings have been dealt with in the most thorough and enlightening way: Michel Florisoone, *Manet* (Monaco: Documents d'Art, 1947); Léon Rosenthal, "Manet et l'Espagne," *Manet aquafortiste et lithographe* (Paris: Le Goupy, 1925), pp. 107–120; Bazin, "Problème de l'originalité de Manet par rapport

à la tradition," *L'Amour de l'Art* (May 1932), pp. 151 ff.

[2] Rosenthal shows that Manet's early formation in a society sharing a fashionable taste for everything Spanish is one of several factors which contributed to the "Spanish look" of many of his paintings of the early sixties. L. Rosenthal, *Manet aquafortiste et lithographe*, p. 112.

44

FIGURE 29 (*Cat. No. 6*).

with new confidence and freedom.

The works which Manet chose to record in drawings during his visit to European cities included a large number of Florentine frescoes, which amply document his stay in Florence. To a Parisian artist, confronted with the restricting practices of academic training at home and the staleness of the salons, and stimulated also by the vigorous but heavy-handed realism of Courbet's painting, the Florentine experience must have been a revelation. Manet saw the frescoes in their original architectural settings. Here was a monumental art devoid of pomposities, youthful, optimistic, pure in form, and frank in color—a sheer delight to his sophisticated eye. The drawings give a measure of his elated response and reveal his preferences for the art of Fra Angelico,

Ghirlandaio, Andrea del Sarto, Fra Bartolomeo, and Luca della Robbia in Florence; Perugino and Raphael in Perugia and Rome.

Our catalogue lists five drawings based on Fra Angelico's fresco of the *Mystical Crucifixion* in San Marco, Florence (figs. 29, 60, 61, 63, 65).[3] *Moine agenouillé* (fig. 65) belongs to this series. It represents the St. Francis of the *Crucifixion*. The quiet form of the figure is described in its broadest contours and developed with a line of uniform thickness throughout. Such a line is normally associated with a transfer procedure such as tracing. Manet's approach, however, is anything but mechanical. A close examination reveals two distinct steps. The figure is first drawn with a faint pencil line which remains visible in the finished drawing. This delicate preliminary sketch or impression of the original fresco is executed freely and rapidly. It serves to locate the major directions of the contours of the original, but involves some degree of trial and error. The second step is a spirited outlining of the light shorthand sketch with a line of uniform width and light value, which synthesizes and strengthens the forms. It is not a mere tracing but a selective clarification of the faint drawing beneath it. There is no longer any hesitancy or approximation in this second and final step, nor does it take any liberties with the model in the form of a facile stylization or second-thought elaborations. It pulls the figure firmly together. Manet forgoes modeling. The spatial relationships are indicated by the overlap of contour lines. These are interrupted wherever a change in plane occurs, leaving a pause, a stretch of bare paper between the overlapping lines. This openness of the lines does away with

---

[3] Precise references to the originals from which the drawings were made are given in the catalogue

whenever such sources have been ascertained.

the need for varying their accentuation and thickness, as is commonly done to suggest spatial and tactile values, and thus allows all lines and graphic accents to retain a uniform emphasis. Another result is the "cleanliness" of the image as a whole, which is also a characteristic of Fra Angelico's style. The similarity extends to less technical aspects as well: the works of both Manet and Fra Angelico manifest a distinctive blend of sophistication and naïveté. Manet deliberately sought to respond as innocently as possible to the immediate sensations he perceived while confronting his model. That these responses were conditioned by the lessons he had learned from the masters did not make them less spontaneous at the time of execution. Manet's approach to his subject or model became increasingly free from conventional, learned responses or methods—a phenomenon which is also apparent in the works of other nineteenth-century "learned innocents," such as David, Ingres, or Cézanne.

Manet's drawings of details of Ghirlandaio's frescoes in Santa Maria Novella in Florence (figs. 30, 31, 66, 68, 72) were also executed with the two-step method: a faint sketch, and a more accented and deliberate final drawing over it (fig. 30). But each drawing interprets a different facet of the original, and does so in a distinct calligraphic idiom.

Mary and Elizabeth (fig. 30)—a detail from the central portion of Ghirlandaio's fresco the *Visitation*—are portrayed in the most abridged form. The triangular pattern of the two women linking arms in the action of embracing predominates; details of features and costume are barely indicated. The profile, formed by an almost unbroken line, makes one shape of the two figures; but the inflections of the line, and its qualification of

the blank areas of paper are such that the volume of the bodies is unmistakably implied. The spontaneity of the action of greeting is heightened in Manet's interpretation by the impetuous calligraphy.

In contrast, the two figures from the quieter scene of the *Birth of the Virgin* (fig. 68) are transcribed with more emphasis on their bulk and on the variety of surface patterns of their costumes. The graphic vocabulary is correspondingly more varied and elaborate. Parallel hatchings, bound by assertive linear contours, establish the major overlapping planes of general body masses, and delicate swirling patterns suggest the embroidered surfaces of the courtly dresses. This is perhaps the most delicately rich drawing of the whole series after Ghirlandaio. It comes closest to presenting a graphic equivalent of the pictorial qualities of the original.

FIGURE 30 *(Cat. No. 7)*.

A second drawing (fig. 31), based on the *Birth of the Virgin*, responds to still another facet of Ghirlandaio's style. It represents the servant girl pouring water, but insists upon her action rather than her features or accouterments. A combination of spiral contours and fanning diagonals captures a moment of impending movement. The originality of the drawing may be measured by the vigor which it imparts to the more staid and monumental figure in Ghirlandaio's fresco.

The copies after sixteenth-century models —primarily frescoes by Raphael and Andrea del Sarto—are also versatile transpositions of a variety of stylistic sources, and each is an interpretation of a limited set of the formal characteristics of the original fresco. This simplification is due in part to practical necessity (the inherent limitations of the drawing technique and media), but also to Manet's deliberate choice of dominant formal features from each source.

In two drawings based on Raphael's fresco of the *Trinity* in Perugia (figs. 86, 87, 88), Manet interprets the Umbrian's early style. As a result, these drawings are somewhat similar in technique to the copies of quattrocento frescoes discussed earlier: the medium is lead pencil; the line is uniform in thickness; the contours place the stress on continuous silhouettes; overlaps are intimated by reserved areas of paper interrupting the contour lines; and the form and gesture of the hands are summarized with a zigzag or scalloped contour which deemphasizes their mass—a mannerism found in a great number of Manet's drawings (figs. 29, 70, 143). The spatial relationships of the figures within a semicircular niche formed by the tectonic arrangement of the bodies themselves and the casual blending of each figure within the stately group are the main objects of Manet's study in these two drawings.

FIGURE 31 *(Cat. No. 10)*.

FIGURE 32 *(see Cat. No. 10)*.

47

The isolation of a group of three figures on the page, and the realization of a compositional and spatial unity in the figures themselves, without the usual props of landscape or interior backgrounds, are significant exercises in the light of later stylistic developments in Manet's original drawings or paintings. These copies of the *Trinity* already indicate possible solutions to a problem of composition which presented particular difficulties to Manet throughout his career (see pp. 29 ff. and p. 71).

Another drawing after Raphael, *Porteuse d'eau* (figs. 89, 90), representing the water carrier found in the right foreground of the *Incendio* fresco, is technically and stylistically quite different from the *Trinity* drawings. Manet emphasizes the sculptural plasticity and monumentality of his model. Adapting the red crayon medium to this end, he transposes the strong chiaroscuro of the fresco by alternating areas of white paper with shadowed planes defined by thick hatchings. The contours, reinforced by parallel lines, establish the boundaries of the volumes in thicks and thins, and impart a strong spiraling movement to the whole body. Manet retains the blocky proportions of the original figure and its rhythmical sequence of ovoid forms, but he strengthens the dynamic contrast between the body curves and the rectilinear hatchings of receding planes. The intrusion of the white paper throughout and the repeated breaks in the contours create a luminous atmosphere around the figure, which is quite unlike the airless space in the *Incendio* fresco.

The relatively large number of drawings based on the frescoes by Andrea del Sarto in the cloister of the Scalzo and the church of the Annunziata in Florence (we list twenty-nine drawings after Sarto in our catalogue) show Manet's personal attrac-

FIGURE 33 *(Cat. No. 129).*

tion to the art of the Florentine master. Single figures (figs. 111, 131) or groups (fig. 99) are technically similar to the *Porteuse d'eau* after Raphael (fig. 89). The forms are modeled in broad planes in light or shadow, but the contours are more abrupt and angular. Manet understands that the stateliness and, occasionally, the grandiloquence of Sarto's figure style have their source in the complex patterns of drapery folds which amplify the breadth of a figure and link it dynamically to others in solemn, processional groups. Indeed, some of Manet's drawings

48

stress this rhythmical movement of drapery patterns almost exclusively (fig. 95) by strengthening the verticals and slow curves with vigorous dark accents, thus dramatizing the solemn tone, the elegant formality, and the introspective mood of the originals.

La Sainte Famille (fig. 110), a drawing copy of Sarto's *Madonna del Sacco*, is the only one in the series which reproduces almost in its entirety the composition on which it is based. It is also the most faithful transposition of the pictorial subtleties of the original: the dramatic alternation of light and dark planes, the foreshortened pyramidal perspective, and the sophisticated balance of solids and voids. Manet does not include the entire background area of the fresco which is semicircular in shape, but chooses a rectangular format instead. However, the curved frame is partially indicated, and this is sufficient to imply its original span, and to give to the figures the scale and placement which are theirs in Sarto's composition. With the exceptions of a greater range of values and emphasis on the proto-baroque contrast of silhouetted dark shape (Joseph) with fully plastic forms (Mary), Manet's graphic vocabulary is similar to that of other drawings of isolated figures or groups from Sarto's frescoes (figs. 95, 99), which have been commented upon.

There is extant another drawing copy of the same group, *La Sainte Famille* (fig. 108), in the Louvre. But its interpretation of the original is very different. The Virgin and Child on the right have been reinforced with red crayon over a preliminary lead pencil sketch, while the figure of Joseph, with the exception of the head, is drawn in the original faint line. In contrast to the more complete version (fig. 110), the Louvre drawing is sketchier and its form is more calligraphic. The value contrasts are fewer

FIGURE 34 *(Cat. No. 129)*.

and no longer dominant, with a more restless effect of light. The lines are short and broken, the contours summary and open. It is in this latter vein that the series of drawings done after the "mother and child" in Andrea del Sarto's fresco of *The Birth of the Virgin* are executed (figs. 2, 5, 103, 104, 105, 107). (In these drawings, Manet depicts the traditional "Mother and Child" theme, whereas in Sarto's fresco the figures actually represent family members and servants attending the child Mary, and not Mary and the Christ child.)

49

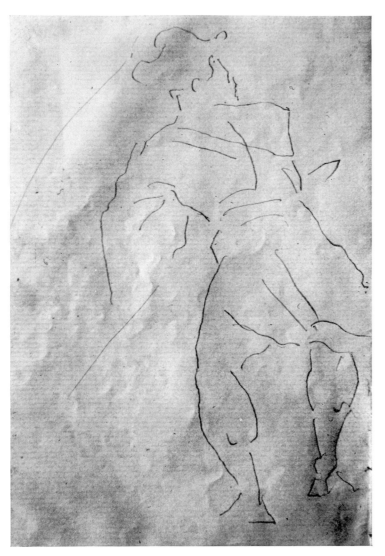

FIGURE 35 *(Cat. No. 129)*.

A number of early copies stress the *movement* of figures more exclusively, with or without specific dramatic overtones. The preferred medium for such drawings is lead pencil, and the graphic mode is rapid and energetic. The three related drawings of the *Soldat avec une lance* (figs. 33, 34, 35) illustrate this category. They are in all probability copies of originals by a Renaissance master but are transposed inventively into purely linear images. The contours are broken up into a series of tense S curves, V

signs, and undulating motifs. These graphic symbols directly convey the tension of the figure's action. One of the drawings (fig. 35) is a tracing of another of the same subject (fig. 34), and appears on the verso of the latter, thus reversing it. In this case, the procedure followed in the copies mentioned so far is not followed. The two versions—original or preliminary drawing, and tracing or final version—are not superposed as two distinct steps in a single drawing. Nevertheless, these related drawings shed light on the "tracing" procedure favored by Manet. The earlier drawing (fig. 34) constitutes the original sketch and is already an all-inclusive and complete image in itself. The tracing procedure of the second drawing further clarifies the graphic vocabulary of the first, through elimination and synthesis, and gives it a definitive and semi-caricatural cast. The movement of the figure, no less dramatic than in the first drawing, is rigidly stamped into this new graphic form. All the linear accents are variations on a cedilla-shaped, reversed curve motif.

Manet chose this spirited linear mode as the most adequate for decorative mythological or allegorical subjects. In *Musique* and *Danse* (figs. 185, 184) it gives to the figures a rococo restlessness and aerial grace. Transparent watercolor washes in pastel tonalities, applied in broad areas of uniform intensity, add a note of gaiety and luminosity. In the buoyant figure of *Musique*, the zigzag linear motif predominates. In the *Danse* Manet develops the forms with delicate curvilinear accents in cedilla or S shapes.

The drawing *Putto et masque* (fig. 36), probably derived from a detail of a Renaissance composition, is interpreted with such a spirited staccato sequence of crisp graphic signs in playful combinations that at first sight these variations might appear gratuitous. The puzzle quickly takes form before one's eyes, and these independent landmarks of the form (cedillas, hook lines, zigzags, S curves) fall into a coherent graphic configuration without a single superfluous accent. This festive linear shorthand is Manet's signature, and appears in its purest form in numerous drawings (see figs. 121, 144, 152, 153, 174).

During his stay in Florence Manet made a series of sketches of individual figures and groups from the relief panels of Luca della Robbia's *Cantoria* (figs. 37 and 77–85). The subject of the carefree young boy appears frequently in Manet's oeuvre, and therefore

it is easy to understand his attraction to Luca's masterpiece. The *Cantoria* panels depict boys and girls performing music and responding to it in a variety of ways. Manet selects the more uninhibited of Luca's figures, those who express the wild abandon of the dance; this is his choice in four of the six drawings. Even the lute player (*Enfant jouant du luth*, fig. 37) does not have the wistful and absorbed expression of its model but seems rather mischievous. In this same spirit, Manet's graphic transposition of the sculptural forms loosens the draperies from the bodies and appears to free the bodies from their forced confinement in the crowded panels of the *Cantoria*. The drawings present the figures in a deeper perspective, with light and air about them, and with no restricting ground line. The volumes of the forms are expressed with a simplified modeling. The transitions between planes in light and in shadow are indicated by abrupt linear contours which are as clearly patterned as the silhouette lines of general profiles. On the other hand, the children drawn by Manet lack the fluid and eurythmic formal character and the emotional nuances of their prototypes. They are relatively awkward of body and their actions appear to be more instantaneous and individualized. In only one drawing (fig. 84) does Manet represent more than one figure.

Of the three included in the drawing, two are from one panel ("Choro") of the *Cantoria*, and the third, on the left, from another ("Cymbalis jubilationis"). It is therefore a composite image rather than one which has been directly lifted from a single composition. This confirms the impression, which drawings of single figures from the same source convey, that Manet was at all times conscious of making his pictorial or

FIGURE 36 (*Cat. No. 119*).

51

FIGURE 37 (*Cat. No. 20*).

FIGURE 38 (*see Cat. No. 20*).

sculptural models his own by casting them into new molds—the drawing copies; and that ready-made compositional arrangements were not his concern.

During these early years Manet employed the media of ink wash and watercolors for more elaborate copies of originals in the Louvre. *Les Petits cavaliers* and *L'Infante* (fig. 199 and Cat. No. 142) are essentially paintings based on originals by Velasquez and the School of Velasquez. *Le Cerf attaqué par des chiens* (fig. 192) is traceable to

the background scene of Titian's *Jupiter and Antiope*, a painting which Manet also copied in its entirety. In this watercolor the decorative and remote animal group of Titian's painting is singled out, brought to the foreground, and made violently active. The dramatic effects of the directional brush strokes against the white field of the paper are exploited to this end, and pictorial nuances are deliberately excluded. The reduction of the image to a limited vocabulary of strokes and broad spottings of wash is analogous to the process of graphic simplification which we have observed in the pencil-drawing copies. In both, the effect of instantaneity results.

Manet did not produce drawing copies after 1858, which is the *terminus ad quem* of his second European tour. Other drawings of the period consist primarily of studies from the model made in and out of Couture's studio.

Pierrot ivre (fig. 39) is believed to represent one of Manet's shipmates, merrymaking, on the merchant ship *Le Havre et Guadeloupe*.[4] Indeed, some aspects of this watercolor and pen drawing may be attributable to the boldness and experimentalism of an early style. The redundant spottings with wash, and the variety of graphic devices, in both pen and brush technique, are signs of early hesitancy and conscious seeking after multiple effects. However, this early drawing already possesses stylistic traits which are consistently found in mature works as well, namely, the caricatural form, the insistent contours revealing the silhouette of the entire figure and isolating it on the page, and the abrupt juxtaposition within this expressive contour of contrasting elements or configurations such as the clownish hat, the hanging sleeve, and the large buttons.

The teachings of Couture were a positive factor in Manet's early career and they may be detected in drawings of this period such as the two versions of *Modèle habillé debout* (figs. 186, 187) and *Portrait de femme assise* (fig. 40). Couture repeatedly emphasized to his students the need for concentration or massing of the greatest light and shadow,

FIGURE 39 *(Cat. No. 1)*.

FIGURE 40 *(Cat. No. 138)*.

---

[4] A. Tabarant, *Manet et ses oeuvres*, p. 22; E. Moreau-Nélaton, *Manet raconté par lui-même* (Paris: Laurens, 1926), I, 14.

53

the definition of the form by its contour, and boldness of execution. He also prescribed charcoal for drawings done as preliminaries to a painting.[5] Couture had in mind a charcoal drawing on a toned canvas which, in a broad manner, would establish contours and shadowed planes. During the painting stage, the reserved light areas would receive the successive color glazes for maximum glow and brilliancy. Manet's two drawings of the model (figs. 186, 187) conform to this general type. The concision and architectonic quality of the figure style also reflect Manet's studies of Renaissance fres-coes. The contours and shadow areas, accented and clearly delineated, reserve the major lighted planes as areas of the paper left intact. These reserved surfaces of paper are the equivalent of the areas of light in a preliminary drawing on canvas which, as prescribed by Couture, would have received transparent color glazes. The indirect influence of the masters of the Renaissance, whom Couture repeatedly offered as models to his students, and whom Manet so assiduously copied, is also prevalent here. It is reflected in the concision and monumentality of the forms.

III. 1859–1863 SPANISH INTERLUDE AND MASTERY OF DRAFTSMANSHIP

The drawings of these four years are extremely varied in form and content. Manet was still open to the solicitations of the art treasures of the museums—primarily the Louvre collections. He also drew inspiration from prints of all periods, and from their more popular forms such as current periodical illustrations.[6] He shared the taste of his Parisian contemporaries for Spanish things—a passing vogue which came to a climax in the summer of 1862, when a Spanish ballet troupe performed in Paris. At that time he made the ballet group and its individual performers the subject of a series of well-known paintings. But no matter how diverse his sources, and whether his subject matter was derived from artistic precedents or drawn from his immediate environment, he demon-strated an overriding concern for modernity. His awareness of contemporary life and his own active share in it color every work by his hand. We observe in them all a unique combination—not yet a complete synthesis—of sound traditional values of composition and of a modern and personal artistic idiom into which the former are transposed.

Some of the earliest drawings of these years owe much to mythological and pastoral subject matter and formal concepts of the past. The figures occupy the foreground plane, and an idyllic landscape background fills the page beyond. The series of paintings entitled *La Nymphe surprise* (fig. 183) and the drawings *La Pêche* (fig. 193) and *La Découverte de Moïse* (fig. 41) cling to this convention.[7] *La Découverte de Moïse* is

---

[5] Thomas Couture, *Entretiens d'atelier* (Paris, 1867), p. 32.

[6] See N.G. Sandblad, *Manet, Three Studies in Artistic Conception* (Lund: The New Society of Letters at Lund, 1954), pp. 17 ff.

[7] *La Découverte de Moïse* (fig. 41), which exists only as a drawing, is the first image in a series dealing with the problem of figures in landscape. The subsequent versions (paintings) are *La Nymphe surprise* of 1861, *Le Déjeuner sur l'herbe* of 1863, and *Baigneuses* of 1874. The concept of the drawing is still related to Venetian precedents; but, in subsequent versions of this general theme, Manet draws more and more directly from nature, thus transforming his subject matter, and to a large degree rejects precedents for compositional devices.

closely related in technique and figure style to the earlier drawing copies, but its execution is less summary. The pen and wash overlay a preliminary pencil sketch. These media reinforce each other. The pen line is descriptive while brush strokes give plastic fullness to the forms, distribute the light over them, and clarify the sequence of planes in depth in alternating dark and light areas. The pyramidal composition focuses on the foreground figure. The opening into a deep, illuminated landscape to the right calls to mind Venetian sixteenth-century models. Manet is striving to attain unity of design by adapting Renaissance devices. The historical subject provides the basic elements of figure and landscape with which to develop a classical composition.

The drawing *La Pêche* (fig. 193) represents a similar search for composition along traditional lines. It is related to the painting *La Pêche* (Jamot, no. 30) of 1860–1861 which repeats the motif of the standing figure in the bark. Stylistically, the drawing is related to the brush drawing *Cerf attaqué par des chiens* (fig. 192). The same dual function of the brush, pictorial and calligraphic, is present in both. Manet strives here, as he does in the corresponding painting *La Pêche*, for baroque illumination and spatial effects by distributing the major value contrasts for maximum unity of composition.

The drawing *Philippe IV* of 1860 (fig. 197), preliminary to an etching, is based on the seventeenth-century copy in the Louvre of the original portrait by Velasquez. Its date marks the outset of Manet's interest in the art of the Spanish master. The drawing is not a mere copy or reproduction, but a concise interpretation of Velasquez's concept of form—one which bears a remarkable affinity to Manet's own artistic vision up to that time. The emphasis Manet places on the

silhouetting contours, the absence of consistent modeling of the masses contained within the encircling outlines are physical qualities found in the works of both artists. Line merely establishes the abstract boundary of a mirror image since it tends to reveal shape and surface rather than volume.

Both Velasquez and Manet thought of form as a means to an end—their primary aim being the realization of an all-inclusive optical effect. Manet's drawing *Philippe IV* is a shortcut to that end.

Related in style and in technique to *Philippe IV* are a few portrait studies: *Auguste Manet* (fig. 196); *M. et Mme. Auguste Manet* (fig. 20); *Profil de femme*

FIGURE 41 *(Cat. No. 144)*.

(fig. 194); *Portrait de Roudier* (fig. 195). But the problem facing Manet in these early portraits was more complex since two different intentions had to be reconciled: first, characterization of the model's individuality of features and expression; and second, the visual unity of form referred to above. Manet's solution is only partially successful in these drawings. His interpretation of personality is somewhat limited by the emphasis given to the image's formal coherence of closed silhouettes, emphatic contours, and broad distribution of lighted and shadowed areas.

Manet's frequent use of pure tracings can be understood in the light of what has been said of the function of line as a device which isolates and crystallizes the data of optical impressions. *L'Enfant à l'épée* (fig. 7) is a tracing which enabled Manet to transfer the developed image of a painting to the etching plate. In spite of the mechanical process and abstraction involved, the tracing preserves the expressive nuances of the painting. The head of the boy, for instance, loses none of its juvenile physical traits, its expression of childlike curiosity, and its unself-consciousness. Daumier alone among French nineteenth-century artists could give mere tracings such intrinsic artistic value. However, Daumier sometimes "uses tracings to 'play about' with a composition. . . ."[8] Manet never did. His tracing transfers the formal components of the painting (minus color) practically unchanged. The figure of the boy, once caught in a precise configuration in one medium, is no longer subject to change. The tracing method is therefore best adapted to such faithful transfer and its graphic style

rigidly conforms to that of the original painting.

During these years, in a number of isolated instances, Manet experiments in the graphic medium in a bolder manner which foretells later developments. *L'Enfant au chien* (fig. 206), a quill pen drawing on which a corresponding etching is based, forgoes, for the sake of spontaneity, the more uniform and composed technical execution of such drawings as *Philippe IV* (fig. 197). We readily recognize the zigzags, commas, and other graphic accents which were characteristic of the pencil line in many of the early copies, but now this same vocabulary recreates with greater immediacy visual sensations of light, mass, textures, and movement. The subject is still reminiscent of Spanish genre by Velasquez or Murillo but interpreted with a bolder and freer hand.

The contrast of the "old" and "new" within this period is offered by two drawings related to paintings executed three years apart. The first, *Buveur d'absinthe* (fig. 201) of 1859, still possesses a Spanish picaresque character, but the second, *Musique aux Tuileries* (fig. 22) of 1862, has the local color of Manet's own environment. The technical bravado and the unconventional bohemian subject matter of the painting *Buveur d'absinthe* struck the public as an insult at the time. The watercolor drawing, derived from the painting, retains these qualities, but it is primarily a technical experiment (the genre attributes of the figure are less prominent than in the painting) and it demonstrates Manet's debt to his teacher Couture. In *Musique aux Tuileries* (fig. 22), Manet takes radically new steps stylistically. The drawing is not derived from a com-

---

[8] K. E. Maison, "Further Daumier Studies—I: The Tracings," *Burlington Magazine* (May 1956),

pp. 162–166.

pleted painting but is the basis for one. It is executed in ink wash over a preliminary pencil sketch. The composition no longer takes into account the traditional Renaissance or baroque space. It is based on a juxtaposition of elements: the figures and the trees. There is no overall geometric integration or grouping of the figures as there is to a degree in the subsequent painting, nor are they arranged to stress a common action. Each figure is studied independently, and remains a distinct graphic pattern within the whole. This applies as well to the interpretation of the background of trees and foliage, which is not experienced as "one" with the figures. Compositional unity depends upon the distribution of graphic accents and spots. The tree trunks, frock coats, top hats, and so on, are further integrated by the white field of the paper which weaves all these separate entities into one pattern or texture and conveys a sense of light and air. A small drawing, *Coin du jardin des Tuileries* (fig. 210), which is not a compositional sketch, is equally fresh and direct in its transcription of the outdoor scene and uses similar contrasts of washes against the white paper to evoke the locale and its atmosphere. In these wash drawings Manet is increasingly concerned with the relatively unpremeditated expression of natural aspects of the contemporary scene.

Perhaps the finest group of drawings ever produced by Manet dates from the years 1862 and 1863. *Lola de Valence* (figs. 214 and 216), *La Toilette (1)* (fig. 218), and *Olympia* (fig. 228) are classic works which hold their own in the company of the best drawings of Delacroix, Ingres, and Degas.

The first mentioned, *Lola de Valence* (fig. 214), was derived from the Louvre painting by that title (fig. 215) and an etching was based on it in turn.

The model is one of the ballerinas of the Spanish troupe which performed in the Paris Hippodrome in August 1862. The painting shows the ballerina standing backstage with a background of props. The drawing reproduces the pose of the figure and her costume with fidelity. The background, a later addition to the painting which gives it a more precise local color, is not found in the drawing. The calligraphic economy of the drawing is most effective against the plain white page. This technical transposition of the painting's image shows that Manet did not intend a replica of his own work but a variant of it.

Technically, the drawing is a combination of pencil, pen, ink wash, watercolor, and gouache, but there is no stress on color per se. Rather, Manet has interpreted the image in an emphatically graphic idiom. Visible in many parts of the drawing is the preliminary pencil line over which the artist applied a black ink wash indicating the color of the hair mass, the accents of major folds in the skirt, and the shadow cast on the ground. Watercolor touches of blue, green, and pink were then very sparingly added to the shawl, the lips, the jewelry, the pattern of the skirt. Finally pink and white gouache accents were brushed in, bringing the subdued color to a climax in the upper part of the figure. In spite of the variety of media, each performs a distinct function without redundancy, and the total effect is of an open, uncluttered image. Individual strokes of the pencil, pen, or brush are consistent with transparency and glitter of the overall pattern. The impress of the particular tool is everywhere in evidence. The assurance of the artist's hand reveals the clarity of his concept of a form envisioned in its totality.

This work represents a classical climax among Manet's early drawings. Subsequent

57

drawings reach greater simplicity, and forgo some of the baroque richness of the *Lola*; but its mastery is never surpassed, if by "mastery" we understand a complete and unhesitant response of the artist's hand to a personal vision or concept.

Around this drawing can be grouped, on a stylistic basis, a number of other water-color drawings with Spanish subject matter. They are *Lola de Valence* (the version belonging to the Harvard University collection) (fig. 216); *Le Bailarin* (fig. 213); *Le Ballet espagnol* (Cat. No. 176); *Complainte moresque* (Cat. No. 169); *Victorine Meurend en costume d'espada* (fig. 8). In the last drawing Manet gives an equal place to graphic and purely pictorial values, and therefore the form is more dependent on the corresponding painting than is the case in *Lola*. The second version of *Lola de Valence* (fig. 216) is based on the Louvre drawing rather than on the painting. Every idiosyncrasy of line in this variant corresponds to one found in the earlier drawing (fig. 214). In spite of this close dependence, the second drawing introduces new formal and expressive elements. While we may notice in it some loss of strength and structural solidity in comparison to the Louvre version, it appears gayer in spirit and paradoxically more spontaneous in execution. This change may be the result of the greater selectivity of graphic means and of the more detached interpretation of the subject which are possible in a second transcription of an original model. These differences might be tentatively summed up by saying that if the Louvre drawing is the baroque version, the Harvard drawing is its rococo paraphrase.

Another outstanding drawing is *La Toilette (1)* of 1862 (fig. 218). Manet derived an etching from it (Guérin, no. 26), but there exists no corresponding painting.

FIGURE 42 *(Cat. No. 164)*.

However, the theme of the seated nude bather with an attendant figure standing in the background attracted Manet at this time. It is interpreted in a more classical vein in a painting sketch, *La Nymphe surprise* (Nationalgalleriet, Oslo), *ca.* 1860 (Jamot, no. 54). Manet could have drawn inspiration from many Renaissance and baroque precedents in which this motif appears. A painting by Tintoretto in the Louvre, *Suzanne au bain* (Inventory no. 1464) may be mentioned as a prominent example among other likely sources. As late as 1874 Manet reinterprets this basic compositional theme in the painting *Baigneuses* (Jamot, no. 264) and in the corresponding watercolor drawing by that title (Cat. No. 430).

Also stylistically, the drawing *La Toilette (1)* (fig. 218) is indebted to tradition—principally to the drawings of Ingres. Both Manet and Ingres placed great emphasis on clearly delineated contours whose expressive power stems from a logical form of abstraction. In the drawings of both artists the linear arabesque imparts a certain volume to the forms: smooth and relief-like in Ingres; more subordinated to pictorial effects, flexible and plastic in Manet. Both Ingres and Manet give careful consideration to the arabesque or two-dimensional coherence of the drawing.

However, Ingres refines and transforms optical data into abstract and decorative linear patterns, and does so by undertaking many successive studies, each asserting more independence from the original model, whereas Manet's abstraction of the human form intensifies his initial optical impression of the model. The definitive character of the contours and the deliberate omission of interior lines—as in the fingerless right hand of the figure (fig. 218), or the lower hem of the drapery—suggest that Manet may have been working from a tracing of a previous study, as was his common practice, strengthening its inherent pattern. Manet made other drawings on the theme of *La Toilette* (figs. 3, 43, 44, 218), but each one is derived from a different set of initial impressions of the model.

La Toilette (1) has still much in common with the style of earlier drawings such as *La Sainte Famille*, after Andrea del Sarto (fig. 110), and the *Portrait of Roudier* (fig. 195). The stress on heavy contours, the massing of shadows in dramatic contrasts and as form-defining devices still prevail. But the artist's power of synthesis has increased, and his technique is more flexible, adapting itself to a greater variety of experiences. Three

other drawings (figs. 3, 43, 44) are closely related in content and style to *La Toilette (1)*, but were not carried out in etching form. The first is the ink wash drawing *Baigneuse* (fig. 3) of which there exists a replica (not by Manet's hand) in the Boymans Museum. It is executed in a combination of pen-and-ink and ink wash techniques over a summary preliminary drawing in crayon, parts of which are still visible on the arm and breasts of the figure. Accented contours and flat wash areas of shadow create a vigorous and dramatic illumination. The ink washes reduce the head to a dark silhouetted shape and merge the shadowed planes of the right side of the body into one mass. These frank coloristic shapes contrast with the bright, blank areas of paper. The brusqueness of these transitions of light and the boldness of the contrasts of the line with

FIGURE 43 *(Cat. No. 184)*.

59

FIGURE 44 *(Cat. No. 186)*.

tonal areas appear in many drawings of these years such as *L'Enfant au chien* (fig. 206) and *Musique aux Tuileries* (fig. 22). In this original way, Manet adapts artistic devices favored by artists of the baroque period.

The drawing *La Toilette (2)* (fig. 44), in the Guérin collection, is the most Ingresque of the seated nude figures in this series. The contours are inflected in such a way that throughout the image one is conscious of the movement of the linear arabesque as such, and, simultaneously, of its descriptive function (defining the relief of the forms). But, whereas in many drawings by Ingres this subtle balance of representation and abstraction appears as an end in itself and is the primary source of aesthetic pleasure, in this drawing by Manet, both of these functions of the form—descriptive and ornamental—are subordinate and wedded to the expression of a dominant visual sensation. This sensation is manifested in a graphic pattern which is all-embracing—the whole, and not the individual parts of the figure, is evoked —and is not subject to detailed analysis. Thus, when we describe such a drawing, we are tempted to refer to the major silhouette of the figure and to its spotty illumination. In contrast, the drawing of a figure by Ingres invites the comparison of profiled forms and their relative flatness with the relief projection of others within the same figure. So, the pleasure which a drawing by Ingres can give us depends upon our gradual recognition of its complementary aspects. Our reaction to a Manet drawing is more

dramatic, since the image tends to provoke a sudden shock of immediate and total recognition.

One of the most frequently illustrated drawings in Manet monographs is a sanguine drawing in the Louvre—*Olympia* (fig. 225). The model was Victorine Meurend, studied in a pose closely resembling that of the model in the painting *Olympia*. The primary pictorial source of the painting's composition is generally acknowledged to be Titian's *Venus of Urbino*, in the Uffizi. But a number of related drawings, produced up to this time, show Manet's awareness of other well-known precedents on the theme of the reclining nude figure in an interior.

Jeanne Duval (fig. 223), *Jeune femme étendue en costume espagnol* (fig. 209), *Femme étendue* (fig. 45), and *Femme nue et chat noir* (Cat. No. 191), the first two of which are watercolor drawing versions of corresponding paintings, appear to have been inspired by Goya's *Majas* (nude and clothed). A frank erotic note and an attempt to stress the *femme fatale* element in the interpretation of the nude or clothed model remind us of Goya, and also of Baudelaire.[9] A fluid brush technique accents the sensuous contours of the bodies whose pallor is deliberately contrasted to the darker surrounding tones. "Correspondences" have justly been pointed out between Manet's *Olympia* and some of Baudelaire's poems.[10] However, these affinities of spirit and artistic outlook between painter and poet can easily be exaggerated. Far more than the *Olympia*,

---

[9] G. H. Hamilton, *Manet and His Critics* (New Haven: Yale University Press, 1954), p. 62, n. 23, gives evidence that Baudelaire showed interest in Goya's prints as early as 1859. This date, as far as we know, is that of Manet's acquaintance with the poet whose portrait appears in *La Musique aux Tuileries* of 1862. One of the drawings

listed in this group, in which we detect Goya's influence, represents Jeanne Duval, Baudelaire's mistress; this drawing corresponds to a painting of 1862. It appears likely therefore that Baudelaire was instrumental in encouraging Manet's study of Goya's oeuvre as early as 1862.

[10] G. H. Hamilton, *Manet and His Critics*, p. 80.

FIGURE 45 (*Cat. No. 189*).

the wash drawings call to mind the morbid and exotic beauty of Baudelaire's images, and yet even they cannot give the equivalent of the poet's fatalism. They may have been produced under the spell of Baudelaire's verses and of Goya's images which appealed to the poet. Manet's indulgence in this vein of inspiration was short-lived, however, and did not have profound effects. Renaissance and baroque models still loomed large in his artistic horizon in these years, and the lesson of Goya did not radically affect his artistic concepts until his trip to Spain in 1865. *Olympia* then, compared to the would-be *femmes damnées* of the wash drawings, is Manet's own creature, not dreamed of but observed. She shocked Manet's contemporaries and fascinates the modern observer by her uncompromising truth to life. The drawing (fig. 225) is serene. The purity of

its lines evokes the boyish but feminine body of Victorine Meurend. Its intrinsic artistic worth resides in its illuminating power.

An isolated drawing, *Odalisque* (fig. 222), from which Manet composed an etching (Guérin, no. 64), reflects a different tradition which had prominent nineteenth-century exponents. Its Oriental theme of the languorous harem beauty lives in works of Ingres, Delacroix, Renoir, and Matisse. Manet paid his homage to it in this watercolor drawing. The technique reminds us of that of *Lola de Valence* (fig. 214). On a lead pencil drawing which is still visible in places, heavy contour lines are brushed in black wash. The hair mass, the shadow of the body, the stripes on the couch and the background area establish the principal tonal contrasts. Touches of gouache—white, pink, and yellow—are used sparingly. They add

62

warmth and depth to the image. So does the brownish field of the paper which acts as a fourth color, primarily in the flesh areas.

The date of the watercolor can be tentatively set as 1862 on the basis of its exotic subject matter and the classical poise of its style. The broad and reposeful contour lines show affinities with the silhouettes of *La Toilette (1)* (fig. 218). In both drawings the dark background is in vigorous contrast to the entire figure, which owes its *éclat* and plasticity to this device. The Oriental costume and attributes of the *Odalisque* figure relate this composition to the odalisques of Delacroix and Ingres; but the economy of the technique and the abstract vigor of the forms give it a modern accent. The *Olympia* drawing and the corresponding painting in the Louvre, which we believe the *Odalisque* precedes, relinquish all romantic associations.

IV. 1864–1868 THE LURE OF ACTUALITY

We know of relatively few drawings produced by Manet during these four years. Those few reveal a great variety of subject matter and of technical characteristics. Under these circumstances it may seem arbitrary to present them under a special heading and thus to distinguish them from the drawings of the early 1860's. However, certain stylistic innovations and novel orientations in the choice of subject matter do prevail, which had appeared only sporadically in Manet's earlier production. A general pattern emerges. A parallel trend is seen in the paintings of these same years, and a passing reference to them will help us define its general outlines.

Manet's interest shifts more exclusively to the spectacles of the contemporary scene. He takes an obvious delight in them and assimilates them in his art. He frequents the outdoors, preferably localities in which crowds habitually gather—the racetrack, or the seashore resorts of Boulogne, Arcachon, and Berck. Many paintings belong to the traditional genres—portraits, still lifes, historical compositions (*L'Exécution de Maximilien*, Jamot, no. 141), or compositions of figures and objects prearranged in the artist's studio (*Le Déjeuner*, Jamot, no. 149). But within the limitations of these genres, Manet observes the familiar and natural aspects of his figures and their setting. He continues to favor a picturesque dressing up of his models by juxtaposing disparate and colorful objects (*Portrait de Zola*, Jamot, no. 146; *Le Déjeuner*, Jamot, no. 149), but only in so far as the picturesque profusion of the forms and colors do not impair the general impression of a casual scene. Studio paraphernalia gradually disappear from his compositions.

Manet continues to consult the masters—Spanish painters in particular. He retains an interest in figure types and compositions derived from well-known paintings by Zurbaran (*Moine en prière*; Jamot, no. 117), by Velasquez (*Philosophe*; Jamot, no. 111), and by Goya (*Le Balcon*; Jamot, no. 150), but reinterprets them freely. When the subject itself is Spanish (*Combat de taureaux*; Jamot, no. 121), it is Spanish actuality, rather than Spanish lore, that is stressed.

Another symptom of Manet's new orientation is his growing understanding of the Japanese mode of vision. The artist pays homage to Japanese prints by reproducing

FIGURE 46 *(Cat. No. 199)*.

one in the background of his *Portrait de Zola* (Jamot, no. 146). But the portrait as a composition, the rigid physical qualities of its forms, and the luminous thrust of its colors are related also, on a deeper level, to Japanese aesthetics.

A refreshing contact with the contempo-

rary scene, a deepening understanding of Spanish models, and an affinity with the Japanese artistic concepts are all symptoms of Manet's absorption with the technical problem of transcription of visual experience. The drawings give their own testimony of this major concern.

Le Christ aux anges (fig. 231) and *Le Christ insulté* (fig. 46) are drawings related to religious paintings of 1864 and 1865. These large compositions intended for the salons are Manet's farewell to the past. The artist's ambition still seems to be to rival the masters of the Renaissance by his choice of a noble humanistic theme, treated in monumental scale. There are interesting points of resemblance between *Le Christ insulté* (fig. 46)[11] and the earlier drawing *La Toilette (2)* (fig. 44). In both works the central figure, studied directly from the model, stands out, while the secondary ones are thrown in semidarkness and are more sketchily indicated. The technique of pen and brush in *Le Christ insulté* recalls the *Composition vénitienne* (fig. 191) and the *Baigneuse* of 1862 (fig. 3). A nervous line accentuates the straining movement of the principal figure.

The drawings related to paintings of outdoor scenes, the race track in particular, break new ground stylistically. A watercolor and gouache replica of the painting *Les Courses à Longchamp*[12] is a composite work based on a number of sketches made on the scene. The most interesting among these direct studies is *Chevaux en course* (fig. 1), which is also integrated in the well-known

---

[11] See A. de Leiris, "Manet's *Christ Scourged* and the Problem of His Religious Painting," *The Art Bulletin*, XLI (June 1959), 198, for a study of the sources of this painting.

[12] This painting, sometimes erroneously re-

ferred to as *Les Courses au Bois de Boulogne*, was cut in three sections by Manet after completion. Two of these sections are extant. (See Jean Collins Harris, "Manet's Racetrack Paintings," *The Art Bulletin*, XLVIII [March 1966], 78–82.)

lithograph *Les Courses* (fig. 237). The lead pencil drawing (fig. 1), executed with a thin line of uniform breadth and intensity throughout, is tinted with watercolor. Each of the four jockeys stands out in a distinct hue—brown, violet, pink, and mauve-blue respectively. The character of the lines suggests that the drawing was based on a tracing of an original sketch, more freely and directly drawn. This is pure speculation, but our earlier observations on Manet's use of tracings leads us to this tentative conclusion. Manet retains in the drawing those elements which convey the action of the entire group and avoids lingering on descriptive passages. The dominant expressive means is a starlike pattern, with no central focus. The viewer cannot apprehend it as a sum of parts but as an integral shape articulated from without by its outer delineating silhouette. Hatchings are introduced within the all-encompassing contour line, but they bridge the entire gap of the blank area within, with little regard for distinctions of individual rider or horse. The drawing gives a telescopic view of the group caught in full motion. In some respects it prefigures the results of speed photography, which was to appear in the 1880's following the invention of sufficiently sensitive films. But unlike the speed photograph which records every visible detail, with the resultant effect of *arrested* time, Manet's drawing condenses visual data to such a degree that the idea of *continuity* of motion in time and space is manifest in the explosive linear pattern of the racing horses.

Another aspect of the races that appealed to Manet was the variegated crowds of strollers and spectators (fig. 235). He juxtaposes the two most striking spectacles of the racetrack, the horses in motion and the colorful group of idlers and carriages on the

sidelines, in the large watercolor version (fig. 233). This composition is repeated, but reversed, in the lithograph.

Aux Courses (fig. 235) is one of a number of initial sketches (e.g., fig. 47) from which the larger composites (watercolor and lithograph) were derived. The accentuation of pure line throughout imposes a specific viewing distance between the observer and the spectacle since all the less optically striking details are left out. In this drawing the perspective is no longer the close-up view, but one experienced at a comfortable distance. These two distinct perspectives are juxtaposed in the lithograph.

Two conclusions may be drawn from our analysis of a few key works of the racetrack

FIGURE 47 *(Cat. No. 211)*.

series. Even the smallest and sketchiest drawing represents a process of synthesis and organization and therefore is an end in itself. Manet takes care to preserve its form in the composite images derived from it. This indicates a trend away from the monumental type of drawing which he had produced up to this time. We can also detect an impressionistic orientation in the strict reliance of the sketch on an unpremeditated visual impression. The Impressionists, ten years hence, will be concerned with the

65

ephemeral aspects of atmosphere which affect one's optical perception of a subject. Manet, however, records the characteristic and the typical in the subject itself.

In the same year, 1864, Manet produced the watercolor *La Sortie du port de Boulogne* (fig. 48). A version of the subject in oils is listed by Jamot (no. 92). A bulbous steamer pouring smoke from its stack creates a wake on the calm expanse of sea. A small sailboat contrasts, in its elegant form and untamed swiftness, with its domesticated but bad-mannered cousin, the steamer. Manet presents this visual antithesis in a subtly humorous way. This interest in objects as such and in the humorous, semi-caricatural interpretations they lend themselves to is foreign to a purely impressionistic point of view. Manet also gives precise shape to the relatively formless phenomena of light, air, and smoke, and evokes the variety of sights, noises, and movements of the port scene.

The watercolor is applied directly without the support of a sketch. A few pencil lines were then added to the silhouette of the steamer for greater precision. The color is delicately descriptive and gives a sense of the liquid element and airy spaces: a blue-green for the sea, a light blue for the sky with areas of buff paper showing through and giving a warm tone to the entire page.

In 1865, following these ventures in outdoor sketching and a gradual emancipation from Renaissance models and museum compositions, Manet went to Spain. The art of

Velasquez and Goya made a deep impression upon him. Velasquez's paintings appeared to him to have solved problems similar to his own, such as the rendering of direct optical data by the most economical means.[13] He admired the ease with which Velasquez could give, with a minimum of modeling, the illusion of ambient air and daylight in full-length figure compositions without losing the clarity and vitality of the silhouettes. Goya's art impressed him also, but he had reservations: "Et Goya! le plus curieux après le maître qu'il a trop

FIGURE 48 (*Cat. No. 202*).

imité. . . ."[14] In this letter, written in Madrid and addressed to Fantin-Latour shortly after his first major encounter with Goya's works,

---

[13] From the beginning of his career Manet had sought technical help, and not merely subject matter, from his Spanish sources. He had been particularly impressed by the simplicity of the forms in these models. While copying *Les Petits cavaliers* (Jamot, no. 7, fig. 18), around 1855, he is reported to have commented, "Ah, ça c'est net! . . . Voilà qui dégoute des ragoûts et des jus . . ."

(Antonin Proust, *Edouard Manet, souvenirs*, A. Barthélemy, ed. [Paris: H. Laurens, 1913]), a saying which qualifies Manet's attraction to Spanish models as something more than the sharing of the then reigning vogue for Spanish subjects.

[14] Manet quoted in *Manet raconté par lui-même et par ses amis*, ed. Pierre Cailler (Geneva, 1945), p. 43.

66

Manet was reserving judgment until he had had other opportunities to view Goya's paintings.[15] But the impact of Goya on Manet was to be a lasting one. Here was an art at once bold in execution and subtle in content as was his own. Here was Spain, true Spain, which confirmed both his renunciation of the Spain he had interpreted in his Paris studio and his determination to choose his subject matter in his own environment. Here was defiant handling of the brush and a predilection for few major contrasts as a basis for composition—a predilection which was already Manet's own. Therefore, the examples of Velasquez and of Goya helped him to develop his style along the course which it had already set for itself. The independent development of Manet's style manifests itself best in works which are inspired by Spanish compositions or have Spanish subjects. For example, there is little of Velasquez's effect of atmospheric depth in *Le Fifre* (Jamot, no. 126) and none of Goya's dramatic chiaroscuro and tension in *Combat de taureaux* (Jamot, no. 121) or in *L'Exécution de Maximilien* (Jamot, no. 141).

The drawings identifiable as works brought back from Spain are few. Duret recalls the times when he and Manet went together to the bullfights in Madrid, and speaks of sketches made on the spot and subsequently used by Manet in his painting versions of the bullfight upon his return.[16] The watercolor sketch of a bullfight scene (Cat. No. 220), which is illustrated in the monograph by Kurt Martin,[17] is undoubtedly one of the Spanish sketches. The violent action is interpreted in a vigorous technique, but the fervor is controlled by an objective observation of local color and by the natural quality of light on the scene. The watercolor medium overlays a free pencil sketch which offers an opportunity for the concentration and conciseness of the final brush work.

Memories of Goya's graphic works live on in two sepia ink drawings to be dated about 1865, *Le Montreur d'ours* (fig. 246) and *Les Saltimbanques* (fig. 12). The ink wash does not merely accentuate the lines of the preliminary pencil sketch, but places emphasis on each of the relatively stumpy figures in turn, and thus deliberately disrupts the continuity of action and spatial milieu. But when compared to Goya's dramatic groupings of figures by means of major contrasts of black, white, or grey, Manet's oppositions of individual figures appear tame and dispassionate. The street scenes are observed objectively by one who is alert to their humorous aspects as spectacles rather than events.

Drawings of circus or street performers by Daumier also bear a superficial resemblance to Manet's depictions of similar subjects and to *Les Saltimbanques* (fig. 12) in particular. Unlike Daumier's performers, Manet's arc expressive puppets whose poses have been arrested. There is little hint of continuity in the gestures and general movement of the figures, nor any suggestion of what came before or what is to follow the frozen moment of action represented.

---

[15] "Ce que j'ai vu de lui jusqu'ici ne m'a pas plu énormément. Je dois en voir ces jours-ci, une magnifique collection chez le duc d'Ossuna." Quoted from *Manet raconté par lui-même et par ses amis*, p. 44.

[16] Théodore Duret, *Histoire d'Edouard Manet et de son oeuvre* (Paris: Fasquelle, 1906), p. 62.

[17] *Edouard Manet, Aquarelle und Pastelle* (Basel: Phoebus, 1958), fig. 8.

Stylistically, the wash drawing *Edgar Allan Poe* (fig. 18) can be dated around 1865, and is based on a photograph.[18] Manet chooses to transcribe some of the accidental effects of light and cast shadow which the photograph mechanically records. The irregularities of the modeling of the face exist also in the original photographic print. This propensity of the camera to fix accidental optical effects has its counterpart in Manet's habits of observation. His drawings often reveal the unexpected selection of unforeseen and odd shadow patterns for the sake of characterization. However, Manet does not rely only on the keenness of his eye. The portrait of Edgar Allan Poe confirms this. Unlike the photograph from which it was derived, the wash drawing singles out outstanding features such as the untamed mass of hair, the triangular shape of the head, the uncommonly high forehead, and the small intent eyes. Details of costume are also prominent. The brush technique is unusually timid if compared to that of *Les Saltimbanques*. This limitation was probably accepted by Manet as the price of faithful resemblance to the model.

The cat appears frequently as a motif in Manet's works. In 1868 it is the exclusive subject of a lithograph and poster, *Le Rendez-vous des chats* (fig. 49), and of an etching (Guérin, no. 52). The poster form and its technique of color lithography lend themselves to a stylized interpretation of the subject and Manet's originality in this mode is sustained by the example of Japanese prints. By emphasizing a closed contour of flowing and flat shapes, he deliberately adapts Oriental calligraphic devices to his own ends. The poster, and the corresponding watercolor

(fig. 50), owe their humorous content to this frank stylization. The curvilinear but tense silhouettes of the animals prefigure the tendrils of art-nouveau motifs and the frozen floral arabesques with which a Lautrec will interpret the stem of a bass fiddle or the indented shape of a gloved hand in his own posters of the early 1890's. But the synthetic character of Manet's composition and of the individual shapes throughout does not represent a caricatural transposition of the subject. It suggests, rather, Manet's amused response to the accidental confron-

FIGURE 49 *(see Cat. No. 227).*

---

[18] See note 31, chap. II.

68

FIGURE 50 *(Cat. No. 227)*.

tation of oddly contrasting objects and forms in a familiar situation. These elements of close observation and witty interpretation of common sights are found in other drawings of the period, such as *Chat sous une chaise* (fig. 243). The artist exploits the juxtaposition of the spindly, angular frame of the chair with the shape of the lethargic cat under it. By restricting his design to these two contrasting elements he gives to each its maximum dramatic value.

A group of drawings with a genre flavor can be assigned to this period (late 1860's) on the basis of their stylistic affinity with the examples above. Among them are *Femme cousant* (fig. 249), with its verso *Nurse et enfant sur un banc* (fig. 248). The drawings of these years gain in flexibility and vitality what they lack of the earlier monumentality. The latter quality survives in the paintings which now require fewer or no preparatory drawings. The drawings produced independently acquire a quickened life pulse in the lighter vein which is now theirs.

69

V. 1869–1874 THE IMPRESSIONIST EXPERIENCE

Manet's travels away from Paris are now more frequent. His art benefits from these changes of scenery which encourage original ventures. The seashore has a special attraction for him dating back perhaps to his early experiences in the merchant marine. We find him in Boulogne in 1869 and in Berck in 1873. In 1870–1871 his activity as a painter was interrupted by the war and by his participation in the defense of Paris. Following the armistice of February 1871, he rejoined his family in Oloron-Sainte-Marie near Arcachon where he was also compelled to break with his normal studio habits and procedures. After a brief stay in Bordeaux and Arcachon he returned to Paris in the midst of the insurrection which was to last until May of that year.

In Arcachon Manet painted port scenes, seascapes, landscapes, and interiors, which are faithful but summary records of visual impressions. The landscapes done during his trip to Holland in 1873 show his exhilarated response to the wide Dutch skies and insistent horizons, and also to the brilliant technique of Franz Hals. Finally, he spent many a day in 1874 on the banks of the Seine, at Gennevilliers, or in nearby Argenteuil, observing and painting gaily attired city-dwellers whose colorful silhouettes he set against shimmering waters and bright hazy skies. Such were the external circumstances which played a prominent role in the evolution of a personal form of Impressionism.

The drawing *Au Café* (fig. 250) of 1869 interprets a complex scene in an informal vein, and the open work of the quill pen lines conveys Manet's heightened interest in problems of natural illumination in spite of the fact that the light sources are arbitrarily distributed. This apparent departure from a naturalistic point of view (the shadow in the back of the left foreground figure would seem to contradict the illumination of the faces of the three men seated at the opposite side of the table) follows a logical system of composition based on contrasts and the selection of a few color accents. The novelty is the function given to these devices. They contribute to an illusion of animated conversation among the figures and bring figures and setting together in a luminous milieu.

The pencil sketches preparatory to the painting *Sur la Plage de Boulogne* of 1869 (figs. 251 through 259) record visual data with equal verve and informality. These thumbnail drawings are swiftly executed in a thin pencil line, with a minimum of descriptive detail, but with a pointed emphasis on the descriptive function of summary contours which distinguish young and old, male and female, in a variety of groupings, poses and actions. Manet introduces most of them in the composite painting of the beach, but retains the identity and integrity of each by reproducing it essentially unaltered on the canvas (fig. 254),[19] resulting in relative looseness of the painting's composition. This loss is balanced by the sharper and more uniform grasp of visual impres-

---

[19] A fuller analysis of the Boulogne drawings and the related seascape can be found in the article by A. de Leiris, "Manet: *Sur la Plage de Boulogne*," *Gazette des Beaux-Arts* LVII (January 1961).

sions in every motif issuing directly from an original sketch.[20]

From the war year of 1870 on, we can detect in Manet's drawings an even bolder interpretation of visual data. *Au Paradis* (fig. 283) is an example. Instead of singling out individual figures within the group, Manet concerns himself with the all-inclusive aspect of a scene suggesting his own passing glance at it. The bare field of the paper, substituted for any definition of locale or background, does produce an effect of spatial depth about the individual figure and the entire group. The focus is more exclusively on one plane than before, and this plane is brought closer to the foreground. The lines encompass the combined profiles of a number of distinct parts of one or more objects or figures, and they are reinforced by the contrast of bold hatchings which relate the interior masses to their graphic contours.

A parallel trend toward a bolder solution to composition is to be traced in paintings of the early 1870's. Manet's new approach consists of a reduction of planes with a stress on the foreground plane which is more freely organized two-dimensionally on a triangular or rectilinear grid. The background provides a unified field and an atmospheric foil for large overlapping foreground forms which are the principal elements of the composition. This trend is first evident in half-length portraits where the problem of composition is a simpler one.[21]

The examples we have just considered—drawings and paintings related stylistically—show a trend, increasingly obvious from 1870 on, toward independence of drawings from paintings. The reason seems clear. The use of preparatory sketches was a necessity as long as Manet thought of sketches as isolated elements and of his paintings as composite juxtapositions of these elements (*Sur la Plage de Boulogne*). But as soon as this distinction could no longer be made and Manet's approach to the subject became equally final and all-inclusive in both sketch and painting, the artist developed his paintings directly. The independent sketch had a similar finality and in most cases was not incorporated in a painting.

In the light of this trend leading to the complete independence of the sketch as a final form and image, a few drawings such as *La Barricade* (fig. 287) and *Intérieur à Arcachon* (fig. 51) suggest a transitional stage. Both combine drawing with watercolor. In *Intérieur à Arcachon*, lines and washes are closely interrelated, and the result is a diffused atmospheric effect; in *La Barricade*, ink wash predominates (with minor accents of red on the caps and the breeches of the soldiers). It emphasizes nuances and contrasts of value rather than color, creating a convincing effect of outdoor light. Each is faithfully transcribed in a different medium: oils and lithography respectively. *La Barricade* still constitutes a composite of independently defined elements: the city architecture, the Goyesque haggard faces of the victims, and the firing

---

[20] During these years (1869–1874) Manet produced a number of brief outdoor sketches similar to Boulogne sketches in style and function. Manet utilized them as documents for such paintings as *Départ du bateau de Folkestone*, *La Jetée de Boulogne*, *Clair de lune sur le port de Boulogne*, and *Partie de croquet à Boulogne* (Jamot, nos. 159, 161, 162, 197).

[21] Any of the portraits of 1872 could serve as examples of this type of composition: *La Femme à l'ombrelle* (Jamot, no. 201). In 1873 the same novel principles of composition are applied to outdoor scenes with more than one figure: *Sur la Plage* (Jamot, no. 224), and *Le Bateau goudronné* (Jamot, no. 222).

FIGURE 51 *(Cat. No. 379)*.

squad which is derived from the group of soldiers in *L'Exécution de Maximilien* (Jamot, no. 141). However, in the process of juxtaposing these component parts Manet insists on the textural unity of the entire composition. The distribution of light contrasts, the differentiation of receding planes in atmosphere give the drawing its pictorial compactness, and enhance the impression of visual immediacy and dramatic nearness of the action portrayed. But light does not invade and destroy Manet's synthetic contours of objects; it creates a new movement about the contours which indirectly enlivens them.

The drawings of the years 1873 and 1874

mark a climax in the stylistic development, outlined above, which corresponds to experiments in *plein-air* painting. Manet worked at Berck-sur-Mer on the Normandy coast in 1873, and at Argenteuil and nearby Gennevilliers on the Seine in 1874.

The drawings which Manet executed during his sojourn at Berck were both watercolors and lead pencil sketches (Cat. Nos. 390 ff.). The watercolors (fig. 316) are done with an economy of brush strokes, and the shapes of sailboats, contrasting with the broad, uniform expanse of sea and sky, create informal but uniform patterns. The composition is of a vignette type with the sub-

72

FIGURE 52 *(Cat. No. 431)*.

ject centered on the sheet. The white field of the paper evokes a light-filled depth. The pencil sketches show a similar impressionistic quality (figs. 301, 325). The use of summary hatchings which bridge the shapes of figures and objects with their natural environment, and the openness of the forms wherever they are seen in strong light (figs. 323, 325) are symptoms of this orientation.

In portraiture, as in the drawing *Théodore de Banville* (fig. 334), Manet insists on an illusion of transience in the pose and expression of his model, and also on the suggestion of specific effects of natural illumination. However, as this portrait drawing indicates, in one major respect Manet's Impressionism differs from Monet's or Sisley's of the same years. The atmospheric effects, which give a greater textural unity to the page, never compromise the precision of descriptive lines. This might also be said of some of Degas's drawings, but Manet's characterization of his model differs in that it is deliberately limited to what his eye could grasp from a single perspective angle.

The formal structure of a drawing by Degas establishes a tenuous, not to say unstable, equilibrium among parts of a figure —a head, a hand, or even an eye or an ear— which appear to have been observed singly and from individual points of view. Manet chooses to study his model from a comfortable distance so as to embrace the entire silhouette in his field of vision. Thus his preference for full face or profile views. The poet Banville, as he appears in the draw-

ing, is aware of the presence of the painter who confronts him squarely. His half-length figure is stable; it is centered on the rectangle of the sheet, and the moment chosen is an unambiguous pause in his action—writing. The drawing *Le Procès de Bazaine* of 1873 (fig. 332)[22] is a composite drawing, comprising a number of abbreviated silhouettes. The uniform distribution of hatchings is an impressionistic device which gives the illusion of a single embracing glance at the crowded courtroom from an ideal vantage point.

Women acquaintances in fashionable city or country attire are the subject of numerous wash drawings from the mid-1870's onward. They are done in a swift brush technique in ink with occasional use of watercolor (fig. 52). They constitute a distinct genre within the general category of portraiture. The artist emphasizes the formal values of pattern and color and almost entirely disregards character analysis and expression. In *Femme au chapeau à brides* (fig. 52) Manet evokes the breezy outdoors and the bright light by the exclusion of all the features of his model which are not visible either as a dense pattern of color or as an abrupt cast shadow. Nevertheless the spottiness of the image— a technical aspect so often found in clumsy imitations of the master's drawings—never compromises the structural soundness of the form in space. The blank intervals of the paper are as functional in this respect as the positive strokes of the brush which adapt themselves to finest nuances of modeling.

---

[22] A tracing of this drawing (fig. 333), which selects the major silhouettes from it and includes two additional figures to the left, reveals that the drawing was probably composed with a lithograph or an etching in mind. This had already been the case with the drawings related to the subject of a political character: the execution of Maximilien.

VI. 1875–1878 THE EXPANDING BRUSH STROKE

Manet's works of the late 1870's assert anew their independence from the aesthetics of Impressionism to which they owe much technically. The paintings are more vibrant in color, the brush technique is swifter and more fluid, and the directness of the sketch is present even in large canvases such as *L'Artiste* and *Le Linge* (Jamot, nos. 259 and 249).

However, the linear components of Manet's compositions are once more vigorously emphasized. Paintings as different as *Portrait de Mallarmé* and *Le Skating* (Jamot, nos. 265 and 279) are composed of large and assertive foreground shapes occupying nearly the entire breadth and height of the picture plane on which they are deliberately centered.

All the genres and subjects which are in Manet's earlier work are still prevalent in his paintings of this period—the single standing figure, double portraits, the figure in half length, and the still life. But he develops a predilection for typical scenes of city life: the street, the stage, and the café, which we have already encountered in drawings.

Similarly, the drawings of these years reveal both a shift away from purely impressionistic values and a more assertive formal pattern, while their subject matter becomes predominantly urban in character.

The example of Japanese graphic art still plays an important role[23] in this evolution, although it is no longer possible to claim—

as was accurately said of the illustrations for Champfleury's *Chats* of 1869—that these later drawings carry a perceptible "parfum japonais."[24] Other earlier influences, such as Italian and Spanish art, have a lasting effect on Manet's style, but are also more fully assimilated by this time.

Desboutin (fig. 53) and *La Convalescente* (fig. 13), a watercolor and a drawing in red crayon respectively, would appear, on stylistic evidence, to have been done at the outset of this period. The impressionistic effects of illumination enhance the naturalness of pose and expression and create a luminous environment for the figures. Broken and predominently linear accents, produced by short crayon or brush strokes, suggest the play of light and shadow over the forms. The apparent rapidity of the strokes and their crisscrossing patterns produce vibrant surfaces which animate the figures themselves. The instantaneity of the actions portrayed—the suspended gesture of the hand of the sewer (*La Convalescente*) and the momentary pause of the hand grasping the pipe (*Desboutin*)—also contributes to the dominant effect of transience that is one of the more superficial symptoms of Impressionism. These drawings also give hints of the emotional states of the sitters. Desboutin is portrayed at a moment of reflection and questioning, and the model of *La Convalescente* in one of absorption and daydream.[25] The revelation of the mental state

---

[23] For a comprehensive and discerning discussion of Japanese influences on French nineteenth-century art, see Ernst Scheyer, "Far Eastern Art and French Impressionism," *Art Quarterly*, VI, 2 (Spring, 1943).

[24] *Ibid.*, p. 125.

[25] The title *La Convalescente*, which is universally accepted and is that of the corresponding

etching (Guérin, no. 65), does not seem to apply to the subject represented here. While the elderly woman is comfortably seated in a deep armchair or chaise lounge, there is here nothing to suggest that she might be convalescing. The title "Couseuse" (Woman Sewing) would have been more appropriate.

FIGURE 53 *(Cat. No. 450)*.

of his models, no matter how subdued (as in these examples), is a relatively rare occurrence in Manet's work and, as could be expected, is to be found primarily in portraits of close friends or relatives.

The composition of these two works centers the figure freely on the page and deliberately cuts the silhouettes by the frame. Concentrating on a single motif, Manet enlarges it by these devices. As a result, the model appears to stand within close range of the spectator, occupying the entire field of his vision. The series of drawings of Théodore Duret's dog Tama (figs. 347, 348) further concentrates the image on the one object and eliminates any description or suggestion of a physical setting. The vividness of these canine faces and profiles is striking. This quality results not so much from the technical virtuosity of the pencil line but from its discipline throughout and its precise characterization of the subject. The pattern is fluid but economical. The drawings captivate the attention by their heightened response to our expectation. We recognize the external aspect of a Pekinese, but we also sense, simultaneously, the native restlessness of this particular ill-tempered beast with the large staring eyes within a moppy wig.

The illustrations for Mallarmé's *Après-midi d'un faune* (figs. 14, 349)—woodcuts executed directly from Manet's pen drawings on wood—display another mood with equal intensity. The tonality of the lines is light, almost airy, and conveys precisely the spirited rhythm of Mallarmé's verses. The versatility of Manet's draftsmanship is demonstrated by the contrast of the blunt and thrusting strokes of the *Tama* drawings which transcribe the fascinating grotesqueness of the Pekinese mask, with the sophisticated lines of the melodious vignette illustrations of *Après-midi d'un faune*.

The autographic drawings illustrating Mallarmé's translation of Poe's *The Raven* have been included in the catalogue because the lithographic process of reproduction does not alter the quality of the original brush work that makes them essentially wash drawings.

Manet employs the brush and ink technique with increasing frequency in these years. His early use of it, as in *Lola de Valence* (fig. 214), had often introduced pictorial effects of texture and color. In the illustration series for *Le Corbeau—A la Fenêtre* (fig. 343) will serve as an example —Manet restricts himself to three basic values of pure white, black, and an intermediary grey obtained by dry brush technique and some scraping of the stone. The greys introduce effects of atmospheric light but do not intrude as transitional values with a modeling function. The bird against the sky, the hand with fingers extended are dramatized in luminous blacks and white. These visual shocks require an economy of technical means. The summary silhouette of his earlier drawings, in which pictorial and purely linear elements often were juxtaposed, has now merged with the color spot within. The stroke of the brush combines the functions of the brush and of the pencil or pen which had remained distinct in the majority of the drawings up to this time.

In *Le Corbeau sur le buste* (fig. 15) the deep blacks visually link the bird and the reclining head below, which are the main protagonists in the poem. The grey diagonal strokes establish a pattern of shadow between them. Manet had seldom given this degree of attention to vagrant shadows before. But in the poem's context shadows do loom large. They are agents of foreboding and fear:

... et mon âme, de cette ombre qui gît

flottante à terre, ne s'élèvera—jamais plus.

Manet gives shadows the equivocal quality of transparency but never lets them obscure the objects they surround.

Scenes of city life and cityscapes are frequent subjects in sketches of the late 1870's. The Impressionists were also drawn to them, but not as exclusively. Degas's interest in urban themes is akin to Manet's, but unlike Degas, Manet seldom introduces the element of portraiture as the focus of interest. His curiosity is drawn to the more general aspects of the café, the theater, or the street which he observes with amused detachment. His drawings record café scenes whose

FIGURE 54 *(Cat. No. 499)*.

habitués are caught in familiar occupations or in relaxed attitudes (figs. 54, 263). Manet frequents the concert hall and the theater (figs. 368, 369, 376) and also records the familiar sights of the street such as carriages, construction workers, and shopping housewives (figs. 24, 380). Viewed as a group,

these sketches interpret the sights which any idle stroller might come upon. The subject matter is prosaic, but the understatement of its interpretation in the sketch is often poetic in a humorous way (figs. 338, 367). The point of view from which the motifs are observed is not particularly dramatic. Unlike Degas in this respect, Manet appears to be a detached and orthodox observer, but his visual grasp of the scene of his choice is nevertheless acute.

In a number of drawings the human figure assumes prominence as the sole motif. In *Audience et chef d'orchestre* (fig. 27) three large silhouettes occupy the foreground. The figures are cut off below the shoulders. This suggests that they are seen close-to by a member of the audience. They form a tightly knit group by virtue of the continuous and uncluttered arabesque which circumscribes them. This leaves little room for details descriptive of physical environment.

Another compositional solution of these years consists of a balanced distribution of bold spottings on the page. This is the basis of the pattern in *Le Bouchon* (fig. 379) and *La Rue Mosnier au bec-de-gaz* (fig. 24). The distribution of a limited number of black accents on the white page (the equivalent of color areas in contemporaneous paintings by Manet) appears as casual as the initial observation it records, and combines the compactness of a two-dimensional pattern with openness of design. By these technical means, Manet conveys a total impression of the scene—an effect obtained by the Impressionists in the seventies by sweeping perspective views.

The basic formal motifs of the drawings considered here are the "spot" (a solid-color shape or a broad brush mark) and the line. The spot assumes a number of expressive values depending upon the context of the scene represented. It can be an emphatic accent, standing for both the color and the shape of single objects—its specific role as it describes the hat of the standing man in *Le Bouchon* (fig. 379), or the music stand in *Chef d'orchestre* (fig. 376), or the skirt ribbon of the singer in *La Belle polonaise* (fig. 338). Another role of the spot, in drawings representing a vast outdoor scene with a number of figures, is to transcribe and simultaneously articulate an array of figures and objects into a coherent and vibrant pattern: *La Rue Mosnier* (fig. 380) is a characteristic example of this interpretation. The figures, lamp posts, vehicles are all transcribed as summary color accents or spots which suggest the distribution of musical symbols on a music sheet. Finally, a single spot can describe an entire figure and its characteristic gesture as in *Chef d'orchestre* (fig. 376). The oneness of color and contour in this figure explains the immediacy of its impact on the eye. In this role it is the instrument of visual drama at its purest. It is toward this end that Manet's graphic work progresses; the "spot" increasingly assimilates and dominates the descriptive and impressionistic elements of the image.

The line in these drawings is exploited with the same virtuosity as the spot. Its caricatural power is revealed in *Tête de femme* (fig. 55). The pen line travels, almost uninterruptedly, around the profile of head and shoulders, conforming to the irregularities of the individual's features. It does so without undue insistence on their grotesque or odd aspects, and thereby avoids the exaggerations and distortions on which pure caricature is based. However, as is the case in caricature, the line brings out only the most striking traits of physiognomy and avoids insistence on those features of the form which the mind of the observer can

FIGURE 55 *(Cat. No. 461)*.

supplement. Such physical qualities as the roundness of a cheek or neck are deliberately understated in *Tête de femme* (fig. 55), but no weakness of structure results.

There is perhaps no better way of summarizing here our observations on the role of the spot and of the line in drawings of the late 1870's than to consider two drawings with the same title, *Audience et chef d'orchestre* (figs. 27, 28). The first is an initial sketch in pencil (fig. 27), and the second, a brush drawing derived from it (fig. 28). Manet gives a measure of his versatility in the two techniques. The pencil drawing is executed with calligraphic zest and humor, but is faithful to the initial visual stimulus. In the brush drawing Manet relies on the shock power of color contrasts and on the swiftness of execution which brush work makes possible, but his ultimate expressive goal remains the same in both versions.

VII. 1879–1883 THE OBJECT-IMAGE

These last four years of Manet's life are marked by the decline of his health with gradually increasing paralysis of his legs, entailing great suffering and frequent interruptions in his work. During the winters, Manet is feverishly at work, since he can only devote a limited time to painting. His summers are now plagued by the necessity of following time-consuming and immobilizing health treatments away from his beloved Paris. These summers are spent on the outskirts of the city, at Bellevue in 1879 and 1880, at Versailles in 1881, and at Rueil in 1882. But while his health becomes a real impediment to uninterrupted activity, Manet's production shows no decline in quality, with the possible exception of some of his pastel profile portraits of women, which occasionally betray a facile repetitiousness. But even they retain the serenity of content which marks earlier works. Pure visual experience remains the live source of Manet's art in these trying years, but it is, of course, more boldly shaped into personal patterns formed by habit. Beginning in 1882 the artist's physical endurance is sharply curtailed; he is repeatedly confined to his studio and, in the summer, to the gardens of the villas he occupies on the outskirts of Paris for his rest and health cures. Painting has become to him a physical need as never before. He sings, with color, his joy at the sight of familiar objects, faces, silhouettes, and the many patterns of life which he finds nearby, within the confines of a now restricted environment. His physical handicap and forced immobility affect his choice of techniques as

well: he makes more frequent use of pastels and watercolors. These media lend themselves to more rapid execution than oils. With a new dash and verve, his pencil, pastel stick, or brush record coquettish, beribboned feminine heads or profiles as well as trifles such as the spiral of a snail shell on its boneless glide, or the glory of a single flower in a crystal vase.

Manet was already familiar with pastels. He had employed them from time to time throughout his career. His first important group of works in this medium is a series on the subject of women at their toilette dated about 1878.[26] These have a pronounced affinity to similar works by Degas. Following that year, 1878, the majority of Manet's pastels are portrait heads. For large compositions oils are still his preferred medium. We conclude that pastels were not simply a lesser substitute which Manet was forced to adopt by circumstances. It was a technique ideally suited to certain categories of works, such as portraiture, which were less demanding of the artist's time and efforts. Manet had always endeavored to attain—in portraiture in particular—a quality of ease and grace in the finished work, even at the cost of numerous erasures and new starts. Pastels were best suited to these aims and procedures. In contemporary drawings he employed kindred media to the same ends. But in the more direct drawing techniques erasures are seldom found.

During this final period of his career Manet's drawing media still include pencil, pen and ink, ink wash, and watercolor. He

---

[26] Tabarant and Jamot give different dates for the series—1878 and 1880 respectively. See A. Tabarant, *Manet et ses oeuvres*, p. 422, for a defense of his dating. The year 1878 is probably the correct

dating since these pastels are related stylistically to paintings in oil of the same year, namely *La Serveuse de bocks* (Jamot, no. 335, fig. 156) and other canvases on the same theme.

80

no longer works in red crayon or autographic lithography. A large majority of the late brush drawings are watercolors; relatively fewer are in black and white. The repetition of a single motif in a number of media is a frequent occurrence. The usual sequence is the pencil sketch followed by a version or versions in wash or watercolor.

These pairs or series of related drawings are the results of a variety of procedures. Two drawings may be based on the same subject with minor changes in angle of view or interpretation as is the case of *Mlle. Marguerite* (Cat. Nos. 563, 564). The pencil

a literary work. The two drawings of *La Dormeuse* (figs. 16, 17) are examples. In other instances the second version is a pen and ink drawing (figs. 56 and 57), or a watercolor (figs. 25 and 404). Many such watercolors illustrate Manet's letters to family and friends.

Drawings belonging to these series and the majority of independent drawings frequently interpret a single object or figure. The verbal content of subject matter is therefore reduced to a minimum, and the fusion of natural motif and formal pattern is complete. The simplest object suffices for

FIGURE 56 *(Cat. No. 479)*.

FIGURE 57 *(Cat. No. 552)*.

drawing represents the figure from the waist up with the head in full profile. The brush drawing is a study of the same model with the same costume and hat, but shows only the shoulders and head in three-quarters profile. In other cases the first drawing is also a pencil drawing and a direct study from nature, but the second version, in brush technique, is a more dramatic and imaginative version, better adapted to the illustration of

the purpose—a flag, a single flower or fruit, a woman's hat. Their background is the white page itself. The term "object-image" refers to the economy of means and concentration on the one object in this category of drawings.

Femme en robe bleue (fig. 413) is among the most accomplished drawings of this type. It is one of a series of watercolors on the same pattern representing a single female

81

figure in three-quarters length (figs. 412, 413). The head is in full profile. The body is turned slightly on its axis. With this choice of pose Manet reconciles the simplicity of the silhouetted features with a natural poise in the figure as a whole. It also enables him to expand the width of the body area so that it effectively balances the blank spaces surrounding it. The color is subdued, consisting of the transparent blue wash of the dress, very few black accents of varying value and the white of the paper. The simplicity of the means, the freedom and economy of brush technique, and the clarity of the two-dimensional pattern make of this image more than a record of a transient visual impression. It is an icon of feminine coquettishness and grace.

In the same category, and based on similar choices of composition and technique, *Isabelle plongeant* (fig. 4) makes its humorous comment by means of the whimsical lines and spots with which the figure is described.

Portrait heads are also interpreted as "object-images." *Tête de femme au col de dentelle* (fig. 382), a pen drawing, reveals Manet's basic approach in this genre. He does not probe the model's individuality deeply. The pattern combines the crisp, undulating line of the collar, the biting lines of the face and hair, and the tight dark knots of the features in which the pen lines are purposely fused. With tongue in cheek the artist has likened this feminine face to the ruffled and staring mask of the Pekinese dog Tama (fig. 346), with its wild but vacuous expression. He expresses in this portrait of a woman a combination of smugness, curiosity, and sensuality which appears in many similar ones by his hand. However, there is no bitterness or satire. Manet's respect for truth in visual data controls his ready wit.

Many feminine profiles executed in the less biting and incisive technique of the brush conform to a certain decorative convention analogous to that of the standing figure type. It consists, in *Tête de femme* (fig. 409), of a particular choice of contrasting silhouettes: the head is shown in near profile while the bust is turned to a more frontal view. The features are generalized, but not to the point of complete anonymity. The type is a fashionable Parisienne with self-conscious bearing. What distinguishes this virtuoso drawing from a slick fashion plate is its acuity of observation implicit in the sureness with which the form is constructed, and the absence of a prior stylization.

In *Tête de femme* (fig. 409), the hat and the ribbon are given a decorative importance equal to that of the features of the face. This aspect of the drawing makes it an intermediary type between the portrait drawings and drawings of woman's fashionable frills (figs. 26, 415, 417). Manet sprinkles these vignettes, like petals, on the pages of his letters to decorous women sitters and to family and friends. His delight in these colorful oddities of fashion is communicated with zest and flamboyance in gaily colored patterns.

Manet wrote these brief illustrated messages during summer periods of confinement away from the stimulating life of Paris for which he was longing. In the letters, Manet carries on light conversations with his Parisian friends and begs them to brighten his day by visiting him. In the walled garden of his Bellevue villa, with brush in hand, he never tired of adding to his collection of vignettes the pattern of a rose, a daisy, a snail, a watering can, and many other similar tidbits. These notations appear again, having lost nothing of their initial freshness, as the frontispiece or the tailpiece of a letter. Occasionally they are inserted in the text as an illustration: for example, *Mirabelle* (fig. 400).[27] They serve also as a decorative background which the words overlay: *Rose* (Cat. No. 523). A few stand isolated on the page with little or no written accompaniment: *Philippine* (fig. 399). In all cases the watercolor spots and the calligraphy complement one another decoratively on the page.

FIGURE 58 (*Cat. No. 556*).

Economy of means and graphic virtuosity reach a climax in these spots. However, no technical formula emerges. The quality of the brush stroke, the fluidity of the color washes, the direction and speed of lines are adapted to the transcription of an infinite number of physical qualities and nuances which Manet observes in the objects he chooses as motifs. Manet differentiates, in this limpid style, the velvety exterior and the sharply undercut interior of an almond in *Philippine* (fig. 399); the sun-spotted and shiny surface of a watering can in *Arrosoir* (fig. 58); the vibrating flight pattern of a bee in *Marguerite et abeille* (Cat. No. 526).

Two elaborate compositions are exceptions among the less ambitious sketches which characterize the trend of late drawings. They are *Pertuiset, le chasseur de lions* (fig. 428) and *Printemps* (fig. 423). Both are based on paintings, and are themselves the sources of etchings with corresponding titles. The originality of the pen and ink technique—with some brushwork in *Printemps*—makes these drawings definitive images in their own right. The vibrant graphic pattern against the white of the paper in *Printemps* creates a sparkling tonality which interprets visually, rather than allegorically, the theme of spring. We recognize in the motif and the pose a convention frequently used by Manet for the representation of the standing female figure. We have encountered it in *Femme en robe bleue* (fig. 413). The figure assumes a static and hieratic pose and is contained within a schematic profile pattern occupying the entire page. What differentiates the *Printemps* is not the character of the pose or its human expression but the nature of the calligraphic vocabulary. Manet renews the latter with each new version of a familiar motif, and within the self-imposed limitation of a personal compositional convention.

---

[27] "A Isabelle cette Mirabelle et la plus belle c'est Isabelle" (text of a letter: Cat. No. 542).

VIII. MANET AND FRENCH DRAWING

To speak of a French tradition in drawing is to refer to a long history of outstanding contributions by artists as different in personal outlooks and styles as Watteau and Delacroix. On many occasions exhibitions entitled "French Drawings" have demonstrated the persistence of a native strain through a great diversity of styles, historical and individual.

For our present purpose, which is to comment on the affinities existing between Manet's drawings and those of his predecessors, we may restrict ourselves to certain types of drawings, namely direct studies from nature. For this same reason we shall forgo consideration of the more complex category of compositional studies, which, being more deliberately planned works, reflect to a greater extent a social ambiance and a period taste. With this selection in mind, we could bring together works by Clouet, Poussin, Watteau, and Daumier, with the understanding that works of many other outstanding draftsmen could be included as well. A sampling of drawings by Manet would not be out of place among representative achievements by these masters. If we should choose a drawing selected at random from this hypothetical group exhibition—a direct study of the model, or of a particular object or scene—as a representative example, we would find that the form of the drawing reflects a deep-seated respect for the *facts* of visual experience. We would also find that the drawing's objective reference to these observed facts is made subtly, by understatement. These characteristics exclude *a priori* stylizations or distortions systematically carried out. Stylization implies

aesthetic detachment and distortions, a subjective point of view. Neither of these two attitudes is likely to be found in its more extreme form among French draftsmen. To exploit form as a vehicle for ideas at the expense of a reality confirmed by sensory impressions runs generally counter to French taste. Expressionistic tendencies are rare in French drawings because they are inimical to an attitude of "friendly" familiarity with the object portrayed. The Frenchman, so touchy on all that appears to infringe upon his rights as an individual, seems, as an artist, intent on preserving analogous "rights" for the external aspects of things as he perceives them empirically.

Seen in this light, Manet's drawings are in the native tradition. Manet's originality is in the quality of his perception of the external character of things; in his power to transmute objects into finite and extremely readable images. His ability for understatement results from a constant disciplining of the hand which is trained to answer without hesitation or delay the dictates of an intuitive perception: "*Quand ça y est, ça y est. Et quand ça n'y est pas on recommence. Tout le reste est de la blague.*"[28] A drawing by Manet channels the observer's attention to a few essentials, and, be it cursive or elaborate, manifests two paradoxically complementary qualities discovered in the most ordinary and familiar scenes: the obvious and the rare. The pleasure we derive from the drawing (that aesthetic pleasure which Berenson has defined as "the exhilarating sense of increased capacity in the observer") is in no small measure the realization that it makes us witness a spectacle of everyday life or a

---

[28] A. Proust, *Edouard Manet, souvenirs*, p. 30.

84

familiar object in an "unnaturally" vivid light. Ultimately, it is this experience which the most adroitly faked drawing cannot give us.

The universal appeal of a drawing by Manet stems from its qualities of frankness and good humor, which are reflections of the nature of the artist and of the man.

CATALOGUE
OF THE DRAWINGS
OF MANET

CATALOGUE
OF THE DRAWINGS
OF MANET

INTRODUCTION

THIS catalogue lists all the drawings—including watercolors—known to the author. The majority of these drawings were made available by their owners for direct study.

The drawings whose present ownership is not known are recorded with the date of the *latest bibliographical reference* to a given collection, followed by the mention "present location unknown." In such cases, the physical characteristics of the drawing (medium, size, marking) and information relating to its past history have been collected indirectly, from bibliographical sources. One major source of such information has been *Manet et ses oeuvres*, by A. Tabarant (Paris: Gallimard, 1947), and an earlier work by the same author, *Manet, histoire catalographique* (Paris: Montaigne, 1931), which includes a nearly complete catalogue of Manet's watercolors and wash drawings.

The large fund of drawings from the former Pellerin collection, acquired by the Louvre in 1954, is listed in its entirety. All factual data

were gathered from a direct study of the originals from the Louvre and are included under each title.

Remarks about individual drawings are included in our catalogue when they do not duplicate text references. An index, following the description of each drawing, refers the reader to the pages of the text where mention is made of the drawing.

All titles are given in French so as to have consistency with the titles already established by tradition for a number of the drawings.

Two monographs under the common title *Graphisme de Manet*, published in 1961 and 1963 by J. Mathey (see bibliography), list and illustrate a number of drawings, found primarily in French private collections, which are attributed to Manet for the first time. The author, with rare exceptions, chooses to list the drawings without reference to provenance or to previous collections. His attributions are based on his identification of the artist's "handwriting" or characteristic calligraphic manner in the drawings themselves and in the written notes, legends, or signatures which appear on a few of them. In support of his conclusions and for comparative purposes Mr. Mathey illustrates details of drawings, paintings, etchings, and lithographs which are securely Manet's. In the majority of cases we have not found these comparisons convincing, and therefore are not ready to accept the conclusions of Mr. Mathey without the support of other, less controversial proof. We do however, tentatively accept the following attributions: numbers 139, 154, 335 of our catalogue, which appear in Mathey, 1961, as figures 28, 52, and 89. These drawings do reveal certain identifiable calligraphic mannerisms in the details. Even more convincing in our view is the verve, frankness, and decisiveness of their overall aspect, which do not suffer from a comparison with the artist's known works.

In order to make more explicit our major points of disagreement with Mr. Mathey's defense of his attributions, we refer the reader to a major drawing (Mathey, 1961, fig. 40) attributed to Manet by Mathey. The evidence which the author presents—in particular his comparison with an earlier lithograph by Manet—is superficially convincing. The head of the boy in the drawing bears a close resemblance to the head of the model in the lithograph. This similarity is in itself puzzling since the figure illustrated in the drawing shows a boy of thirteen, while the model in the lithograph appears to be at least three years younger. Thus, the close dependence of the drawing upon the lithograph for almost every detail of the features would indicate that the lithograph itself was the drawing's source. There exist other, more persuasive reasons to doubt Manet's authorship. The drawing itself is weak and as a result the figure lacks plasticity. We miss entirely the vigor of contours which the earlier lithograph possesses and which lends authority to a similar figure, drawn by Manet, dated around 1868, No. 234 of our catalogue. The author of the drawing illustrated by Mathey was certainly familiar with Manet's style

but, in our view, did not possess his assurance or his visual grasp of the figure as a whole. We know of no figure represented in a relaxed pose drawn or painted by Manet, which slumps as this one does. The weakness and hesitancy of the lines, the mindless accumulation of disparate accents in the folds and shadows contribute to this general effect. We hasten to add that, in the absence of any objective proof, our conclusions, and Mr. Mathey's, are by their very nature controversial.

In the second monograph (Mathey, 1963) the author illustrates a selection of drawings from three sketchbooks also attributed to Manet. They appear to us to be by another hand, being on the whole fussy in technique and too consciously composed for picturesque effects. These are qualities not generally found in Manet's graphic work. However, we recognize that Mr. Mathey attributes these drawings to a very early period of Manet's career, and that they might conceivably be examples of Manet's youthful work. We doubt that this is so, however, because while the drawings are not in the style of his mature work, they do exhibit a very competent and consistent style of their own—this is especially true of the landscapes. It would be arrogant on our part to assert categorically that these sketches could not possibly be the early work of Manet. However, the evidence so far presented is too slight and too problematic to permit a positive attribution.

For further references to this problem we indicate to the reader a review of Mr. Mathey's book published in the *London Times Literary Supplement* of October 1961, and to an article by T. Reff in the *Art Bulletin* of December 1964, page 554, note 21.

We are of course not immune to errors of attributions ourselves. But we have attempted to list and illustrate only the drawings which can be securely attributed to Manet. These include items of greater or lesser interest, but we believe the stamp of Manet's hand is on all of them. Our intent was to offer scholars a useful tool, and to present to the general reader a comprehensive view of Manet's work at its most direct and personal—the drawings.

ABBREVIATIONS

BOOKS AND ARTICLES

Bazire—Edmond Bazire, *Manet* (Paris: A. Quantin, 1884).

Bouchot-Saupique—J. Bouchot-Saupique, "Manet dessinateur," *La Revue du Louvre*, XI, 2 (1961).

Colin—Paul Colin, *Edouard Manet* (Paris: Floury, 1932).

Courthion—Pierre Courthion, *Edouard Manet* (New York: Abrams, 1962).

Duret, 1902—Théodore Duret, *Histoire d'Edouard Manet et de son oeuvre* (Paris: Floury, 1902).

Duret, 1906—Théodore Duret, *Histoire d'Edouard Manet et de son oeuvre* (Paris: Fasquelle, 1906).

Duret, 1919—Théodore Duret, *Histoire d'Edouard Manet et de son oeuvre* (Paris: Bernheim jeune, 1919).

Focillon—H. Focillon, "Manet en blanc et noir," *Gazette des Beaux-Arts* (December 1927).

Florisoone—Michel Florisoone, *Manet* (Monaco: Documents d'Art, 1947).

Glaser—Curt Glaser, *Edouard Manet, Faksimiles nach Zeichnungen und Aquarellen* (Munich: Piper, 1922).

Guérin—Marcel Guérin, *L'Oeuvre gravé de Manet* (Paris: Floury, 1944).

Hamilton—G. H. Hamilton, *Manet and His Critics* (New Haven: Yale University Press, 1954).

Hanson—Anne Coffin Hanson, *Edouard Manet*, exhibition catalogue, Philadelphia Museum of Art—The Art Institute of Chicago, Nov. 1966–Feb. 1967.

Hoetink—H. R. Hoetink, *Franse tekeningen uit de 19e eeuw* (Rotterdam: Museum Boymans-van Beuningen, 1967 [catalogue of French nineteenth-century drawings in the collections of the museum]). Forthcoming.

Jamot—P. Jamot, G. Wildenstein, and M. L. Bataille, *Manet*, 2 vols. (Paris: Les Beaux-Arts, 1932).

Jedlicka—G. Jedlicka, *Edouard Manet* (Zurich: Rentsch, 1941).

Mallarmé, *Le Corbeau*—Translation by S. Mallarmé of Edgar Allan Poe's *The Raven* (Paris: Lesclide, 1875).

Martin—Kurt Martin, *Edouard Manet, Watercolors and Pastels* (London: Faber and Faber, 1959).

Mathey, 1961—J. Mathey, *Graphisme de Manet* (Paris: by the author, 1961).

Mathey, 1963—J. Mathey, *Graphisme de Manet, II: Peintures réapparues* (Paris: by the author, 1963).

Meier-Graefe—J. Meier-Graefe, *Edouard Manet* (Munich: Piper, 1912).

M-N, 1906—E. Moreau-Nélaton, *Manet graveur et lithographe* (Paris: Delteil, 1906).

M-N, 1926—E. Moreau-Nélaton, *Manet raconté par lui-même*, 2 vols. (Paris: Laurens, 1926).

M-N, Catalogue—Summary manuscript catalogue of Manet's oeuvre, Cabinet des Estampes, Bibliothèque Nationale, Paris.

Pataky—Dénes Pataky, *Master Drawings from the Collection of the Budapest Museum of Fine Arts, Nineteenth and Twentieth Centuries* (New York: Abrams, 1959).

Perruchot—Henri Perruchot, *La Vie de Manet* (Paris: Hachette, 1959).

Proust—Antonin Proust, *Edouard Manet, souvenirs*, A. Barthélemy, ed. (Paris: H. Laurens, 1913).

Rewald—John Rewald, *Edouard Manet, Pastels* (Oxford: Cassirer, 1947).

Rey—Robert Rey, *Edouard Manet, choix de soixante-quatre dessins* (Paris: Braun, 1932).

Rey, *Manet*, 1938—Robert Rey, *Manet* (London-Toronto: Heinemann, 1938).

Rey, *Manet*, 1962—Robert Rey, *Manet* (Milan: Vallardi, 1962).

Richardson—John Richardson, *Edouard Manet, Paintings and Drawings* (New York: Phaidon, 1958).

Rio Letters—Edouard Manet, *Lettres de jeunesse*, L. Rouart, ed. (Paris: Louis Rouart et fils, 1929).

Rosenthal—Léon Rosenthal, *Manet aquafortiste et lithographe* (Paris: Le Goupy, 1925).

Sandblad—N.G. Sandblad, *Manet, Three Studies in Artistic Conception* (Lund: The New Society of Letters at Lund, 1954).

Tabarant, 1931—A. Tabarant, *Manet, histoire catalographique* (Paris: Montaigne, 1931).

Tabarant, 1947—A. Tabarant, *Manet et ses oeuvres* (Paris: Gallimard, 1947).

Tschudi—Hugo von Tschudi, *Edouard Manet* (Berlin: Cassirer, 1902).

Vaudoyer—J. L. Vaudoyer, *Edouard Manet* (Paris: Editions du Dimanche, 1955).

Waldmann, 1910—Emil Waldmann, ed., *Edouard Manet* (Berlin: Cassirer, 1910).

Waldmann, 1923—Emil Waldmann, ed., *Edouard Manet* (Berlin: Cassirer, 1923).

EXHIBITIONS

1867—Exhibition organized by Manet of his own work, shortly after the opening of the Exposition Universelle of 1867, in Paris.

1884—Posthumous exhibition of works of Manet at the Ecole Nationale des Beaux-Arts.

Matthiesen, 1928—Exhibition of Manet works at the Matthiesen Gallery, Berlin, Feb.–Mar. 1928.

London, 1932—Exhibition of French art (1200–1900) at the Royal Academy of Arts, Burlington House, London, 1932.

Orangerie, 1932—"Manet: 1832–1883," retrospective centennial exhibition at the Musée de l'Orangerie, Paris, 1932.

Art français, 1937—"Chefs d'oeuvre de l'art français," Palais National des Arts, Paris, 1937.

Wildenstein, 1948—"Manet," loan exhibition, Wildenstein Gallery, New York, Feb. 26–Apr. 3, 1948.

SALES

1884—Posthumous sale of Manet's works from his own estate, Paris, Feb. 1884.

Pellerin, 1926—Anonymous sale of works from the collection of Auguste Pellerin, Hôtel Drouot, Paris, 1926.

Pellerin, 1954—Sale of drawings and watercolors from the collection of Auguste Pellerin, Galerie Charpentier, Paris, June 1954.

OTHER ABBREVIATIONS

Bibl.—Bibliography.

Cat. No.—Refers to numbers in this catalogue.

Coll.—Collection.

Exh.—Exhibition, Exhibited.

Ill.—Illustration, Illustrated.

Guérin, no. . . . —Refers to number in Marcel Guérin, *L'Oeuvre gravé de Manet* (Paris: Floury, 1944).

Jamot, no. . . . , fig. . . . —Catalogue and figure numbers in P. Jamot, G. Wildenstein, and J. L. Bataille, *Manet*, 2 vols. (Paris: Les Beaux-Arts, 1932).

Cab. des Dessins—The Cabinet des Dessins in the Louvre, Paris.

RF—The inventory numbers of the drawings in the Louvre collection.

Cab. des Estampes—The Cabinet des Estampes in the Bibliothèque Nationale, Paris. (Most of the Manet drawings in this fund were once in the collection of E. Moreau-Nélaton.)

Stamp E. M.—The initials (E. M.) which were stamped on the works of Manet found in his studio, prior to the sale of 1884.

Boulogne sketchbook—Sketchbook of drawings done by Manet in Boulogne in 1869 (dimensions 142 x 95 mm.); now in the Cabinet des Dessins, Louvre. Bequest of Moreau-Nélaton, 1927.

Lead—Lead pencil.

Pen—Pen and ink.

Sepia—Sepia wash.

Wash—Ink wash.

THE CATALOGUE

1845–1852

1. PIERROT IVRE (*fig. 39*)
Watercolor and pen; date, *ca.* 1849.
Bibl.: M-N, 1926, I, fig. 2; Tabarant, 1931,
  no. 1.
Coll.: Forget, Paris, 1926 (present location un-
  known).
Text ref.: p. 53.

1852–1858

2. SAINT COSME ET SAINT DAMIEN (*fig. 60*)
Lead; 290 x 212 mm.; stamp E.M.
Coll.: Cab. des Dessins (RF 30 339).
  Derived from Fra Angelico's *Mystical
  Crucifixion*, San Marco, Florence
  (fig. 59). (Detail).
Text ref.: p. 45.

3. SAINT DOMINIQUE ET SAINT JÉRÔME
  (*fig. 61*)
Lead; 290 x 212 mm.; stamp E.M.
Coll.: Cab. des Dessins (RF 30 331).
  Derived from Fra Angelico's *Mystical
  Crucifixion*, San Marco, Florence
  (fig. 62). (Detail).
Text ref.: p. 45.

4. MOINE AGENOUILLÉ (SAINT FRANÇOIS)
  (*fig. 65*)
Lead; 278 x 266 mm.; stamp E.M.
Bibl.: Rey, p. 3 (ill.).
Coll.: E. Rouart, Paris.
  Derived from Fra Angelico's *Mystical
  Crucifixion*, San Marco, Florence
  (fig. 64). (Detail).
Text ref.: pp. 7, 40, 45.

5. SAINT BERNARD (*fig. 63*)
Lead; 290 x 212 mm.; stamp E.M.
Coll.: Cab. des Dessins (RF 30 347).

Derived from Fra Angelico's *Mystical
  Crucifixion*, San Marco, Florence
  (fig. 64).
Text ref.: p. 45.

**6. SAINT JEAN GUALBERTO ET SAINT PIERRE
  MARTYR** (*fig. 29*)
Lead; 290 x 212 mm.
Coll.: Cab. des Dessins (RF 30 326).
  Derived from Fra Angelico's *Mystical
  Crucifixion*, San Marco, Florence
  (fig. 64).
Text ref.: pp. 2, 45, 47.

7. LA VISITATION (*fig. 30*)
Lead; 290 x 212 mm.; stamp E.M.
Coll.: Cab. des Dessins (RF 30 342).
  Derived from Ghirlandaio's *Visitation*,
  Santa Maria Novella, Florence (fig. 67).
Text ref.: pp. 8, 46.

8. DEUX TÊTES DE FEMMES (*fig. 66*)
Lead; 290 x 212 mm.; stamp E.M.
Coll.: Cab. des Dessins (RF 30 345).
  Derived from Ghirlandaio's *Visitation*,
  Santa Maria Novella, Florence (fig. 67).
Text ref.: p. 46.

9. DEUX FIGURES (*fig. 68*)
Lead; 290 x 215 mm.; stamp E.M.
Coll.: Cab. des Dessins (RF 30 379).
  Derived from Ghirlandaio's *Birth of the
  Virgin*, Santa Maria Novella, Florence
  (fig. 69). (Detail).
Text ref.: p. 46.

10. VERSEUSE D'EAU (*fig. 31*)
Lead; 275 x 208 mm.
Coll.: Cab. des Dessins (RF 30 343).
  Derived from Ghirlandaio's *Birth of the
  Virgin*, Santa Maria Novella, Florence
  (figs. 32 and 69).
Text ref.: pp. 2, 8, 46, 47.

11. FEMME PRIANT (NERA CORSI) (*fig. 70*)
Lead; 280 x 212 mm.
Bibl.: Bouchot-Saupique, fig. 3.
Coll.: Cab. des Dessins (RF 30 320).
  Derived from Ghirlandaio's full-figure
    portrait of Nera Corsi, Santa Trinità,
    Florence (fig. 71). (Detail).
Text ref.: p. 47.

12. FEMME TENDANT LES MAINS (*fig. 72*)
Lead; 290 x 212 mm.
Coll.: Cab. des Dessins (RF 30 319).
  Derived from Ghirlandaio's *Birth of John
    the Baptist*, Santa Maria Novella, Florence
    (fig. 73). (Detail).
Text ref.: p. 46.

13. DEUX FIGURES
Lead; 172 x 218 mm.
Bibl.: Rey, p. 4 (ill.).
Coll.: E. Rouart, Paris.
  Derived from Ghirlandaio: left figure de-
    rived from *St. Francis Restores to Life the
    Dead Child of the Spini Family*; right fig-
    ure derived from *The Funeral of St. Fran-
    cis*, both in Santa Trinità, Florence.

14. ENFANT ET TÊTE (*fig. 76*)
Sanguine; 290 x 213 mm.
Coll.: Cab. des Dessins (RF 30 296).
  The child figure is derived from a study for
    the *Madonna del Gatto*, by Leonardo da
    Vinci, Uffizi, Florence (in Manet's draw-
    ing the figure of the child is reversed, in-
    dicating a tracing process). The head in
    profile is derived from a drawing by An-
    drea del Sarto, *Head of a Boy*, in the Uffizi,
    Florence (Uffizi, no. 626E) ill. in S.
    Freedberg, *Andrea del Sarto* [Cambridge,
    Mass.: Harvard University Press, 1962],
    fig. 117).

15. LEONIDAS (*fig. 74*)
Lead; 290 x 212 mm.; stamp E.M.
Coll.: Cab. des Dessins (RF 30 356).

Derived from Perugino's *Fortitude and
    Temperance*, Collegio del Cambio,
    Perugia (fig. 75). (Detail).
Text ref.: p. 8.

16. ENFANT NU (*fig. 77*)
Lead; 157 x 85 mm.
Coll.: Cab. des Dessins (RF 30 461).
  Derived from Luca della Robbia's *Cantoria*
    ("Cymbalis jubilationis" panel), Cathedral
    Museum, Florence (fig. 78). (Detail).
Text ref.: p. 51.

17. ENFANT CYMBALIER (*fig. 82*)
Lead; 156 x 87 mm.; stamp E.M.
Coll.: Cab. des Dessins (RF 30 433).
  Derived from Luca della Robbia's *Cantoria*
    ("Cymbalis benesonantibus" panel), Ca-
    thedral Museum, Florence (fig. 83). (De-
    tail).
Text ref.: p. 51.

18. ENFANT NU DANSANT (*fig. 79*)
Lead; 157 x 88 mm.
Coll.: Cab. des Dessins (RF 30 514).
  Derived from Luca della Robbia's *Cantoria*
    ("Tympanum" panel), Cathedral Mu-
    seum, Florence (fig. 81). (Detail).
Text ref.: p. 51.

19. ENFANT NU DANSANT (*fig. 80*)
Lead; 156 x 92 mm.
Coll.: Cab. des Dessins (RF 30 513).
  Derived from Luca della Robbia's *Cantoria*
    ("Tympanum" panel), Cathedral Mu-
    seum, Florence (fig. 81). (Detail).
Text ref.: p. 51.

20. ENFANT JOUANT DU LUTH (*fig. 37*)
Lead; 157 x 93 mm.
Coll.: Cab. des Dessins (RF 30 519).
  Derived from Luca della Robbia's *Cantoria*
    ("Chordis et organum" panel), Cathedral
    Museum, Florence (fig. 38).
Text ref.: pp. 51, 52.

21. TROIS ENFANTS DANSANT (*fig. 84*)
Lead and sepia; 285 x 218 mm.; stamp E.M.
Bibl.: Mathey, 1961, fig. 16 (dimensions listed
by Mathey, 80 x 215, are incorrect).
Coll.: Cab. des Dessins (RF 30 459).
> This is a composite group. The two figures
> on the right are derived from Luca della
> Robbia's *Cantoria* ("Choro" panel), Ca-
> thedral Museum, Florence (fig. 85). The
> figure on the left is derived from the panel
> "Cymbalis jubilationis" (see Cat. No. 16
> and fig. 78). (Detail).
Text ref.: p. 51.

22. SAINTS MAURUS, PLACIDUS, BENEDICTUS
(*fig. 86*)
Lead; 290 x 212 mm.; stamp E.M.
Coll.: Cab. des Dessins (RF 30 349).
> Derived from Raphael's *Trinity*, San Severo,
> Perugia (fig. 87). (Detail).
Text ref.: p. 47.

23. SAINTS ROMUALDUS, BENEDICTUS,
JOHANNES (*fig. 88*)
Lead; 290 x 212 mm.
Coll.: Cab. des Dessins (RF 30 322).
> Derived from Raphael's *Trinity*, San Severo,
> Perugia (fig. 87). (Detail).
Text ref.: p. 47.

24. PORTEUSE D'EAU (*fig. 89*)
Sanguine; 298 x 218 mm.; stamp E.M.
Coll.: Cab. des Dessins (RF 30 431).
> Derived from Raphael's *Incendio*, Vatican,
> Rome (fig. 90). (Detail).
Text ref.: pp. 8, 41, 48.

25. FIGURE DRAPÉE (*fig. 95*)
Black crayon; 290 x 212 mm.; stamp E.M.
Bibl.: Bouchot-Saupique, fig. 2.
Coll.: Cab. des Dessins (RF 30 337).
> Derived from Fra Bartolomeo's *Circum-
> cision*, Uffizi, Florence.
Text ref.: p. 49.

26. SAINT JEAN ET LE CHRIST ENFANT
(*fig. 93*)
Lead and sanguine; 212 x 290 mm.; stamp E.M.
Coll.: Cab. des Dessins (RF 30 332).
> Derived from Fra Bartolomeo's *St. Ann
> Altarpiece*, San Marco, Florence (fig. 94).
> (Detail).

27. DEUX FIGURES (*fig. 96*)
Sanguine; 290 x 212 mm.
Coll.: Cab. des Dessins (RF 30 302).
> Derived from a drawing by Fra Bartolomeo
> (Uffizi, no. 481), ill. in H. von der Ga-
> belentz, *Fra Bartolomeo und die Floren-
> tiner Renaissance*, 2 vols. (Leipzig: Hierse-
> mann, 1922), II, no. 143.

28. LA VIERGE AGENOUILLÉE (*fig. 97*)
Black crayon; 290 x 212 mm.
Coll.: Cab. des Dessins (RF 30 327).
> Derived from Fra Bartolomeo's *Annuncia-
> tion*, Convento della Maddalena, Le Cal-
> dine. Manet's drawing was very probably
> done from Fra Bartolomeo's drawing
> study for the composition (Uffizi, no.
> 463).

29. SAINT MARTYR DE PROFIL (SAINT
ÉTIENNE) (*fig. 91*)
Black crayon; 290 x 212 mm.
Coll.: Cab. des Dessins (RF 30 325).
> Derived from Fra Bartolomeo's *Madonna
> Enthroned with SS. Stephen and John the
> Baptist*, Lucca Cathedral. The direct
> source of Manet's drawing is a drawing
> study of *Saint Stephen* by Fra Bartolomeo
> (Uffizi, no. 483) (fig. 92). (Detail).

30. FEMME ET DEUX ENFANTS (*fig. 98*)
Sanguine; 113 x 290 mm.; stamp E.M.
Coll.: Cab. des Dessins (RF 30 357).
> Derived from a drawing by Fra Bartolomeo,
> *Madonna and Child and Putto* (Uffizi, no.
> 492E), ill. in F. Knapp, *Fra Bartolomeo
> della Porta u. die Schule von San Marco*
> (Halle a. S.: W. Knapp, 1903), fig. 89.

31. TROIS SAINTS (*fig. 99*)
Black crayon; 290 x 212 mm.; stamp E.M.
Bibl.: Bouchot-Saupique, fig. 8.
Coll.: Cab. des Dessins (RF 30 344).
 Derived from Andrea del Sarto's *Clothing of the Lepers*, Annunziata, Florence (fig. 100).
Text ref.: pp. 8, 48, 49.

32. MOINE ET SOLDAT (*fig. 101*)
Black crayon; 290 x 212 mm.; stamp E.M.
Coll.: Cab. des Dessins (RF 30 335).
 Derived from Andrea del Sarto's *Gamblers Struck by Lightning*, Annunziata, Florence (fig. 102).

33. MÈRE ET ENFANT (*fig. 103*)
Sanguine; 290 x 212 mm.; stamp E.M.
Bibl.: Mathey, 1961, fig. 18.
Coll.: Cab. des Dessins (RF 30 341).
 Derived from Andrea del Sarto's *Birth of the Virgin*, Annunziata, Florence (fig. 106). (Detail). The Louvre collection also includes a counterproof of this drawing.
Text ref.: pp. 10, 49.

34. DEUX FIGURES (*fig. 5*)
Sanguine; 290 x 212 mm.
Coll.: Cab. des Dessins (RF 30 333).
 Derived from Andrea del Sarto's *Birth of the Virgin*, Annunziata, Florence (fig. 6).
Text ref.: pp. 8, 9, 10, 49.

35. MÈRE ET ENFANT (*fig. 2*)
Sanguine; 297 x 219 mm.; stamp E.M.
Coll.: Cab. des Dessins (RF 30 458).
 Derived from Andrea del Sarto's *Birth of the Virgin*, Annunziata, Florence (fig. 106).
Text ref.: pp. 2, 10, 49.

36. MÈRE ET ENFANT (*fig. 104*)
Sanguine; 216 x 290 mm.
Coll.: Cab. des Dessins (RF 30 290).
 Derived from Andrea del Sarto's *Birth of the Virgin*, Annunziata, Florence (fig. 106).
Text ref.: pp. 10, 49.

37. MÈRE ET ENFANT (*fig. 107*)
Sanguine; 206 x 280 mm.
Coll.: Cab. des Dessins (RF 30 298).
 Derived from Andrea del Sarto's *Birth of the Virgin*, Annunziata, Florence (fig. 106).
Text ref.: pp. 10, 49.

38. MÈRE ET ENFANT
Sanguine; 213 x 290 mm.
Coll.: Cab. des Dessins (RF 30 299).
 Derived from Andrea del Sarto's *Birth of the Virgin*, Annunziata, Florence (fig. 106).

39. FIGURE ASSISE (*fig. 105*)
Sanguine; 290 x 212 mm.
Coll.: Cab. des Dessins (RF 30 304).
 Derived from Andrea del Sarto's *Birth of the Virgin*, Annunziata, Florence (fig. 106).
Text ref.: pp. 10, 49.

40. LA SAINTE FAMILLE (*fig. 110*)
Lead and sanguine; stamp E.M.
Bibl.: Rey, p. 2 (ill.); Mathey, 1961, fig. 105.
Coll.: Le Garrec, Paris, 1932 (present location unknown).
 Derived from Andrea del Sarto's *Madonna del Sacco*, Annunziata, Florence (fig. 109). (Detail).
Text ref.: pp. 9, 41, 49, 59.

41. LA SAINTE FAMILLE (*fig. 108*)
Lead and sanguine; 212 x 290 mm.; stamp E.M.
Coll.: Cab. des Dessins (RF 30 359).
 Derived from Andrea del Sarto's *Madonna del Sacco*, Annunziata, Florence (fig. 109). (Detail).
Text ref.: p. 49.

42. FIGURE DRAPÉE (*fig. 111*)
Sanguine; 290 x 219 mm.; stamp E.M.
Bibl.: Bouchot-Saupique, fig. 9.
Coll.: Cab. des Dessins (RF 30 508).
 Derived from Andrea del Sarto's *Arrival of*

the Kings, Annunziata, Florence (fig. 112). (Detail).
Text ref.: p. 48.

43. GROUPE DE FIGURES (*fig. 113*)
Lead; 288 x 212 mm.
Coll.: Cab. des Dessins (RF 30 309).
    Derived from Andrea del Sarto's *Children Healed by San Filippo's Robe*, Annunziata, Florence (fig. 115). (Detail).

44. FEMME AGENOUILLÉE (LUCRETIA DEL FEDE) (*fig. 114*)
Sanguine and black crayon; 170 x 220 mm.
Coll.: Cab. des Dessins (RF 30 372).
    Derived from Andrea del Sarto's *Children Healed by San Filippo's Robe*, Annunziata, Florence (fig. 115). (Detail).

45. DEUX FEMMES EMBRASSÉES (*fig. 118*)
Lead; 290 x 212 mm.; stamp E.M.
Coll.: Cab. des Dessins (RF 30 360).
    Derived from Andrea del Sarto's *Visitation*, Scalzo, Florence (fig. 117). (Detail).

46. DEUX FIGURES (*fig. 116*)
Lead and sanguine; 290 x 212 mm.
Coll.: Cab. des Dessins (RF 30 305).
    The smaller figure, carrying a burden, is derived from Andrea del Sarto's *Visitation*, Scalzo, Florence (fig. 117).

47. L'ARRESTATION DU BAPTISTE (*fig. 119*)
Lead; 290 x 212 mm.; stamp E.M.
Coll.: Cab. des Dessins (RF 30 329).
    Derived from Andrea del Sarto's *Arrest of John the Baptist*, Scalzo, Florence (fig. 120). (Detail).

48. SOLDAT (*fig. 121*)
Lead; 290 x 212 mm.; stamp E.M.
Coll.: Cab. des Dessins (RF 30 351).
    Derived from Andrea del Sarto's *Arrest of*

John the Baptist, Scalzo, Florence (fig. 120). (Detail).
Text ref.: p. 51.

49. DEUX FIGURES EN BUSTE (*fig. 124*)
Lead; 290 x 212 mm.; stamp E.M.
Coll.: Cab. des Dessins (RF 30 366).
    Derived from Andrea del Sarto's *Preaching of John the Baptist*, Scalzo, Florence (fig. 125). (Detail).

50. FIGURE DEBOUT (*fig. 122*)
Lead; 275 x 212 mm.; stamp E.M.
Coll.: Cab. des Dessins (RF 30 334).
    Derived from Andrea del Sarto's *Preaching of John the Baptist*, Scalzo, Florence (fig. 123). (Detail).

51. JUSTICE (*fig. 126*)
Lead; 290 x 212 mm.; stamp E.M.
Bibl.: Bouchot-Saupique, fig. 6.
Coll.: Cab. des Dessins (RF 30 376).
    Derived from Andrea del Sarto's *Justice*, Scalzo, Florence (fig. 127).

52. SOLDAT
Lead; 290 x 210 mm.; stamp E.M.
Coll.: Cab. des Dessins (RF 30 358).
    Derived from Andrea del Sarto's *Decapitation of Saint John the Baptist*, Scalzo, Florence (central figure of the executioner seen from the back in Sarto's composition).

53. FEMME ASSISE (*fig. 128*)
Lead; 283 x 287 mm.; signed lower right "E. Manet."
Bibl.: Rey, p. 11 ("Napolitaine assise") (ill.); Mathey, 1961, fig. 21 ("Italienne assise de profil").
Coll.: Cab. des Estampes (Dc 300d–res. no. 6).
    Derived from Andrea del Sarto's *Naming of John the Baptist*, Scalzo, Florence (fig. 129). (Detail).

54. DEUX ANGELOTS (*fig. 130*)
Black crayon; 290 x 212 mm.; stamp E.M.
Coll.: Cab. des Dessins (RF 30 368).
  Derived from Andrea del Sarto's *Vallom-
  brosa Altarpiece*, Uffizi, Florence.

55. FIGURE DE DOS
Lead; 289 x 212 mm.
Coll.: Cab. des Dessins (RF 30 288).
  Derived from Andrea del Sarto's *Baptism of
  the People*, Scalzo, Florence (fig. 134).
  Same figure as in Cat. No. 56, but more
  roughly blocked out.

56. FIGURE DE DOS (*fig. 131*)
Lead; 290 x 212 mm.
Bibl.: Bouchot-Saupique, fig. 5.
Coll.: Cab. des Dessins (RF 30 295).
  Derived from Andrea del Sarto's *Baptism of
  the People*, Scalzo, Florence (fig. 134).
Text ref.: p. 48.

57. ANGELOTS ET ARBRES (*fig. 132*)
Lead; 290 x 212 mm.; stamp E.M.
Coll.: Cab. des Dessins (RF 30 373).
  Derived from Andrea del Sarto's *Baptism of
  the People*, Scalzo, Florence (fig. 134).

58. DEUX FIGURES (*fig. 133*)
Lead; 290 x 213 mm.
Coll.: Cab. des Dessins (RF 30 311).
  Derived from Andrea del Sarto's *Baptism of
  the People*, Scalzo, Florence (fig. 134).

59. SOLDAT DE DOS (*fig. 137*)
Lead; 290 x 212 mm.
Coll.: Cab. des Dessins (RF 30 293).
  Derived from Andrea del Sarto's *Dance of
  Salome*, Scalzo, Florence (fig. 138).

60. SAINT MARC
Lead; 290 x 212 mm.
Coll.: Cab. des Dessins (RF 30 312).

See Cat. No. 126 for third drawing in this
series of Evangelists.

61. SAINT MATHIEU (*fig. 135*)
Lead; 290 x 212 mm.
Coll.: Cab. des Dessins (RF 30 328).
  See Cat. No. 126 for third drawing in this
  series of Evangelists.

62. BACCHUS ET PUTTI (*fig. 141*)
Watercolor; 217 x 295 mm.; stamp E.M.
Coll.: Cab. des Dessins (RF 30 450).

63. PUTTI ET FAUNE (*fig. 142*)
Lead and watercolor; 105 x 178 mm.
Coll.: Cab. des Dessins (RF 30 317).

64. ESCALIER DE CLOÎTRE (*fig. 139*)
Lead, sepia, and pen; 290 x 212 mm.
Bibl.: Mathey, 1963, fig. 18.
Coll.: Cab. des Dessins (RF 30 363).

65. FAÇADE BAROQUE
Lead; 290 x 212 mm.; stamp E.M.
Coll.: Cab. des Dessins (RF 30 361).

66. INTÉRIEUR VOÛTÉ
Lead; 290 x 212 mm.; stamp E.M.
Coll.: Cab. des Dessins (RF 30 354).

67. VUE D'UNE RUE ITALIENNE (*fig. 140*)
Lead and sanguine; 290 x 207 mm.
Coll.: Cab. des Dessins (RF 30 315).

68. DÉTAIL DE FAÇADE
Lead; 290 x 212 mm.
Coll.: Cab. des Dessins (RF 30 301).

69. PLAN D'ÉGLISE ET DÉTAIL DE CHAPITEAU
Lead and sanguine; 290 x 212 mm.
Coll.: Cab. des Dessins (RF 30 300).

70. LE CHRIST AU MILIEU D'UNE FOULE
    (*fig. 145*)
Lead; 288 x 212 mm.; stamp E.M.
Coll.: Cab. des Dessins (RF 30 338).

71. DEUX FIGURES DRAPÉES (*fig. 147*)
Lead; 290 x 212 mm.
Coll.: Cab. des Dessins (RF 30 324).

72. TROIS TÊTES (*fig. 146*)
Lead; 290 x 212 mm.; stamp E.M.
Coll.: Cab. des Dessins (RF 30 348).

   Two of the heads in this drawing, and one
   of the two figures in the drawing listed
   above (Cat. No. 71), appear in *Le Christ
   au milieu d'une foule* (Cat. No. 70). This
   suggests that the latter drawing is a "composite" composition for which these details were studies, probably derived from
   an original fifteenth-century composition
   (we have not been able to trace these
   drawings to their source).

73. SAINTE MARTYRE AGENOUILLÉE
    (*fig. 143*)
Lead; 290 x 212 mm.
Coll.: Cab. des Dessins (RF 30 323).
Text ref.: p. 47.

74. GROUPE CIRCULAIRE DE DEUX FEMMES
    ET ENFANT (*fig. 144*)
Lead; 290 x 212 mm.
Coll.: Cab. des Dessins (RF 30 321).

   At right angles to the main group, on the
   same page, is drawn a woman, in profile,
   presenting her infant child.
Text ref.: p. 51.

75. MÈRE ET ENFANT, ET DEUX PERSONNAGES
Lead; 290 x 212 mm.
Coll.: Cab. des Dessins (RF 30 318).

76. SAINT PRIANT DEVANT DEUX ANGES
Lead; 290 x 212 mm.
Coll.: Cab. des Dessins (RF 30 316).

77. FIGURE ACCROUPIE DE DOS
Lead; 290 x 212 mm.
Coll.: Cab. des Dessins (RF 30 314).

78. SÉRIE DE CROQUIS DE FIGURES
Lead and sanguine; 290 x 212 mm.
Coll.: Cab. des Dessins (RF 30 313).

79. DEUX FIGURES
Lead; 290 x 212 mm.
Coll.: Cab. des Dessins (RF 30 310).

80. DEUX FIGURES ENCADRÉES
Lead; 290 x 212 mm.
Coll.: Cab. des Dessins (RF 30 308).

81. LE CHRIST ENFANT ET SAINT JEAN
    (*fig. 148*)
Sanguine and lead; 290 x 212 mm.
Coll.: Cab. des Dessins (RF 30 303).

82. PUTTI ET ANGES (*fig. 149*)
Sanguine; 290 x 212 mm.
Coll.: Cab. des Dessins (RF 30 397).

83. FIGURE DANS UN CADRE CIRCULAIRE
Lead; 290 x 211 mm.
Coll.: Cab. des Dessins (RF 30 294).

84. FOI ET CHARITÉ (*fig. 150*)
Sanguine; 288 x 212 mm.
Coll.: Cab. des Dessins (RF 30 292).

85. FEMME EN BUSTE
Sanguine (very faint drawing); 289 x 212 mm.
Coll.: Cab. des Dessins (RF 30 375).

   A counterproof of this drawing exists in the
   same collection (RF 30 291).

86. ENFANT COUCHÉ (*fig. 152*)
Lead; 290 x 212 mm.
Coll.: Cab. des Dessins (RF 30 289).
Text ref.: p. 51.

87. FEMME NUE ASSISE (*fig. 160*)
Lead; 156 x 93 mm.
Coll.: Cab. des Dessins (RF 30 464).
   Very probably a free sketch of the right foreground figure in Domenichino's *Chase of Diana*, Borghese Gallery, Rome (fig. 161). (Detail).

88. FEMME NUE EN BUSTE
Lead; 88 x 154 mm.
Coll.: Cab. des Dessins (RF 30 463).

89. DEUX PUTTI VOLANT
Lead; 157 x 87 mm.
Coll.: Cab. des Dessins (RF 30 462).

90. MÈRE ET ENFANT, ET DEUX PUTTI PORTANT UN FARDEAU (*fig. 162*)
Sanguine; 293 x 217 mm.; stamp E.M.
Coll.: Cab. des Dessins (RF 30 460).

91. CYGNE (*fig. 155*)
Lead; 156 x 91 mm.
Coll.: Cab. des Dessins (RF 30 563).

92. SOLDAT
Lead and pen; 240 x 332 mm.
Coll.: Cab. des Dessins (RF 30 520).

93. FIGURE ALLÉGORIQUE AVEC DRAPEAUX (*fig. 154*)
Lead and wash; 174 x 113 mm.
Coll.: Cab. des Dessins (RF 30 518).

94. GROUPE DE FEMMES AGENOUILLÉES
Lead; 92 x 156 mm.
Coll.: Cab. des Dessins (RF 30 517).

95. MÈRE ET ENFANT (*fig. 156*)
Lead; 157 x 89 mm.
Coll.: Cab. des Dessins (RF 30 516).

96. HERCULE ET LE LION (*fig. 151*)
Lead; 153 x 92 mm.
Coll.: Cab. des Dessins (RF 30 515).

97. FIGURE NUE ASSISE ET FIGURE AGENOUILLÉE (*fig. 153*)
Lead; 205 x 130 mm.
Coll.: Cab. des Dessins (RF 30 512).
Text ref.: p. 51.

98. FIGURE NUE ET PUTTO
Lead; 128 x 199 mm.
Coll.: Cab. des Dessins (RF 30 511).

99. FEMME RELEVANT SA JUPE (*fig. 157*)
Lead and watercolor on grey paper; 153 x 132 mm.
Coll.: Cab. des Dessins (RF 30 510).

100. CHRYSIPPOS (*fig. 169*)
Sanguine and lead on grey paper; 227 x 143 mm.
Coll.: Cab. des Dessins (RF 30 509).
   Derived from a Hellenistic statuette, *Chrysippos*, in the Louvre (Louvre, Salle des Caryatides, Inv. no. 80) (fig. 170).
Text ref.: p. 8.

101. FEMME AU MIROIR DANS UN CADRE OVALE (*fig. 163*)
Lead, watercolor, and pen; 295 x 170 mm.; stamp E.M.
Coll.: Cab. des Dessins (RF 30 507).

102. FEMME DE DOS AVEC DEUX ENFANTS (*fig. 165*)
Lead; 91 x 57 mm.; stamp E.M.
Coll.: Cab. des Dessins (RF 30 443).
   Derived from Franciabigio's *Marriage of the Virgin*, Annunziata, Florence (fig. 164). (Detail).

103. BUSTE D'ANGE
Lead; 156 x 91 mm.; stamp E.M.
Coll.: Cab. des Dessins (RF 30 442).

104. DEUX PUTTI (*fig. 158*)
Lead; 156 x 90 mm.; stamp E.M.
Coll.: Cab. des Dessins (RF 30 441).
   Derived from the cupids of Correggio's *Danaë*, Borghese Gallery, Rome (fig. 159). (Detail).

105. MAIN (*fig. 172*)
Black crayon and white chalk on grey paper; 195 x 122 mm.; stamp E.M.
Coll.: Cab. des Dessins (RF 30 396).

106. TÊTES D'ENFANTS ORIENTAUX (*fig. 168*)
Lead; 170 x 92 mm.; stamp E.M.
Coll.: Cab. des Dessins (RF 30 398).

107. FIGURE ASSISE, LA TÊTE DANS LES MAINS
Lead; 92 x 157 mm.; stamp E.M.
Coll.: Cab. des Dessins (RF 30 444).

108. ANGE VOLANT
Lead; 156 x 90 mm.; stamp E.M.
Coll.: Cab. des Dessins (RF 30 445).

109. DEUX PUTTI (*fig. 174*)
Lead, wash, and pen with sepia ink; 285 x 153 mm.
Coll.: Cab. des Dessins (RF 30 432).
Text ref.: p. 51.

110. GROUPE DE DEUX FEMMES ET ENFANT
Lead and sanguine; 194 x 120 mm.; stamp E.M.
Coll.: Cab. des Dessins (RF 30 399).

111. FIGURE DE FEMME (*fig. 166*)
Lead; 195 x 123 mm.; stamp E.M.
Coll.: Cab. des Dessins (RF 30 397).

112. DEUX TÊTES
Lead; 290 x 212 mm.; stamp E.M.
Coll.: Cab. des Dessins (RF 30 362).

113. TÊTE DE FEMME (*fig. 167*)
Lead with black crayon touches; 290 x 212 mm.
Coll.: Cab. des Dessins (RF 30 374).

114. BAIGNEUSE
Lead; 290 x 212 mm.; stamp E.M.
Coll.: Cab. des Dessins (RF 30 367).

115. FIGURE ALLÉGORIQUE (*fig. 178*)
Lead and watercolor; 175 x 212 mm.; stamp E.M.
Coll.: Cab. des Dessins (RF 30 353).

116. FEMME ET PUTTO (*fig. 175*)
Sanguine; 290 x 212 mm.; stamp E.M.
Coll.: Cab. des Dessins (RF 30 364).

117. GROUPE ALLÉGORIQUE: FEMME ET DEUX PUTTI (*fig. 179*)
Lead; 290 x 212 mm.; stamp E.M.
Coll.: Cab. des Dessins (RF 30 352).

118. MÈRE ET ENFANT, ET AUTRES ESQUISSES (*fig. 176*)
Sanguine; 290 x 212 mm.; stamp E.M.
Coll.: Cab. des Dessins (RF 30 355).

119. PUTTO ET MASQUE (*fig. 36*)
Lead; 290 x 212 mm.
Coll.: Cab. des Dessins (RF 30 371).
Text ref.: pp. 50, 51.

120. SOLDAT EN ARMURE (*fig. 180*)
Lead and watercolor; 290 x 212 mm.
Coll.: Cab. des Dessins (RF 30 370).
Text ref.: p. 9.

121. DEUX FIGURES
Lead; 290 x 212 mm.; stamp E.M.
Coll.: Cab. des Dessins (RF 30 365).

122. ESQUISSES DE TÊTES
Lead; 212 x 290 mm.; stamp E.M.
Coll.: Cab. des Dessins (RF 30 369).

123. SOLDATS LUTTANT
Lead; 290 x 212 mm.; stamp E.M.
Coll.: Cab. des Dessins (RF 30 330).

124. DEUX FIGURES DRAPÉES (*fig. 181*)
Sanguine; 290 x 212 mm.; stamp E.M.
Coll.: Cab. des Dessins (RF 30 340).

125. SERVANTE ET PAGE (*fig. 177*)
Lead; 290 x 212 mm.; stamp E.M.
Coll.: Cab. des Dessins (RF 30 336).

126. SAINT LUC (*fig. 136*)
Lead; 290 x 212 mm.; stamp E.M.
Coll.: Cab. des Dessins (RF 30 377).
   This drawing belongs to the series of Evangelists comprising Cat. Nos. 60 and 61.

127. FIGURE NUE ASSISE (*fig. 182*)
Lead; 178 x 132 mm.; stamp E.M.
Coll.: Cab. des Dessins (RF 11 970).
   It appears likely, from the type and pose, that this drawing was based on a painting. This source remains to be found. Affinities exist between this drawing and the painting *La Nymphe surprise* of 1862 (Jamot, no. 55), and this drawing may have been one of the sources of the painting (see fig. 183).
Text ref.: p. 54.

128. FEMME ASSISE (*fig. 173*)
Black crayon.
Bibl.: Rey, p. 9 (ill.); Rey, *Manet*, 1962, p. 17 (dated in the early 1870's by Rey).
Coll.: M. Guérin, Paris, 1932 (present location unknown).

129. SOLDATS (*figs. 33, 34, 35*)
Lead; 240 x 265 mm.; stamp E.M. Two figures on recto (figs. 33, 34); one figure on verso (fig. 35).
Coll.: P. Benoit, Paris; Cab. des Dessins (RF 11 973).
   These drawings are on two pages which once were part of a sketchbook. The figure which appears on the verso (fig. 35) is a tracing of the corresponding recto figure (fig. 34).
Text ref.: pp. 48, 49, 50.

130. DANSE (*fig. 184*)
Lead and watercolor; 290 x 220 mm.
Bibl.: Rey, p. 6 (ill.).
Coll.: E. Rouart, Paris.
Text ref.: p. 50.

131. MUSIQUE (*fig. 185*)
Lead and watercolor; 290 x 220 mm.
Bibl.: Rey, p. 5 (ill.); Florisoone, pl. 9.
Coll.: E. Rouart, Paris.
Text ref.: p. 50.

132. PROCESSION RELIGIEUSE
Lead and watercolor; 220 x 284 mm.
Bibl.: Rey, p. 38 (ill.).
Coll.: E. Rouart, Paris.

133. TROIS ENFANTS DE CHOEUR (*fig. 190*)
Lead and sepia; 220 x 115 mm.
Coll.: Museum Boymans-van Beuningen, Rotterdam (Inv. no. FII 45).
   H. R. Hoetink, Curator of the Boymans Museum, has identified this drawing as a study of Ghirlandaio's fresco, *The Burial of St. Francis*, in the Cappella Sassetti, Santa Trinità, Florence.

134. ENFANT DE CHOEUR (*fig. 189*)
Sanguine; 346 x 229 mm.
Bibl.: Rey, p. 12 (ill.); Rey, *Manet*, 1962, p. 78.
Coll.: Cab. des Estampes (Dc 300d–res. no. 9).

135. MODÈLE HABILLÉ DEBOUT (*fig. 186*)
Coll.: Hector Brown (present location unknown).
   Reproduced in a photograph belonging to the Photograph Collection, Fogg Art Museum, Harvard University, Cambridge, Mass.
Text ref.: pp. 53, 54.

136. MODÈLE HABILLÉ DEBOUT (*fig. 187*)
Coll.: Hector Brown (present location unknown).
   Reproduced in a photograph belonging to the Photograph Collection, Fogg Art Museum, Harvard University, Cambridge, Mass.
   This drawing is the verso of the preceding drawing (Cat. No. 135).
Text ref.: pp. 53, 54.

137. JOUEUR DE LUTH (*fig. 188*)
Bibl.: Bazire, p. 7 (ill.).
(Location unknown.)

138. PORTRAIT DE FEMME ASSISE (*fig. 40*)
Charcoal; 545 x 410 mm.; signed at lower center "E. Manet."
Bibl.: Hanson, no. 18.
Exh.: Matthiesen, 1928, no. 93; "From Fouquet to Gauguin," London, 1952, no. 106.
Coll.: V. W. van Gogh, Laren, Holland.
Text ref.: p. 53.

139. L'ÉPLUCHEUSE DE LÉGUMES
Conté crayon and chalk on grey paper; 550 x 420 mm.
Bibl.: Mathey, 1961, no. 28.
Coll.: P. Dubaut, Paris.

140. COMPOSITION VÉNITIENNE (*fig. 191*)
Watercolor; 270 x 245 mm.
Bibl.: Tabarant, 1947, p. 22.
Exh.: Wildenstein, 1948, no. 46.
Sale: Degas collection, Georges Petit Gallery,

Paris, March 26–27, 1918, no. 223.
Coll.: Justin K. Thannhauser, New York.
   This composition suggests a Venetian source, direct or indirect.
Text ref.: p. 64.

141. LE CERF ATTAQUÉ PAR DES CHIENS (*fig. 192*)
Watercolor; 205 x 285 mm.; date, *ca.* 1860; stamp E.M.
Coll.: Gallery M. Guyot, Paris (present location unknown).
   Derived from a detail of Titian's painting, *Jupiter and Antiope*, Louvre.
Text ref.: pp. 52, 55.

142. L'INFANTE (MARIE-MARGUERITE)
Lead and watercolor; 310 x 270 mm.
Bibl.: Tabarant, 1931, no. 7; Tabarant, 1947, p. 37; Mathey, 1963, fig. 88 (Mathey gives the year 1883 as the date of the sale); Hanson, p. 41, no. 5.
Sale: 1884, no. 124.
Coll.: M. de Lostalot, Paris, 1884 (present location unknown).
   Derived from Velasquez's portrait, *L'Infante*, in the Louvre.
Text ref.: pp. 11, 52.

1859–1861

143. LA PÊCHE (*fig. 193*)
Watercolor; 210 x 290 mm.
Bibl.: Tabarant, 1931, no. 46; Tabarant, 1947, p. 219; Hoetink, no. 186, "River Landscape"; Hanson, no. 13.
Sale: Camille Pissarro collection, Georges Petit Gallery, Paris, Dec. 3, 1928, no. 68.
Coll.: C. Pissarro, Paris; P. Cassirer, Berlin; F. Koenigs, Haarlem; D. G. van Beuningen, Rotterdam, 1940; Museum Boymans-van Beuningen, Rotterdam (Inv. no. FII 108).
   Tabarant tentatively dates this work, which he reluctantly entitles "Marine," around

1874 and suggests that the motif is Argenteuil.

Text ref.: pp. 54, 55.

144. LA DÉCOUVERTE DE MOÏSE (*fig. 41*)
Lead, wash and pen, squared with sanguine; 333 x 280 mm.
Bibl.: Hanson, p. 49 and no. 14.
Coll.: Museum Boymans-van Beuningen, Rotterdam (Inv. no. FII 105).
Text ref.: pp. 40, 54, 55.

145. ENFANT FAISANT SES PREMIERS PAS
Lead; 155 x 123 mm.
Bibl.: Mathey, 1961, fig. 30.
Coll.: E. Blot, Paris; P. Dubaut, Paris.
   A note by Mathey, 1961, refers to a drawing by Rubens, in the Louvre, as a source for this drawing.

146. LES PETITS CAVALIERS (*fig. 199*)
Watercolor; 220 x 270 mm.
Bibl.: Meier-Graefe, fig. 2; Tabarant, 1947, p. 19; Hanson, under no. 4.
Sale: 1884, no. 133.
Coll.: Bernheim-Jeune, Paris; Prince de Wagram, Paris, 1947 (present location unknown).
   Derived from the painting by this title in the Louvre (School of Velasquez). A proof of the etching, heightened with watercolor, is reproduced in Richardson, fig. 2.
Text ref.: pp. 11, 52.

147. LE BUVEUR D'ABSINTHE (*fig. 201*)
Watercolor; 290 x 190 mm.; date, 1859.
Bibl.: Hanson, p. 43 and no. 8.
Sales: Pellerin, 1926, no. 38; J. Stonborough collection, New York, Oct. 1940.
Coll.: National Gallery, Washington, D. C., Rosenwald Collection.
   Related to the painting by Manet, *Le Buveur d'absinthe*, which was refused at the Salon of 1859, and to the etching, Guérin, no. 9.
Text ref.: pp. 13, 56.

147a. LE BUVEUR D'ABSINTHE
Pen and Wash; 241 x 142 mm.
Bibl.: Hanson, under no. 8.
Coll.: Hill-Stead Museum, Farmington, Connecticut.

148. LE BUVEUR D'ABSINTHE (*fig. 200*)
Autography; related to preceding drawing.
   Produced for the autographic album, *L'Art à Paris*, 1867.

149. AUGUSTE MANET (*fig. 196*)
Sanguine; 170 x 140 mm.; signed and dated "Ed. M. 1860."
Bibl.: Rey, *Manet*, 1962, p. 6 (ill.).
Exh.: London, 1932, no. 970; Orangerie, 1932, no. 100; Art français, 1937, no. 683.
Coll.: E. Rouart, Paris.
   Related to etching, Guérin, nos. 5 and 10.
Text ref.: pp. 26, 55.

150. MONSIEUR ET MADAME AUGUSTE
   MANET (*fig. 20*)
Sanguine; 300 x 325 mm.; date, 1860.
Coll.: E. Rouart, Paris.
Text ref.: pp. 26, 30, 55 (see fig. 21).

151. PHILIPPE IV (*fig. 197*)
Date, 1860.
Bibl.: M–N, 1926, I, fig. 93; Guérin, under no. 7; Mathey, 1963, fig. 51; Hanson, p. 41 and under no. 6.
(Location unknown.)
   Related to the etching, Guérin, no. 7 (see also painting, fig. 198).
Text ref.: pp. 11, 55, 56.

152. PROFIL DE FEMME (*fig. 194*)
Sanguine; 290 x 252 mm.; signed lower right in ink "M."
Bibl.: Rey, *Manet*, 1962, p. 38 (ill.).
Coll.: Cab. des Estampes (Dc 300d–res. no. 10).
Text ref.: p. 56.

153. PORTRAIT DE ROUDIER (*fig. 195*)
Sanguine; 196 x 157 mm.; inscribed "à mon ami Roudier," and signed "Manet."
Exh.: "Exposition rétrospective de l'art français," Amsterdam, 1926, no. 177.
Coll.: R. Koechlin, Paris; Cab. des Dessins (RF 23 340) (bequest of Koechlin, 1932).
Text ref.: pp. 56, 59.

154. HOMME DEBOUT, LA MAIN ÉTENDUE
Sanguine; 350 x 240 mm.
Bibl.: Mathey, 1961, fig. 52 ("Personnage debout, portant une robe ouverte sur le côté").
Sale: Collection of Mme Ménard-Dorian, Georges Petit Gallery, Dec. 2, 1929 (note of Mathey [1961]: "catalogued at the sale under the name Roll").
Coll.: Mme Ménard-Dorian, Paris; P. Dubaut, Paris.

155. L'ENFANT AU PLATEAU
Lead and wash; 210 x 114 mm.; date, 1861.
Bibl.: Tabarant, 1931, no. 11; Tabarant, 1947, p. 37; *Phillips Collection Catalogue* (Washington, D. C., 1952), p. 64; Hanson, no. 24.
Coll.: Phillips, Washington, D. C.
Related to the etching, Guérin, no. 15.

156. L'ENFANT À L'ÉPÉE (*fig. 7*)
Bibl.: Bazire, p. 55 (ill.).
(Location unknown.)
Related to the painting and to the etching, Guérin, no. 12.
Text ref.: pp. 10, 56.

157. L'ENFANT AU CHIEN (*fig. 206*)
Quill pen and sepia ink; date, 1861; signed lower right, "E. Manet."
Bibl.: Waldmann, 1910, p. 142; Mathey, 1961, fig. 31; Hanson, under no. 20.
Coll.: Curt Glaser, Berlin, 1910 (present location unknown).

Related to the etching, Guérin, no. 17.
Text ref.: pp. 17, 56, 61.

158. CHATS
Lead; 780 x 108 mm.; stamp E.M.
Coll.: Cab. des Dessins (RF 30 438).

159. LA MARCHANDE DE CIERGES (*fig. 207*)
Lead; date, 1861.
Bibl.: Rey, p. 45 (ill.); Mathey, 1963, fig. 62; Hanson, under no. 21.
Coll.: Le Garrec, Paris, 1932 (present location unknown).
Related to the etching, Guérin, no. 19.
Text ref.: p. 17.

160. LE CHANTEUR ESPAGNOL (*fig. 205*)
Tracing; date, 1861.
Bibl.: Bazire, p. 11 (ill.); Rosenthal, p. 168; Hanson, under no. 47.
(Location unknown.)
Related to the etching, Guérin, no. 16.
Text ref.: p. 10.

161. LE CHANTEUR ESPAGNOL (*fig. 203*)
Watercolor; 290 x 220 mm.; signed lower left "Manet."
Bibl.: Tabarant, 1947, p. 102; Hanson, under no. 47.
Coll.: A. Proust, Paris, 1864; Faure, Paris; Durand-Ruel, Paris; Eissler, Vienna, 1922 (present location unknown).
Text ref.: pp. 10, 11, 44. (See figs. 202, 204.)

1862–1863

162. PÊCHEUR
Lead; 122 x 183 mm.; stamp E.M.
Coll.: E. Rouart, Paris.

163. FEUILLES ET FLEUR
Sanguine; 306 x 225 mm.; stamp E.M.
Bibl.: Rey, p. 32 (ill.).
Coll.: E. Rouart, Paris.

164. FONTAINE (*fig. 42*)
Lead and watercolor; 156 x 93 mm.
Bibl.: Rey, p. 1 (ill.).
Coll.: Cab. des Estampes (Dc 300d–res. no. 18).
Text ref.: p. 58.

165. LE VIEUX MUSICIEN (*fig. 171*)
Lead, pen, and wash; 240 x 320 mm.; stamp E.M.
Bibl.: Rey, *Manet*, 1938, p. 123 (ill.); Tabarant, 1947, p. 47.
Coll.: Durand-Ruel, Paris, before 1947 (present location unknown).

166. JEUNE FEMME ÉTENDUE EN COSTUME ESPAGNOL (*fig. 209*)
Watercolor; 165 x 235 mm.; stamp E.M.
Bibl.: Duret, 1902, p. 31; Tabarant, 1931, no. 18; *Yale University Art Gallery Bulletin* (Dec. 1962), p. 12; Hanson, no. 53.
Coll.: Et. Bignou, Paris; Dorville, Paris; Yale University Art Gallery, New Haven (gift of John S. Thacher).
  Same subject as the painting (Jamot, no. 63, fig. 319) (fig. 208).
Text ref.: p. 61.

167. ESPAGNOL
Lead and watercolor; stamp E.M.
Bibl.: Rey, p. 36 (ill.).
Coll.: E. Rouart, Paris.

168. ESPAGNOLE À L'ÉVENTAIL
Wash; 215 x 130 mm.
Bibl.: Tabarant, 1931, no. 19 bis; Tabarant, 1947, p. 55.
Sale: 1884, no. 145.
Coll.: Portier, Paris, 1947 (present location unknown).

169. COMPLAINTE MORESQUE
Lead and wash; 200 x 190 mm.; date, 1862.
Bibl.: Tabarant, 1931, no. 20; Tabarant, 1947, p. 56.

Sale: 1884, no. 149.
Coll.: Lehideux, Paris, 1947 (present location unknown).
Text ref.: p. 58.

170. COIN DU JARDIN DES TUILERIES (*fig. 210*)
Wash; 178 x 112 mm.; signed lower right in ink "E.M."; date, *ca.* 1862.
Bibl.: Rey, p. 34 (ill.); Sandblad, pp. 17 ff.; Mathey, 1961, fig. 126.
Exh.: Orangerie, 1932, no. 102.
Coll.: Cab. des Estampes (Dc 300d–res. no. 13).
Text ref.: p. 57.

171. LA MUSIQUE AUX TUILERIES (*fig. 22*)
Lead and wash on two joined pages; 185 x 225 mm.
Bibl.: M–N, 1926, I, 34, fig. 23; Tabarant, 1931, p. 513; Rey, p. 34 (ill.); Martin, pl. 2; Mathey, 1961, fig. 124.
Exh.: Orangerie, 1932, no. 101.
Coll.: E. Rouart, Paris.
Text ref.: pp. 32, 33, 41, 56, 61.

172. PERSONNAGES (*fig. 211*)
Lead; 197 x 126 mm.
Coll.: Cab. des Dessins (RF 30 536).
  Appear to be direct preparatory sketches of figures for the painting *La Musique aux Tuileries* (Jamot, no. 36, fig. 352).

173. PERSONNAGES
Lead; 182 x 110 mm.
Coll.: Cab. des Dessins (RF 30 474).
  Appear to be direct preparatory sketches of figures for the painting *La Musique aux Tuileries* (Jamot, no. 36, fig. 352).

174. DEUX FEMMES
Lead; 184 x 110 mm.; stamp E.M.
Coll.: E. Rouart, Paris.
  Related to the painting *La Musique aux Tuileries* (Jamot, no. 36, fig. 352).

175. COURSE DE TAUREAUX (*fig. 212*)
Watercolor on a fan; signed lower left "E. Manet."
Bibl.: Tabarant, 1931, no. 21; Tabarant, 1947, p. 56.
Exh.: "Manet, trente-cinq tableaux de la collection Pellerin," Bernheim—Jeune Gallery, Paris, June 1910, no. 34.
Sale: 1884, no. 134.
Coll.: Pellerin, Paris, 1947 (present location unknown).

176. LE BALLET ESPAGNOL
Lead, wash and watercolor with gouache; 230 x 410 mm.; signed lower left "Manet."
Bibl.: J. Leymarie, *Manet* (Paris: Hazan, 1952), pl. 11; Richardson, fig. 11; Pataky, no. 40.
Coll.: P. von Majovszky, Budapest; Budapest Museum of Fine Arts.
Text ref.: p. 58.

177. LE BUVEUR D'EAU
Sepia wash; 135 x 95 mm.; signed and dated top right "Manet 2 Avril 1865."
Bibl.: *Zeitschrift für bildende Kunst*, XIX (1884), 251; Tabarant, 1931, no. 24; Tabarant, 1947, p. 51.
Coll.: Stahl, Berlin, 1947 (present location unknown).

178. LOLA DE VALENCE (*fig. 214*)
Lead, pen, wash, watercolor, and gouache; 256 x 174 mm.; date, 1862; signed lower right "Manet."
Bibl.: M–N, 1926, II, fig. 335; Tabarant, 1947, no. 558; Martin, pl. 3.
Coll.: Camondo, Paris; Cab. des Dessins (RF 4102) (bequest of Camondo, 1911).
  Related to etching, Guérin, no. 23 (see figs. 215, 217).
Text ref.: pp. 13, 41, 57, 58, 62, 77.

179. LOLA DE VALENCE (*fig. 216*)
Lead, pen, wash, watercolor and gouache; 253 x 175 mm.; signed lower right "Manet."
Bibl.: Hanson, under no. 45.
Coll.: Grenville L. Winthrop; Fogg Art Museum, Harvard University, Cambridge, Mass. (bequest of Grenville L. Winthrop).
Text ref.: pp. 13, 57, 58.

180. LE BAÏLARIN (MARIANO CAMPRUBI) (*fig. 213*)
Wash and watercolor; 170 x 150 mm.; stamp E.M.
Bibl.: Duret, 1902, pl. 7; Jamot, under no. 47; Tabarant, 1947, p. 54; Hanson, under no. 42.
Sale: 1884, no. 144.
Coll.: Mme Manet, Paris; J. Doucet, Paris; Bernstein, Paris, 1917 (present location unknown).
  Related to etching, Guérin, no. 43.
Text ref.: p. 58.

181. VICTORINE MEUREND EN COSTUME D'ESPADA (*fig. 8*)
Watercolor; 300 x 230 mm.; signed lower right "Manet."
Bibl.: Hanson, under no. 50.
Exh.: Wildenstein, 1948, no. 47.
Coll.: Museum of Art, Rhode Island School of Design, Providence, Rhode Island.
  Related to the etching, Guérin, no. 32 (see figs. 10, 11), and to the painting (see fig. 9).
Text ref.: pp. 12, 13, 41, 58, 67.

182. TÊTE DE MODÈLE (*fig. 219*)
Sanguine.
Bibl.: Bazire, p. 8 (ill.).
(Location unknown.)
  This study of a head is related to the nude study *Baigneuse* (Cat. No. 188).

183. PROFIL DE FEMME (*fig. 220*)
Bibl.: Rewald, p. 6 (ill.).
(Location unknown.)

Probably a likeness of Mme Edouard Manet (see the painting *Mme Manet au piano*, Jamot, no. 142, fig. 125).

184. FEMME SE COIFFANT (*fig. 43*)
Sanguine and lead; 307 x 255 mm.; stamp E.M.
Bibl.: Rey, p. 7 (ill.).
Coll.: Cab. des Estampes (Dc 300d–res. no. 8).
Text ref.: p. 59.

185. LA TOILETTE (first version) (*fig. 218*)
Sanguine; 280 x 200 mm.; date, 1862.
Bibl.: *Vasari Society* (London: Oxford University Press, 1905–1935), 2nd series, XI, no. 15 (ill.); Rey, p. 10 (ill.); A. Mongan, *Great Drawings of All Time* (New York, 1962), under no. 793.
Exh.: London, 1932, no. 999; Orangerie, 1932, no. 107.
Coll.: Guiot, Paris; Leicester Galleries, London; Samuel Courtauld, London; University of London, Courtauld Institute of Art.
  Study for the etching, Guérin, no. 26 (see fig. 221).
Text ref.: pp. 19, 31, 41, 57, 58, 59, 63.

186. LA TOILETTE (second version) (*fig. 44*)
Sanguine; 270 x 195 mm.; signed lower right "E. Manet."
Bibl.: Rey, p. 10 (ill.); Mathey, 1961, fig. 50.
Exh.: Orangerie, 1932, no. 106.
Sale: 1884, no. 177.
Coll.: M. Guérin, Paris; private collection, U.S.A.
  Related to the etching, Guérin, no. 26 (see fig. 221).
Text ref.: pp. 19, 31, 59, 60, 61, 64.

187. LA TOILETTE (second version; tracing)
Tracing done with metal point on mica sheet from preceding drawing (Cat. No. 186);

240 x 160 mm.; stamp E.M.; signed lower right "E.M."
Coll.: Cab. des Dessins.

188. BAIGNEUSE (*fig. 3*)
Pen and wash; 266 x 203 mm.; date, 1862.
Bibl.: *Vasari Society* (London: Oxford University Press, 1905–1935), 2nd series, VIII, no. 16 (ill.); Hanson, p. 49 and no. 15.
Exh.: London, 1932, no. 959.
Coll.: A. Lousada, London.
  A different version of this subject is owned by the Museum Boymans-van Beuningen, Rotterdam (Inv. no. FII 191). It is, in our opinion, not by Manet's hand (a comparison of it with the London drawing brings out its structural weaknesses and the haphazardness of its "spontaneity" of technique). It has been illustrated and mentioned as an authentic Manet in a number of monographs including Huygues, *Le Dessin français au XIXème siècle* (Lausanne: Ed. Mermod, 1956), pl. 86, and Mathey, 1961, p. 18, where it is referred to as "La Femme au bain."
Text ref.: pp. 4, 59, 64.

189. FEMME ÉTENDUE (*fig. 45*)
Wash; 135 x 190 mm.; stamp E.M.
Bibl.: Waldmann, 1910, p. 17 (ill.); Tabarant, 1947, fig. 563; Mathey, 1961, fig. 74 (entitled "Femme assise").
(Location unknown.)
Text ref.: pp. 61, 62.

190. FEMME NUE ET CHAT NOIR (first version)
Sepia and watercolor; 285 x 410 mm.; signed lower right "E.M."
Bibl.: Charles de Tolnay, *History and Technique of Old Master Drawings* (New York: H. Bittner and Co., 1943), fig. 254; Tabarant, 1947, p. 77.
Coll.: T. Duret, Paris; Knoedler and Co., Paris, before 1947 (present location unknown).

191. FEMME NUE ET CHAT NOIR (second version)

Wash; 210 x 275 mm.

Bibl.: Tabarant, 1947, p. 77.

Coll.: A. Beurdeley, Paris, 1920 (present location unknown).

Served as a source for the wood engraving, Guérin, no. 87 (see Guérin, fig. 59).

Text ref.: p. 61.

192. JEANNE DUVAL (*fig. 223*)

Watercolor: 155 x 230 mm.

Bibl.: Rey, p. 13 (ill.); Tabarant, 1947, p. 57; Richardson, fig. 13.

Exh.: Matthiesen, 1928, no. 3.

Coll.: Kunsthalle, Bremen.

Text ref.: p. 61.

193. ODALISQUE (*fig. 222*)

Wash, watercolor, and gouache; 127 x 197 mm.

Bibl.: Meier-Graefe, p. 55, fig. 31; Tabarant, 1931, p. 516, no. 17.

Exh.: Orangerie, 1932, no. 105.

Coll.: A. Pellerin, Paris; Cab. des Dessins (RF 6929) (gift of the Société des Amis du Louvre, 1926).

Text ref.: pp. 18, 62.

194. ÉTUDE POUR L'OLYMPIA (first version) (*fig. 224*)

Sanguine; 224 x 298 mm.

Bibl.: Rey, p. 8 (ill.).

Coll.: Cab. des Estampes (Dc 300d-res. no. 7).

195. ÉTUDE POUR L'OLYMPIA (second version) (*fig. 225*)

Sanguine; 245 x 457 mm.; stamp E.M.

Bibl.: Meier-Graefe, p. 133, fig. 64; Tabarant, 1931, p. 522; F. Mathey, *Olympia* (Paris: Vendôme, 1948), fig. 5.

Coll.: H. Rouart, Paris; J. Doucet, Paris; Cab. des Dessins (RF 24 335) (acquired by the Louvre at a public sale, Hôtel Drouot, Paris, March 30, 1935, no. 42).

Text ref.: pp. 61, 62.

196. OLYMPIA (*fig. 228*)

Watercolor; 200 x 310 mm.; signed lower right "E. Manet."

Bibl.: Tabarant, 1931, no. 27; Richardson, fig. 19; Martin, pl. 5; Rey, *Manet*, 1962, p. 14 (ill.); Hanson, p. 75 and no. 55.

Exh.: Orangerie, 1932, no. 108a.

Coll.: J. Strauss, Paris; G. Bernheim, Paris; A. Mayer, Paris; A. Daber, Paris; D. Morely, London; private collection, Paris.

Related to the etching, Guérin, nos. 39 and 40 (see figs. 226, 227, and 229).

Text ref.: pp. 13, 41, 57.

197. LE DÉJEUNER SUR L'HERBE (*fig. 230*)

Lead and watercolor; 345 x 415 mm.

Bibl.: Tabarant, 1931, no. 25; Tabarant, 1947, no. 568, pp. 72, 513; J. Leymarie, *Manet* (Paris: Hazan, 1952), pl. 14; Richardson, fig. 17; Martin, pl. 4.

Coll.: B. Cassirer, Berlin; M. S. Walzer, Oxford.

1864–1868

198. LE CHRIST AUX ANGES (*fig. 231*)

Lead, quill pen, watercolor, and gouache; 324 x 268 mm.; signed lower right "Manet"; date, 1864.

Bibl.: Tabarant, 1931, no. 31, p. 524; Jamot, under no. 85; Martin, pl. 6; Hanson, under no. 70.

Coll.: Mme E. Zola, Paris; Cab. des Dessins (RF 4520) (bequest of Mme E. Zola to the Louvre, 1918).

Related to the etching, Guérin, no. 34.

Text ref.: p. 64.

199. LE CHRIST INSULTÉ PAR LES SOLDATS (*fig. 46*)

Sepia wash and pen; 267 x 202 mm.; date, 1864.

Bibl.: Florisoone, pl. 30.

Exh.: Matthiesen, 1928, no. 13.

Coll.: Dr. Haans Swarzenski, Cambridge, Mass.

Text ref.: pp. 31, 64.

200. LE TORERO MORT
Black chalk; date, 1864.
Bibl.: Duret, 1906 (ill., facing p. 24); Guérin,
under no. 75.
(Location unknown.)
   Preliminary drawing for the etching (Gué-
   rin, no. 33), and for the lithograph *La
   Guerre Civile* (Guérin, no. 75).

201. LE KEARSAGE
Watercolor; 260 x 350 mm.; date, 1864.
Bibl.: Meier-Graefe, fig. 77, under the title
   "Alabama"; Tabarant, 1931, no. 32; Ta-
   barant, 1947, p. 89; Hanson, under no. 63.
Sale: 1884, no. 128.
Coll.: Dr. Robin, Paris, 1884 (present location
   unknown).

202. LA SORTIE DU PORT DE BOULOGNE
   (*fig. 48*)
Lead and watercolor; 140 x 185 mm. Some use
   of lead pencil is found on outlines and
   overlays the watercolor, in particular on
   the hull of the boat.
Bibl.: Rio Letters (ill.); Mathey, 1963, fig. 41.
Coll.: E. Rouart, Paris.
   There are two pencil sketches on the verso:
   on the left, a sailboat; on the right, a sail.
Text ref.: p. 66.

203. COURSES À LONGCHAMP (*fig. 233*)
Watercolor and gouache; 250 x 560 mm., on
   two joined sheets; signed and dated lower
   left corner "Manet 1864."
Bibl.: Tabarant, 1931, no. 21; Tabarant, 1947,
   p. 100; Martin, pl. 7; Hanson, under nos.
   67, 68, 69.
Coll.: Grenville L. Winthrop; Fogg Art Museum, Harvard University, Cambridge,
   Mass. (bequest of Grenville L. Winthrop).
   Related to the lithograph, Guérin, no. 72
   (see fig. 237).
Text ref.: pp. 6, 65.

204. AUX COURSES
Lead; 120 x 110 mm.; signed lower right "E.
   Manet."
Coll.: Cab. des Estampes (Dc 300d-res. no. 4).

205. AUX COURSES (*fig. 235*)
Lead; 184 x 113 mm.; stamp E.M.
Bibl.: Rey, p. 31 (ill.).
Coll.: E. Rouart, Paris.
   For comparison, see fig. 236.
Text ref.: p. 65.

206. VOITURE AUX COURSES
Watercolor.
Coll.: Baron Von Hirsh, Basel.
   Reproduced in a photograph belonging to
   the Photograph Collection, Fogg Art Mu-
   seum, Harvard University, Cambridge,
   Mass.

207. DESCENTE DE L'OMNIBUS (*fig. 234*)
Lead; 110 x 182 mm.; stamp E.M.
Coll.: Cab. des Dessins (RF 30 453).

208. DEUX HOMMES PANSANT UN CHEVAL
   (*fig. 232*)
Lead; 197 x 123 mm.
Coll.: Cab. des Dessins (RF 30 454).

209. CROQUIS D'HOMME EN BUSTE
Lead; 120 x 182 mm.; stamp E.M.
Coll.: Cab. des Dessins (RF 30 457).

210. GROUPE DE FIGURES
Lead; 157 x 91 mm.
Coll.: Cab. des Dessins (RF 30 499).

211. FOULE AUX COURSES (*fig. 47*)
Lead; 110 x 182 mm.; stamp E.M.
Coll.: Cab. des Dessins (RF 30 452).
Text ref.: p. 65.

212. CHEVAUX EN COURSE (*fig. 1*)
Lead and watercolor; 197 x 269 mm.; stamp
E.M.; date, 1864.
Coll.: Cab. des Dessins (RF 30 451).
Text ref.: pp. 64, 65.

213. LA POSADA
Watercolor; 241 x 406 mm. (frame); stamp
E.M.; date, *ca.* 1865.
Bibl.: Tabarant, 1931, no. 26; Rey, *Manet*,
1938, p. 118 (ill.); Tabarant, 1947, p. 75.
Exh.: 1884, no. 121.
Sale: 1884, no. 131 (dimensions given in sale
catalogue, 420 x 570 mm. [frame], appear
to be erroneous).
Coll.: Gauthier-Lathuille, Paris; Paul Rosen-
berg, Paris; private collection, U.S.A.
Related to the painting, Jamot, no. 123, and
to the etching, Guérin, no. 47. My recent
study of this watercolor leads me to sus-
pect that the watercolor brushwork, which
overlays Manet's pencil drawing, was added by another hand, because it is relatively
inarticulate and lacks consistency.

214. FÉLIX BRACQUEMOND (*fig. 19*)
Special graphic technique (see page 28 of our
text); 169 x 112 mm.; date, 1865.
Bibl.: Rosenthal, p. 74; Guérin, no. 42.

215. EDGAR ALLAN POE (*fig. 18*)
Wash; 303 x 225 mm.; signed "E.M." under
the right shoulder.
Bibl.: Rey, p. 24 (ill.); Hanson, under no. 137.
Coll.: Cab. des Estampes (Dc 300d-res. no. 15).
Related to the etching, Guérin, no. 55.
Text ref.: pp. 26, 27, 68.

216. LE MONTREUR D'OURS (*fig. 246*)
Sepia wash; 145 x 250 mm.; signed lower left
"E.M."; date, *ca.* 1865.
Bibl.: M–N, 1926, I, fig. 30.
Exh.: Orangerie, 1932, no. 104.
Coll.: Moreau-Nélaton, Paris; Cab. des Estam-

pes (gift of Moreau-Nélaton to the Bibli-
othèque Nationale, 1927).
Related to the etching, Guérin, no. 41.
Text ref.: pp. 14, 67.

217. LES SALTIMBANQUES (*fig. 12*)
Lead and sepia wash; 253 x 289 mm.; stamp
E.M.
Bibl.: M–N, 1926, I, fig. 29; Rey, p. 33 (ill.);
Richardson, fig. 5; Martin, pl. 1.
Exh.: Orangerie, 1932, no. 103.
Coll.: Cab. des Estampes (Dc 300d-res. no. 14).
Text ref.: pp. 14, 15, 67.

218. TORERO EN BUSTE (*fig. 238*)
Lead; 117 x 188 mm.
Coll.: Cab. des Dessins (RF 30 505).

219. CHAPEAU ET GUITARE
Lead and watercolor; 333 x 227 mm.
Bibl.: T. Reff, "Manet's Frontispiece Etch-
ings," *Bulletin of the New York Public
Library* (March 1962), pl. 1.
Coll.: New York Public Library.
Study for frontispiece etching, Guérin, no.
62, first plate.

220. COURSE DE TAUREAUX
Watercolor; 192 x 215 mm.; signed bottom
left "E.M."
Bibl.: F. Daulte, *Dessins français de Manet à
Cézanne* (Lausanne, 1954), no. 1; Martin,
pl. 8; Rey, *Manet*, 1962, p. 32 (ill.).
Coll.: Schoeller, Paris; A. Strölin, Lausanne;
private collection, Paris.
Text ref.: p. 67.

221. JAMBES CHAUSSÉES D'ESCARPINS
(*fig. 239*)
Lead; 88 x 155 mm.; stamp E.M.
Coll.: Cab. des Dessins (RF 30 449).

222. ESCARPINS
Watercolor; 76 x 107 mm.

Bibl.: Hanson, no. 41.
Coll.: Mr. and Mrs. Alex M. Lewyt, New York.

223. LE CHIFFONNIER (*fig. 240*)
Watercolor; 156 x 85 mm.
Bibl.: Hanson, under no. 76.
Coll.: Cab. des Dessins (RF 30 495).

224. FLEURS DU MAL (*fig. 244*)
Pen and sanguine; signed lower left "Manet."
Coll.: M. Guérin, Paris (present location unknown).
    Drawn on one of the prints of the etching *Charles Baudelaire*, Guérin, no. 38.
Text ref.: p. 20.

225. CHAT SOUS UNE CHAISE (*fig. 243*)
Lead and wash; 215 x 132 mm.; signed lower right "E.M."
Bibl.: Rey, p. 29 (ill.); Hanson, under no. 88.
Exh.: Orangerie, 1932, no. 112.
Coll.: Cab. des Estampes (Dc 300d-res. no. 11).
    Related to the etching, Guérin, no. 52.
Text ref.: p. 69.

226. LES CHATS (*fig. 245*)
Black crayon; 128 x 97 mm.; stamp E.M.; date, 1868.
Coll.: Cab. des Dessins (RF 30 380).
    Sketches for the etching, Guérin, no. 52.
Text ref.: p. 22.

227. LE RENDEZ-VOUS DES CHATS (*fig. 50*)
Watercolor and gouache; 425 x 320 mm.; signed lower right "E. Manet."; date, 1868.
Bibl.: Rey, p. 30 (ill.); Richardson, fig. 33; Hanson, under no. 90.
Coll.: Le Garrec, Paris, 1932 (present location unknown).
    Related to the poster, Guérin, no. 74 (see fig. 49).
Text ref.: pp. 21, 22, 68, 69.

228. CHATS
Lead and wash; date, 1868.
Bibl.: Guérin, under no. 74; Hanson, under no. 90.
(Location unknown.)

229. DEUX CHATS (*fig. 241*)
Lead; 148 x 100 mm.; stamp E.M.
Coll.: Cab. des Dessins (RF 30 381).

230. CHAT
Lead; 103 x 78 mm.; stamp E.M.
Coll.: Cab. des Dessins (RF 30 434).

231. CHATS (*fig. 242*)
Lead; 103 x 78 mm.; stamp E.M.
Coll.: Cab. des Dessins (RF 30 436).

232. JEUNE HOMME (*fig. 247*)
Sanguine; 325 x 232 mm.; signed lower right "ed. Manet."; date, *ca.* 1868 (in Hoetink, *ca.* 1866).
Bibl.: Museum Boymans-van Beuningen, *Agenda Diary* (1961), no. 43, pl. XLIII; Hoetink, no. 182, "Léon Leenhoff."
Coll.: Museum Boymans-van Beuningen, Rotterdam (Inv. no. FII 104).
    The model for this drawing is very probably Léon Koëlla-Leenhoff, Manet's son (we have revised our earlier dating, quoted by Miss Agnes Mongan in *Great Drawings of All Time* [New York, 1962], under number 794).

233. LE BALCON
Lead and watercolor; 108 x 82 mm.; signed lower left "E. Manet" by the hand of Mme E. Manet.
Bibl.: Tabarant, 1931, no. 34; Tabarant, 1947, fig. 582; Hanson, no. 104.
Coll.: Bernheim-Jeune, Paris; Mr. and Mrs. Alex M. Lewyt, New York.

234. MME MANET AU PIANO
Watercolor; 310 x 220 mm.; lower right, apocryphal signature "Manet."
Bibl.: Tabarant, 1931, no. 35; Tabarant, 1947, fig. 583.
Coll.: Mme Manet, Paris; Cortot, Paris, 1910 (present location unknown).
   Tabarant (1931, p. 155) mentions a replica of this watercolor.

235. NURSE ET ENFANT SUR UN BANC (*fig. 248*)
Lead; 120 x 185 mm.
Bibl.: Hoetink, no. 178; Hanson, no. 154.
Coll.: Museum Boymans-van Beuningen, Rotterdam (Inv. no. FII 46).
Text ref.: p. 69.

236. FEMME COUSANT (*fig. 249*)
Lead; 120 x 185 mm.
Bibl.: Hoetink, no, 178; Hanson, no. 154.
Coll.: Museum Boymans-van Beuningen, Rotterdam (Inv. no. FII 46).
   Verso of Cat. No. 235.
Text ref.: p. 69.

237. DEUX ENFANTS PORTANT UN FARDEAU
Sanguine and lead; 156 x 90 mm.; stamp E.M.
Coll.: Cab. des Dessins (RF 30 435).

1869–1874

238. AU CAFÉ (*fig. 250*)
Quill pen; 295 x 393 mm.
Bibl.: Hanson, no. 92.
Exh.: Wildenstein, 1948, no. 49; "One Hundred Twenty-Five Master Drawings," The Solomon R. Guggenheim Museum, New York, May–July 1962, no. 74.
Coll.: P. J. Sachs, Cambridge, Mass.; Fogg Art Museum, Harvard University, Cambridge, Mass.
   Served as a basis for the autographies, Guérin, nos. 80, 81.
Text ref.: pp. 16, 70.

239. FEMME AUX LONGUES TRESSES
Lead (?).
Bibl.: Bazire, p. 102 (ill.).
(Location unknown.)

240. FEMME ET ENFANT
Lead; from Boulogne sketchbook (see list of abbreviations); date, 1869.
Coll.: Cab. des Dessins.
   See painting *Sur la Plage de Boulogne* (fig. 254) for comparison.
Text ref.: pp. 35, 70.

241. JEUNE GARÇON DE DOS
Lead; from Boulogne sketchbook.
Coll.: Cab. des Dessins.
Text ref.: pp. 35, 70.

242. FEMME COURANT
Lead; from Boulogne sketchbook.
Coll.: Cab. des Dessins.
Text ref.: pp. 35, 70.

243. DEUX ENFANTS
Lead; from Boulogne sketchbook.
Coll.: Cab. des Dessins.
Text ref.: pp. 35, 70.

244. ENFANTS
Lead; from Boulogne sketchbook.
Coll.: Cab. des Dessins.
Text ref.: pp. 35, 70.

245. HOMME SOUS UN PARAPLUIE
Lead; from Boulogne sketchbook.
Coll.: Cab. des Dessins.
Text ref.: pp. 35, 70.

246. JEUNE GARÇON (*fig. 252*)
Lead; from Boulogne sketchbook.
Coll.: Cab. des Dessins.
Text ref.: pp. 35, 70.

247. FEMME ET ENFANT
Lead; from Boulogne sketchbook.
Coll.: Cab. des Dessins.
Text ref.: pp. 35, 70.

248. PERSONNAGES
Lead; from Boulogne sketchbook.
Coll.: Cab. des Dessins.
Text ref.: pp. 35, 70.

249. ÂNE (*fig. 256*)
Lead; from Boulogne sketchbook.
Coll.: Cab. des Dessins.
Text ref.: pp. 35, 70.

250. TROIS FEMMES (*fig. 251*)
Lead; from Boulogne sketchbook.
Coll.: Cab. des Dessins.
Text ref.: pp. 35, 70.

251. BARQUE À VOILE
Lead; from Boulogne sketchbook.
Coll.: Cab. des Dessins.
Text ref.: pp. 35, 70.

252. FEMME ASSISE
Lead; from Boulogne sketchbook.
Coll.: Cab. des Dessins.
Text ref.: pp. 35, 70.

253. JEUNE FEMME (*fig. 255*)
Lead; from Boulogne sketchbook.
Coll.: Cab. des Dessins.
Text ref.: pp. 35, 70.

254. ENFANT À CHEVAL
Lead; from Boulogne sketchbook.
Coll.: Cab. des Dessins.
Text ref.: pp. 35, 70.

255. ENFANT PORTANT UN SAC
Lead; from Boulogne sketchbook.
Coll.: Cab. des Dessins.
Text ref.: pp. 35, 70.

256. ENFANT À CHEVAL DE FACE (first version)
Lead; from Boulogne sketchbook.
Coll.: Cab. des Dessins.
Text ref.: pp. 35, 70.

257. ENFANT À CHEVAL DE FACE (second version) (*fig. 259*)
Lead; from Boulogne sketchbook.
Coll.: Cab. des Dessins.
Text ref.: pp. 35, 70.

258. FEMME DE DOS ET CABINE
Lead; from Boulogne sketchbook.
Coll.: Cab. des Dessins.
Text ref.: pp. 35, 70.

259. CABINE (*fig. 258*)
Lead; from Boulogne sketchbook.
Coll.: Cab. des Dessins.
Text ref.: pp. 35, 70.

260. HOMME PANSANT UN CHEVAL
Lead; from Boulogne sketchbook.
Coll.: Cab. des Dessins.
Text ref.: pp. 35, 70.

261. FEMME DE DOS
Lead; from Boulogne sketchbook.
Coll.: Cab. des Dessins.
Text ref.: pp. 35, 70.

262. ENFANT DE DOS
Lead; from Boulogne sketchbook.
Coll.: Cab. des Dessins.
Text ref.: pp. 35, 70.

263. JEUNE FILLE
Lead; from Boulogne sketchbook.
Coll.: Cab. des Dessins.
Text ref.: pp. 35, 70.

264. FEMME ASSISE
Lead; from Boulogne sketchbook.
Coll.: Cab. des Dessins.
Text ref.: pp. 35, 70.

265. FEMME ASSISE, LISANT
Lead; from Boulogne sketchbook.
Coll.: Cab. des Dessins.
Text ref.: pp. 35, 70.

266. ENFANT AU CAPUCHON
Lead; from Boulogne sketchbook.
Coll.: Cab. des Dessins.
Text ref.: pp. 35, 70.

267. JEUNE GARÇON ASSIS
Lead; from Boulogne sketchbook.
Coll.: Cab. des Dessins.
Text ref.: pp. 35, 70.

268. PERSONNAGE DEBOUT
Lead; from Boulogne sketchbook.
Coll.: Cab. des Dessins.
Text ref.: pp. 35, 70.

269. HOMME AU CHAPEAU MELON (*fig. 253*)
Lead; from Boulogne sketchbook.
Coll.: Cab. des Dessins.
Text ref.: pp. 35, 70.

270. CIEL ET LUNE (*fig. 257*)
Watercolor; from Boulogne sketchbook.
Coll.: Cab. des Dessins.
Text ref.: pp. 35, 70.

271. FEMME DE PROFIL
Lead; from Boulogne sketchbook.
Coll.: Cab. des Dessins.
Text ref.: pp. 35, 70.

272. JETÉE
Watercolor; from Boulogne sketchbook.
Coll.: Cab. des Dessins.
Text ref.: pp. 35, 70.

273. MARINE
Lead; from Boulogne sketchbook.
Coll.: Cab. des Dessins.
Text ref.: pp. 35, 70.

274. COUPLE EN PROMENADE
Lead; from Boulogne sketchbook.
Coll.: Cab. des Dessins.
Text ref.: pp. 35, 70.

275. GROUPE DE FEMMES
Lead; from Boulogne sketchbook.
Coll.: Cab. des Dessins.
Text ref.: pp. 35, 70.

276. INTÉRIEUR DE CAFÉ (*fig. 263*)
Lead; from Boulogne sketchbook; drawn over
    two pages.
Coll.: Cab. des Dessins.
Text ref.: pp. 35, 70, 78.

277. FEMME DEBOUT
Lead; from Boulogne sketchbook.
Coll.: Cab. des Dessins.
Text ref.: pp. 35, 70.

278. JEUNE FILLE DE PROFIL
Lead; from Boulogne sketchbook.
Coll.: Cab. des Dessins.
Text ref.: pp. 35, 70.

279. FEMME ASSISE DE PROFIL
Lead; from Boulogne sketchbook.
Coll.: Cab. des Dessins.
Text ref.: pp. 35, 70.

280. PERSONNAGES SUR LA JETÉE
Lead; from Boulogne sketchbook.
Coll.: Cab. des Dessins.
Text ref.: pp. 35, 70.

281. BARQUE AVEC PERSONNAGES
Lead; from Boulogne sketchbook.

Coll.: Cab. des Dessins.
Text ref.: pp. 35, 70.

282. LE DÉPART DU BATEAU DE FOLKESTONE
    (*fig. 260*)
Lead; 197 x 126 mm.; date, 1869.
Coll.: Cab. des Dessins (RF 30 537).
    Study for the painting (Jamot, no. 162, fig.
    330).
Text ref.: p. 35.

283. HOMME DE PROFIL (*fig. 262*)
Lead; 103 x 64 mm.
Bibl.: Hanson, under no. 91.
Coll.: Cab. des Dessins (RF 30 543).
    Study for the central figure of the painting
    Départ du bateau de Folkestone (Jamot,
    no. 163, fig. 313).

284. FEMME DE DOS AVEC OMBRELLE
    (*fig. 261*)
Lead; 197 x 121 mm.; stamp E.M.
Coll.: Cab. des Dessins (RF 30 400).
    Verso: study for the figure of the captain in
    the painting *Départ du bateau de Folke-
    stone* (Jamot, no. 162, fig. 330).

285. DEUX FEMMES AVEC OMBRELLE
Lead; 197 x 127 mm.; stamp E.M.
Coll.: Cab. des Dessins (RF 30 401).

286. ESQUISSES DE PERSONNAGES ET DE TÊTES
Lead; 182 x 110 mm.; stamp E.M.
Coll.: Cab. des Dessins (RF 30 425).

287. HOMME AVEC OMBRELLE
Lead; 198 x 127 mm.; stamp E.M.
Coll.: Cab. des Dessins (RF 30 426).

288. GROUPE DE FIGURES
Lead; 197 x 126 mm.
Coll.: Cab. des Dessins (RF 30 427).

289. HOMME ET JEUNE GARÇON (*fig. 264*)
Lead; 197 x 125 mm.; stamp E.M.
Coll.: Cab. des Dessins (RF 30 429).

290. UNE FOULE
Lead; 100 x 65 mm.; stamp E.M.
Coll.: Cab. des Dessins (RF 30 530).

291. DEUX PERSONNAGES (*fig. 266*)
Lead; 198 x 115 mm.
Coll.: Cab. des Dessins (RF 30 533).

292. CINQ PERSONNAGES (*fig. 265*)
Lead; 197 x 123 mm.
Coll.: Cab. des Dessins (RF 30 534).

293. TROIS PERSONNAGES (*fig. 267*)
Lead; 197 x 126 mm.
Coll.: Cab. des Dessins (RF 30 535).

294. HOMME COURANT
Lead; 100 x 63 mm.; stamp E.M.
Coll.: Cab. des Dessins (RF 30 541).

295. TROIS FEMMES
Lead; 102 x 63 mm.; stamp E.M.
Coll.: Cab. des Dessins (RF 30 542).

296. HOMME DE DOS
Lead; 102 x 64 mm.; stamp E.M.
Coll.: Cab. des Dessins (RF 30 544).

297. HOMME DE FACE
Lead; 97 x 62 mm.; stamp E.M.
Coll.: Cab. des Dessins (RF 30 545).

298. HOMME PORTANT DES LORGNONS
Lead; 100 x 64 mm.; stamp E.M.
Coll.: Cab. des Dessins (RF 30 546).

299. HOMME S'APPUYANT SUR SA CANNE
    (*fig. 271*)

Lead; 98 x 64 mm.; stamp E.M.
Coll.: Cab. des Dessins (RF 30 547).

300. HOMME, BRAS CROISÉS DANS LE DOS
    (*fig. 269*)
Lead; 102 x 63 mm.; stamp E.M.
Coll.: Cab. des Dessins (RF 30 548).

301. PROUE DE BATEAU (*fig. 268*)
Lead; 125 x 192 mm.
Coll.: Cab. des Dessins (RF 30 552).

302. GOUVERNAIL DE BATEAU (*fig. 270*)
Lead; 100 x 63 mm.; stamp E.M.
Coll.: Cab. des Dessins (RF 30 560).

303. HOMME AU GOUVERNAIL (*fig. 272*)
Lead; 98 x 63 mm.; stamp E.M.
Coll.: Cab. des Dessins (RF 30 561).

304. TROIS PERSONNAGES DE DOS
Lead; 198 x 127 mm.
Coll.: Cab. des Dessins (RF 30 470).

305. GROUPE DE PERSONNAGES
Lead; 197 x 126 mm.
Coll.: Cab. des Dessins (RF 30 471).

306. HOMME ET FEMME AVEC OMBRELLE
    (*fig. 277*)
Lead; 197 x 118 mm.
Bibl.: Bouchot-Saupique, fig. 12.
Coll.: Cab. des Dessins (RF 30 472).

307. DEUX FEMMES
Lead; 127 x 198 mm.
Coll.: Cab. des Dessins (RF 30 473).

308. HOMME AVEC CANNE À PÊCHE
    (*fig. 274*)
Lead; 100 x 63 mm.; stamp E.M.
Coll.: Cab. des Dessins (RF 30 480).

309. HOMME AVEC FARDEAU SOUS LE BRAS
Lead; 100 x 62 mm.; stamp E.M.
Coll.: Cab. des Dessins (RF 30 481).

310. HOMME DE DOS
Lead; 100 x 63 mm.; stamp E.M.
Coll.: Cab. des Dessins (RF 30 482).

311. HOMME APPUYÉ SUR SA CANNE
    (*fig. 273*)
Lead; 100 x 64 mm.; stamp E.M.
Coll.: Cab. des Dessins (RF 30 483).

312. DEUX PERSONNAGES (*fig. 276*)
Lead; 103 x 64 mm.
Coll.: Cab. des Dessins (RF 30 484).

313. COUPLE DE FACE
Lead; 102 x 64 mm.; stamp E.M.
Coll.: Cab. des Dessins (RF 30 485).

314. TROIS PERSONNAGES
Lead; 100 x 65 mm.; stamp E.M.
Coll.: Cab. des Dessins (RF 30 486).

315. DEUX HOMMES (*fig. 275*)
Lead; 100 x 63 mm.; stamp E.M.
Coll.: Cab. des Dessins (RF 30 487).

316. ESQUISSE DE PAYSAGE
Lead; 63 x 98 mm.; stamp E.M.
Coll.: Cab. des Dessins (RF 30 490).
    Verso: *Femme de dos.*

317. DEUX FEMMES DE PROFIL
Lead; 63 x 100 mm.; stamp E.M.
Coll.: Cab. des Dessins (RF 30 489).

318. PERSONNAGE DE FACE
Lead; 98 x 63 mm.; stamp E.M.
Coll.: Cab. des Dessins (RF 30 493).

319. TÊTE DE FEMME ET TÊTE D'HOMME
    (*fig. 280*)
Lead; 99 x 63 mm.; stamp E.M.
Coll.: Cab. des Dessins (RF 30 494).

320. PERSONNAGES ACCOUDÉS À UN
    BASTINGAGE
Lead; 126 x 197 mm.
Coll.: Cab. des Dessins (RF 30 506).

321. CROQUIS DE PLAGE
Lead; 185 x 119 mm.; stamp E.M.; upper part
    of sheet, figures in a row boat; lower part
    of sheet, houses on a cliff.
Coll.: E. Rouart, Paris.

322. COUPLE BOURGEOIS
Lead; 142 x 93 mm.
Bibl.: Rey, p. 40 (ill.).
Coll.: E. Rouart, Paris.

323. FORTS DES HALLES
Lead; 142 x 93 mm.
Bibl.: Rey, p. 40 (ill.).
Coll.: E. Rouart, Paris.

324. TÊTE D'HOMME À CASQUETTE (*fig. 281*)
Black crayon; 136 x 83 mm.
Coll.: Cab. des Dessins (RF 11 972).

325. PERSONNAGE BOSSU
Black crayon; 142 x 93 mm.
Coll.: E. Rouart, Paris.

326. DEUX PERSONNAGES SUR LA PLAGE
    (*fig. 278*)
Lead and sepia; 64 x 99 mm.
Coll.: Cab. des Dessins (RF 30 488).

327. DEUX PERSONNAGES SUR LA PLAGE
    (*fig. 279*)
Lead; 63 x 100 mm.; stamp E.M.
Coll.: Cab. des Dessins (RF 30 491).

328. CHATS
Six sketches, five in wash, one in lead; 300 x
    230 mm.
Bibl.: Tabarant, 1931, no. 37; Tabarant, 1947,
    p. 170.
Sales: Pellerin, 1926, no. 39; André Saint col-
    lection, Hôtel Drouot, Paris, Feb. 1932,
    no. 34.
Coll.: André Saint, Paris, 1932; A. Tabarant,
    Paris, 1947 (present location unknown).

329. TROIS CHATS
Lead; 142 x 95 mm.; from the Boulogne sketch-
    book.
Coll.: Cab. des Dessins.

330. CHAT ET PERSONNAGES
Lead; 195 x 125 mm.
Coll.: Cab. des Dessins (RF 30 551).

331. PORTE OUVERTE SUR L'INTÉRIEUR D'UN
    CAFÉ
Lead; 100 x 65 mm.; stamp E.M.
Coll.: Cab. des Dessins (RF 30 529).

332. BUSTE D'HOMME À FAVORIS
Bibl.: Bazire, p. 88 (ill.).
(Location unknown).

333. LEÇON DE MUSIQUE (*fig. 282*)
Lead; 112 x 185 mm.
Bibl.: Rey, p. 40 ("Les Musiciens") (ill.).
Coll.: E. Rouart, Paris.

334. SOLDATS SE RENDANT AUX AVANT-POSTES
    (*fig. 286*)
Lead and blue-black wash; 185 x 240 mm.;
    stamp E.M.; date, 1870.
Bibl.: Rey, p. 37 (ill.).
Coll.: E. Rouart, Paris.

335. CONVOI MILITAIRE
Conté crayon; 200 x 260 mm.
Bibl.: Mathey, 1961, no. 89.
Coll.: P. Dubaut, Paris.

336. STRUCTURES URBAINES
Lead; date, 1870.
Bibl.: Rey, p. 37 (ill.).
Coll.: Le Garrec, Paris, 1932 (present location
　unknown).

337. SOLDATS D'INFANTERIE (*fig. 284*)
Lead; 185 x 119 mm.; stamp E.M.
Bibl.: Rey, p. 43 ("Au Café") (ill.).
Coll.: E. Rouart, Paris.

338. AU PARADIS (*fig. 283*)
Lead; 215 x 272 mm.; stamp E.M.
Bibl.: Rey, p. 38 (ill.).
Coll.: Cab. des Estampes (Dc 300d-res. no. 5).
Text ref.: pp. 16, 71.

339. FEMME AU CARLIN
Lead; 127 x 105 mm.; stamp E.M.
Bibl.: Rey, p. 41 (ill.).
Coll.: E. Rouart, Paris.

340. TÊTE D'HOMME À FAVORIS
Lead; 184 x 113 mm.; stamp E.M.
Coll.: Cab. des Dessins (RF 11 971).
　On the verso appear sketches of a head and
　of a scene showing a circus tent next to a
　clump of trees.

341. VUE D'UNE RUE (*fig. 288*)
Lead; 171 x 109 mm.; stamp E.M.
Coll.: Cab. des Dessins (RF 30 503).

342. LA BARRICADE (*fig. 287*)
Wash with some touches of watercolor; 460 x
　335 mm.; stamp E.M.; date, 1871.
Bibl.: Tabarant, 1931, no. 41; Tabarant, 1947,
　p. 190; Richardson, fig. 38; Martin, pl. 10;
　Pataky, no. 41; Hanson, no. 115.
Coll.: P. von Majovszky, Budapest; Budapest
　Museum of Fine Arts.
　Study for the lithograph, Guérin, no. 76.
Text ref.: pp. 16, 71.

343. L'EXÉCUTION DE MAXIMILIEN (*fig. 285*)
Lead; 230 x 320 mm.; date, 1867.
Bibl.: Pataky, no. 42.
Coll.: P. von Majovszky, Budapest; Budapest
　Museum of Fine Arts.
　This is a tracing related to the lithograph,
　Guérin, no. 73. It appears on the verso of
　the preceding drawing (Cat. No. 342) and
　was used in transparency for the firing
　squad on the recto (*La Barricade*).
Text ref.: p. 16.

344. MAISON ET QUAIS
Lead; 113 x 172 mm.; stamp E.M.
Coll.: E. Rouart, Paris.

345. DEUX PERSONNAGES
Black crayon; 105 x 172 mm.; stamp E.M.
Coll.: E. Rouart, Paris.

346. FEMME DE PROFIL (*fig. 289*)
Lead; 100 x 63 mm.; stamp E.M.
Coll.: Cab. des Dessins (RF 30 409).

347. FEMME DE PROFIL (*fig. 291*)
Lead; 100 x 63 mm.; stamp E.M.; date, 1871.
Coll.: Cab. des Dessins (RF 30 410).
　Sketch for the painting *La Partie de croquet
　à Boulogne* (Jamot, no. 197, fig. 355).
Text ref.: p. 35.

348. FEMME DE PROFIL, LA MAIN LEVÉE
Lead; 98 x 65 mm.; stamp E.M.
Coll.: Cab. des Dessins (RF 30 411).
　Sketch for the painting *La Partie de croquet
　à Boulogne* (Jamot, no. 197, fig. 355).

349. FEMME DE DOS (*fig. 290*)
Lead; 101 x 64 mm.; stamp E.M.
Coll.: Cab. des Dessins (RF 30 412).
　Sketch for the painting *La Partie de croquet
　à Boulogne* (Jamot, no. 197, fig. 355).
Text ref.: p. 35.

350. FEMMES JOUANT AU CROQUET
Lead; 100 x 64 mm.; stamp E.M.
Coll.: Cab. des Dessins (RF 30 538).
  Sketch for the painting *La Partie de croquet
  à Boulogne* (Jamot, no. 197, fig. 355).

351. FEMME JOUANT AU CROQUET
Lead and watercolor; 100 x 64 mm.
Coll.: Cab. des Dessins (RF 30 539).
  Sketch for the painting *La Partie de croquet
  à Boulogne* (Jamot, no. 197, fig. 355).

352. FEMME JOUANT AU CROQUET (*fig. 298*)
Lead; 100 x 64 mm.
Coll.: Cab. des Dessins (RF 30 540).
  Sketch for the painting *La Partie de croquet
  à Boulogne* (Jamot, no. 197, fig. 355).
Text ref.: p. 35.

353. GROUPE DE FEMMES (*fig. 297*)
Lead; 99 x 64 mm.; stamp E.M.
Coll.: Cab. des Dessins (RF 30 413).

354. HOMME PORTANT UN SCEAU
Lead; 100 x 64 mm.; stamp E.M.
Coll.: Cab. des Dessins (RF 30 414).

355. GROUPE DE PERSONNAGES
Lead; 100 x 64 mm.; stamp E.M.
Coll.: Cab. des Dessins (RF 30 415).

356. FEMME AVEC OMBRELLE (*fig. 293*)
Lead; 98 x 63 mm.; stamp E.M.
Coll.: Cab. des Dessins (RF 30 416).

357. HOMME DE DOS
Lead; 98 x 63 mm.; stamp E.M.
Coll.: Cab. des Dessins (RF 30 417).

358. FEMME JOUANT AU CROQUET (*fig. 294*)
Lead; 102 x 64 mm.; stamp E.M.
Coll.: Cab. des Dessins (RF 30 418).
  Sketch for the painting *La Partie de croquet
  à Boulogne* (Jamot, no. 197, fig. 355).

359. HOMME DE DOS
Lead; 100 x 63 mm.; stamp E.M.
Coll.: Cab. des Dessins (RF 30 419).

360. HOMME DE DOS
Lead; 104 x 64 mm.; stamp E.M.
Coll.: Cab. des Dessins (RF 30 420).

361. FEMME AVEC OMBRELLE (*fig. 292*)
Lead; 103 x 67 mm.; stamp E.M.
Coll.: Cab. des Dessins (RF 30 421).

362. FEMME DEBOUT
Lead; 98 x 63 mm.; stamp E.M.
Coll.: Cab. des Dessins (RF 30 422).

363. FEMME PENCHÉE EN AVANT
Lead; 100 x 63 mm.; stamp E.M.
Coll.: Cab. des Dessins (RF 30 423).

364. FEMME DE PROFIL
Lead; 100 x 63 mm.; stamp E.M.
Coll.: Cab. des Dessins (RF 30 424).

365. HOMME JOUANT AU CROQUET
Lead; 99 x 63 mm.; stamp E.M.
Coll.: Cab. des Dessins (RF 30 478).
  Sketch for the painting *La Partie de croquet
  à Boulogne* (Jamot, no. 197, fig. 355).
Text ref.: p. 35.

366. GROUPE DE PERSONNAGES
Lead; 197 x 124 mm.
Coll.: Cab. des Dessins (RF 30 475).

367. HOMME JOUANT AU CROQUET
  (*fig. 296*)
Lead; 103 x 63 mm.
Coll.: Cab. des Dessins (RF 30 476).
  Sketch for the painting *La Partie de croquet
  à Boulogne* (Jamot, no. 197, fig. 355).
Text ref.: p. 35.

368. VIEILLE FEMME AVEC CANNE (*fig. 295*)
Lead; 172 x 90 mm.
Coll.: Cab. des Dessins (RF 30 496).

369. HOMME PORTANT UNE HOTTE
Lead; 98 x 63 mm.; stamp E.M.
Coll.: Cab. des Dessins (RF 30 479).

370. HOMME PORTANT UN SCEAU
Lead; 100 x 64 mm.; stamp E.M.
Coll.: Cab. des Dessins (RF 30 477).

371. SILHOUETTE DE FEMME SUR LA PLAGE
(*fig. 311*)
Lead; 138 x 89 mm.
Coll.: Cab. des Dessins (RF 30 497).

372. PLAGE
Lead; 115 x 185 mm.; stamp E.M.
Coll.: E. Rouart, Paris.

373. CAVALIER ET FEMME SUR UNE ROUTE
(*fig. 313*)
Lead; 174 x 113 mm.; stamp E.M.
Coll.: Cab. des Dessins (RF 30 498).

374. FEMME PORTANT UN FARDEAU
(*fig. 312*)
Lead; 180 x 110 mm.; stamp E.M.
Coll.: Cab. des Dessins (RF 30 440).

375. BOSQUET D'ARBRES (*fig. 314*)
Lead; 100 x 146 mm.; stamp E.M.
Coll.: Cab. des Dessins (RF 30 501).

376. ARBRE (*fig. 315*)
Lead; 146 x 97 mm.; stamp E.M.
Coll.: Cab. des Dessins (RF 30 502).

377. MARINE AU CLAIR DE LUNE (*fig. 309*)
Wash; 197 x 179 mm.
Bibl.: Mathey, 1963, fig. 12.
Coll.: Cab. des Dessins (RF 30 504).

378. FEMME ASSISE AU CLAIR DE LUNE
(*fig. 310*)
Wash; 270 x 188 mm.
Bibl.: Mathey, 1963, fig. 128.
Coll.: Cab. des Dessins (RF 30 465).

379. INTÉRIEUR À ARCACHON (*fig. 51*)
Lead, pen, and wash; 184 x 235 mm.; date, 1871.
Bibl.: M–N, 1926, I, fig. 146; Tabarant, 1947,
   no. 587; Hanson, no. 117.
Coll.: P. Romanelli, Paris; W. G. Russell Allen,
   Boston; Fogg Art Museum, Harvard Uni-
   versity, Cambridge, Mass. (bequest of
   W. G. Russell Allen, 1957).
   Represents Mme E. Manet and her son at
   Arcachon (Tabarant). Related to the
   painting (Jamot, no. 193, fig. 334).
Text ref.: pp. 33, 71, 72.

380. À ARCACHON (*fig. 308*)
Black crayon and bluish wash; 120 x 185 mm.
Bibl.: Tabarant, 1931, no. 39; Tabarant, 1947,
   p. 189; Hanson, under no. 117.
Sale: Pellerin, 1926.
Coll.: Stonborough, 1926 (present location un-
   known).

381. FEMME SOUS LA LAMPE (*fig. 305*)
Black crayon and bluish wash; 170 x 120 mm.
Bibl.: Tabarant, 1931, no. 40; Rey, p. 39 (ill.).
Sale: Pellerin, 1926.
Coll.: Le Garrec, Paris, 1926 (present location
   unknown).

382. FEMME LISANT (*fig. 306*)
Lead; 185 x 120 mm.; stamp E.M.
Coll.: E. Rouart, Paris.
   The model is the artist's mother (informa-
   tion given by Mme E. Rouart).

383. BUSTE D'HOMME BARBU
Lead; inscribed below the bust "Lalain."
Bibl.: Rey, p. 23 (ill.).
Coll.: Kunsthalle, Bremen.

384. FEMME AU PIANO (*fig. 307*)
Lead and wash; 157 x 103 mm.; stamp E.M.
Coll.: Cab. des Dessins (RF 30 430).

385. FEMME AU PIANO
Watercolor; 152 x 114 mm.
Coll.: Mr. and Mrs. Alex M. Lewyt, New
York.
  Corresponds in most respects to Cat. No.
  384, but shows the figure wearing a
  plaid dress. This watercolor does not correspond to any described by Tabarant
  (1947, p. 155) under the title *Mme Manet
  au piano* of 1868. Its style suggests the ap-
  proximate date of 1874.

386. LE PORT DE BORDEAUX
Lead and watercolor; 180 x 240 mm.
Bibl.: Tabarant, 1947, no. 586; Martin, fig. 9.
Coll.: Private collection, France.

387. PORTRAIT DE BERTHE MORISOT
Lead; 175 x 140 mm.
Bibl.: R. Huygue, "Manet peintre," *L'Amour
  de l'Art* (May 1932), p. 179, fig. 76; F.
  Daulte, *Le Dessin français de Manet à
  Cézanne* (Lausanne, 1954), no. 2.
Coll.: Roger-Marx, Paris; private collection,
  Paris.

388. VUE DE VILLAGE (*fig. 299*)
Lead; 108 x 167 mm.; stamp E.M.; date, *ca.*
  1872.
Coll.: Cab. des Dessins (RF 30 446).

389. PAYSAGE AU MOULIN À VENT (*fig. 300*)
Lead; 104 x 155 mm.; stamp E.M.; date, *ca.*
  1872.
Coll.: Cab. des Dessins (RF 30 447).

390. TROIS BARQUES À VOILE (*fig. 301*)
Lead; 91 x 142 mm.; stamp E.M.
Coll.: Cab. des Dessins (RF 30 556).
  Probably done at Berck in 1873.
Text ref.: pp. 72, 74.

391. PROUE D'UN BATEAU
Lead; 125 x 122 mm.
Coll.: Cab. des Dessins (RF 30 555).
Text ref.: p. 72.

392. DEUX VOILIERS (*fig. 302*)
Lead; 91 x 141.; date, 1873.
Coll.: Cab. des Dessins (RF 30 554).
  Related to the painting *La Plage à Berck à
  marée basse* (Jamot, no. 228, fig. 315).
Text ref.: p. 72.

393. BARQUES À VOILE (*fig. 303*)
Lead; 127 x 85 mm.; stamp E.M.
Coll.: Cab. des Dessins (RF 30 553).
Text ref.: p. 72.

394. BARQUE À VOILE
Lead; 123 x 120 mm.; stamp E.M.
Coll.: Cab. des Estampes (Dc 300d-res. no. 2).
Text ref.: p. 72.

395. BARQUE À VOILE
Watercolor; 143 x 92 mm.
Exh.: Orangerie, 1932, no. 113 (3).
Coll.: Cab. des Estampes (Dc 300d-res. no. 17).
Text ref.: p. 72.

396. BARQUE À VOILE (*fig. 316*)
Watercolor and gouache; 135 x 81 mm.
Exh.: Orangerie, 1932, no. 113 (1).
Coll.: Cab. des Estampes (Dc 300d-res. no. 19).
Text ref.: p. 72.

397. MER AGITÉE (*fig. 318*)
Watercolor; 150 x 235 mm.; stamp E.M.; date,
  1873.
Bibl.: Tabarant, 1931, no. 48; Florisoone, pl. 55;
  Martin, pl. 11.
Exh.: Matthiesen, 1928, no. 29.
Coll.: Faure, Paris; Mrs. Ash, New York.
Text ref.: p. 72.

398. MARINE
Watercolor; 205 x 240 mm.
Bibl.: *Marées Gesellschaft* portfolio (Munich,
    1922), pl. IX; Glaser, no. 9; Tabarant, 1931,
    no. 43; Tabarant, 1947, p. 218.
Sale: Beurdeley collection, Georges Petit Gal-
    lery, Paris, 1920, no. 312.
Coll.: Dr. Hans R. Hahnloser, Berne.
Text ref.: p. 72.

399. MARINE (*fig. 317*)
Watercolor.
Bibl.: Tabarant, 1931, no. 45; photograph in
    Moreau-Nélaton Fund, folio 4, Cab. des
    Estampes.
(Location unknown.)
Text ref.: p. 72.

400. MARINE
Watercolor; 250 x 300 mm.; signed lower left
    "Manet."
Bibl.: Tabarant, 1931, no. 44; photograph in
    Moreau-Nélaton Fund, folio 5, Cab. des
    Estampes.
(Location unknown.)
Text ref.: p. 72.

401. MER CALME
Watercolor; 160 x 230 mm.; stamp E.M.
Bibl.: Tabarant, 1931, no. 47.
Exh.: "Collection Faure," Durand-Ruel Gal-
    lery, Paris, March 1906, no. 15.
Coll.: Faure, Paris, 1906 (present location un-
    known).
Text ref.: p. 72.

402. BARQUE (*fig. 321*)
Lead and watercolor; 93 x 143 mm.; stamp
    E.M.
Coll.: Cab. des Dessins (RF 30 550).
Text ref.: p. 72.

403. BARQUE (*fig. 322*)
Lead; 60 x 143 mm.; stamp E.M.

Coll.: Cab. des Dessins (RF 30 557).
Text ref.: p. 72.

404. BARQUE (*fig. 320*)
Lead; 60 x 143 mm.; stamp E.M.
Coll.: Cab. des Dessins (RF 30 558).
Text ref.: p. 72.

405. LA BARQUE ÉCHOUÉE (*fig. 324*)
Lead; 62 x 120 mm.; stamp E.M.
Exh.: Orangerie, 1932, no. 114 (4).
Coll.: Cab. des Estampes (Dc 300d-res. no. 1).
Text ref.: p. 72.

406. CHEVAUX SUR LA PLAGE (*fig. 325*)
Lead; lower right, the word "alezan."
Bibl.: Rey, p. 39 (ill.); Mathey, 1963, fig. 40.
Coll.: Le Garrec, Paris, 1932 (present location
    unknown).
Text ref.: p. 74.

407. PERSONNAGE DANS UNE BARQUE
    (*fig. 319*)
Lead; 64 x 100 mm.; stamp E.M.
Coll.: Cab. des Dessins (RF 30 559).
Text ref.: p. 72.

408. DEUX PERSONNAGES SUR LA PLAGE
    (*fig. 328*)
Lead and watercolor; 100 x 65 mm.; stamp
    E.M.
Coll.: Cab. des Dessins (RF 30 549).
Text ref.: p. 72.

409. JEUNE GARÇON DEBOUT, DE DOS, SUR
    LA PLAGE
Lead; 179 x 109 mm.; stamp E.M.
Coll.: Cab. des Dessins (RF 30 439).
Text ref.: p. 72.

410. PERSONNAGES SUR LA PLAGE
Lead; 180 x 242 mm.; stamp E.M.; date, 1873.
Coll.: E. Rouart, Paris.

Related to *Marine* (Jamot, no. 223, fig. 302).
Text ref.: p. 72.

411. AU SALON (*fig. 327*)
Lead and watercolor; 147 x 100 mm.
Bibl.: Mathey, 1961, fig. 120.
Coll.: Cab. des Dessins (RF 30 528).
 The painting *Sur la Plage* (Jamot, no. 224, fig. 173) can be seen on the background wall.

412. TÊTE D'HOMME (*fig. 330*)
Lead; 102 x 63 mm.; stamp E.M.
Coll.: Cab. des Dessins (RF 30 405).

413. TÊTE D'HOMME (*fig. 329*)
Lead; 100 x 64 mm.; stamp E.M.
Coll.: Cab. des Dessins (RF 30 406).

414. TÊTE DE FEMME (*fig. 331*)
Lead; 88 x 50 mm.; stamp E.M.
Coll.: Cab. des Dessins (RF 30 407).

415. TÊTE D'HOMME
Lead; 90 x 63 mm.; stamp E.M.
Coll.: Cab. des Dessins (RF 30 408).

416. POLICHINELLE
Lead and watercolor; 340 x 235 mm.
Bibl.: Tabarant, 1931, no. 49; Hanson, under no. 140.
Coll.: Brodin, Paris.

417. COUPLE ASSIS SUR UN BANC (*fig. 323*)
Lead; 120 x 184 mm.
Bibl.: Hoetink, no. 179.
Coll.: Museum Boymans-van Beuningen, Rotterdam (Inv. no. FII 47).
Text ref.: p. 74.

418. LE PROCÈS DE BAZAINE (*fig. 332*)
Lead; 185 x 238 mm.; stamp E.M.; date, 1873.
Bibl.: Hoetink, no. 185.

Coll.: Museum Boymans-van Beuningen, Rotterdam (Inv. no. FII 107).
 Verso: study of a detail of the large drawing, and sketch of a cat.
Text ref.: p. 74.

419. LE PROCÈS DE BAZAINE (*fig. 333*)
Lead; 179 x 319 mm.; stamp E.M.; date, 1873.
Coll.: Cab. des Dessins (RF 30 466).
 Tracing of Cat. No. 418.
Text ref.: p. 74.

420. PORTRAIT OF VICTORINE MEUREND (*fig. 339*)
Pen; 152 x 114 mm.
Exh.: Santa Barbara Museum, Santa Barbara, California, 1959; "One Hundred Twenty-Five Master Drawings," The Solomon R. Guggenheim Museum, New York, May–July 1962, no. 75.
Sale: Camille Pissarro collection, Georges Petit Gallery, Paris, Dec. 3, 1928, no. 69.
Coll.: C. Pissarro, Paris, 1928; C. E. Slatkin, New York.
 In support of our dating is the correspondence between this portrait and that of Victorine Meurend in the painting *Le Linge* of 1873.

421. THÉODORE DE BANVILLE (*fig. 334*)
Lead; 185 x 120 mm.; date, 1874.
Bibl.: Rey, p. 18 (ill.).
Coll.: E. Rouart, Paris.
Text ref.: pp. 27, 28, 74.

422. THÉODORE DE BANVILLE (*fig. 335*)
Lead, wash, and pen; 183 x 118 mm.; stamp E.M.; date, 1874.
Bibl.: Hanson, under no. 138.
Coll.: Cab. des Dessins (RF 30 378).
 Related to the etching *Le Rêve du marin*, Guérin, nos. 60, 61 (see fig. 336).
Text ref.: pp. 27, 28.

423. PORTRAIT DE M. VIGNAUX
Pen; 198 x 143 mm.; signed lower left "Manet."
Bibl.: Bazire, p. 31 (ill.); Tabarant, 1947, fig.
668, under the erroneous title "Pertuiset,
le 'Chasseur de lions' "; Hanson, no. 147.
Coll.: E. Degas, Paris; Baltimore Museum,
Cone Collection.
The model is H. Vignaux, novelist and friend
of Manet.

424. TROIS VITRIERS
Pen.
Bibl.: Bazire, p. 107 (ill.).
(Location unknown.)

425. PÉNICHES EN SEINE
Watercolor; 250 x 350 mm.; signed lower right
"Manet."
Bibl.: Tabarant, 1931, no. 54; Tabarant, 1947,
p. 248.
Sales: 1884, no. 129; Haviland collection, Hô-
tel Drouot, Paris, Dec. 7, 1922.
Coll.: Haviland, Paris, 1922; Knoedler and Co.,
Paris (present location unknown).

426. PÉNICHES EN SEINE
Watercolor; 250 x 350 mm.; stamp E.M.
Bibl.: Tabarant, 1931, no. 55; Tabarant, 1947,
p. 248.
Sale: 1884, no. 130.
Coll.: Durand-Ruel, Paris, 1884 (present loca-
tion unknown).

427. VILLA AU BORD DE LA SEINE
Watercolor; 180 x 240 mm.; date, 1874.
Bibl.: Tabarant, 1931, no. 57.
Sale: Pellerin, 1926, no. 43.
Coll.: Bucher, Paris, 1926 (present location un-
known).

428. ÉTUDES DE VOILIERS
Watercolor; 250 x 350 mm. (eight sketches on
one sheet).

Bibl.: Tabarant, 1931, no. 56; Tabarant, 1947,
p. 249.
Sale: Degas collection, Hôtel Drouot, Paris,
Nov. 15–16, 1918, no. 219.
Coll.: Fiquet, Paris, 1918 (present location un-
known).

429. EN BATEAU
Pen; date, 1874.
Bibl.: Waldmann, 1910, p. 135 (ill.); Hanson,
under no. 125.
(Location unknown.)
Related to the painting (Jamot, no. 244).
The drawing illustrated in Mathey, 1961,
fig. 135, appears to us to be a clumsy copy
of this drawing by another hand.

430. BAIGNEUSES
Wash and watercolor; date, 1874.
Bibl.: Tabarant, 1947, no. 606.
Coll.: A. Pellerin (present location unknown).
Related to the painting (Jamot, no. 264, fig.
63).
Text ref.: p. 58.

431. FEMME AU CHAPEAU À BRIDES (fig. 52)
Watercolor; 185 x 120 mm.
Bibl.: Hoetink, no. 184; Hanson, no. 160.
Coll.: Museum Boymans-van Beuningen, Rot-
terdam. (Inv. no. FII 106).
Text ref.: pp. 73, 74.

432. FEMME EN CHAPEAU ACCOUDÉE
Pen and wash; 175 x 115 mm.; stamp E.M.
Bibl.: Tabarant, 1931, no. 62; Tabarant, 1947,
p. 259 (ill.).
Sale: Degas collection, Georges Petit Gallery,
Paris, March 26–27, 1918, no. 224.
Coll.: Schöneger, 1918 (present location un-
known).

433. FEMME AU CHAPEAU ROUGE
Watercolor; 170 x 110 mm.
Bibl.: Tabarant, 1931, no. 60; Tabarant, 1947,
p. 259.

125

Sale: G. Viau collection, Durand-Ruel Gallery, Paris, March 1907, no. 143.

Coll.: G. Viau, Paris, 1907 (present location unknown).

434. BERTHE MORISOT À L'ÉVENTAIL (fig. 304)

Watercolor; 205 x 165 mm.; date, 1874.

Bibl.: *Marées Gesellschaft* portfolio (Munich, 1922), pl. x; Tabarant, 1931, no. 59; Martin, pl. 12; Hanson, no. 110.

Exh. "De Delacroix à Picasso," Hugo Perls Gallery, Berlin, Feb. 1925.

Coll.: Durieux-Cassirer, Berlin; M. Oppenheim, Berlin; The Art Institute of Chicago, The Joseph and Helen Regenstein Collection.

435. COUSEUSE À CONTRE-JOUR

Watercolor; 180 x 140 mm.; stamp E.M.

Bibl.: Tabarant, 1931, no. 63; Tabarant, 1947, p. 260.

Coll.: Vollard, Paris; G. Viau, Paris, 1942; M. Walther.

436. FEMME ASSISE

Watercolor; 180 x 125 mm.

Bibl.: Tabarant, 1947, p. 260 (ill.).

Sale: Hôtel Drouot, Paris, March 6–7, 1935, no. 130.

(Location unknown.)

1875–1878

437. CORBEAU (fig. 341)

Black crayon; date, 1875.

Bibl.: Rey, p. 28 (ill.).

Coll.: E. Rouart, Paris.

438. LE CORBEAU

Wash; in oval format; date, 1875.

Bibl.: Hanson, under no. 133.

(Location unknown.)

Sketch for the *ex libris* autographic drawing of the same subject, Guérin, no. 86.

439. LE CORBEAU

Wash; date, 1875.

Bibl.: Duret, 1906 (ill., facing p. 228); Hanson, under no. 133.

(Location unknown.)

This drawing is similar in technique to Cat. No. 441, but the head of the bird is not represented in pure profile view.

440. LE CORBEAU (fig. 340)

Autographic wash; drawing size, 60 x 240 mm.

Ex libris of Edgar Allan Poe, *Le Corbeau*, translated by S. Mallarmé (Paris: Richard Lesclide, 1875); catalogued by Guérin, no. 86.

Text ref.: p. 41.

441. LE CORBEAU, TÊTE DE PROFIL (fig. 342)

Autographic wash; drawing size, 250 x 320 mm.

Bibl.: Mallarmé, *Le Corbeau* (ill.).

Catalogued by Guérin, no. 85.

Text ref.: p. 23.

442. LE CORBEAU ET TAMA

Autographic wash; drawing size, 250 x 320 mm.

Catalogued by Guérin, no. 84.

443. LA CHAISE (fig. 344)

Autographic wash; 290 x 276 mm.; signed lower left "E.M."

Bibl.: Mallarmé, *Le Corbeau* (ill.).

Catalogued by Guérin, no. 86d.

444. SOUS LA LAMPE (fig. 345)

Autographic wash; 275 x 375 mm.

Bibl.: Mallarmé, *Le Corbeau* (ill.).

Catalogued by Guérin, no. 86a.

445. À LA FENÊTRE (fig. 343)

Autographic wash; 385 x 300 mm.; signed lower left "E.M."; date, 1875.

Bibl.: Mallarmé, *Le Corbeau* (ill.).

Catalogued by Guérin, no. 86c.

Text ref.: pp. 22, 77.

446. LE CORBEAU SUR LE BUSTE *(fig. 15)*
Autographic wash; 475 x 316 mm.; signed lower right "E.M."
Bibl.: Mallarmé, *Le Corbeau* (ill.).
  Catalogued by Guérin, no. 86b.
Text ref.: pp. 23, 77.

447. TAMA *(fig. 348)*
Lead; 83 x 110 mm.
Coll.: Kunsthalle, Hamburg (Inv. No. 1924/437).
  Related to the autographic wash, Guérin, no. 84.
Text ref.: pp. 36, 77.

448. TAMA *(fig. 346)*
Lead; 81 x 109 mm.
Bibl.: Rey, p. 27 (ill.).
Coll.: Kunsthalle, Hamburg (Inv. No. 1924/438).
  Related to the autographic wash, Guérin, no. 84.
Text ref.: pp. 36, 82.

449. TAMA *(fig. 347)*
Lead; 159 x 110 mm.
Bibl.: Rey, p. 26 (ill.).
Coll.: Kunsthalle, Hamburg (Inv. No. 1924/439).
  Related to the autographic wash, Guérin, no. 84.
Text ref.: pp. 36, 77.

450. DESBOUTIN *(fig. 53)*
Watercolor; 228 x 140 mm.; signed lower right "E.M."
Bibl.: Tabarant, 1931, no. 64; Rey, p. 20 (ill.); Martin, pl. 14.
Coll.: Fogg Art Museum, Harvard University, Cambridge, Mass.
Text ref.: pp. 6, 75, 76.

451. MLLE DODU (first version) *(fig. 350)*
Lead; 176 x 177 mm.

Bibl.: Rhode Island School of Design, *Museum Bulletin*, XIX, 4 (Oct. 1931), 69.
Coll.: Scott & Fowles, New York; Museum of Art, Rhode Island School of Design, Providence, Rhode Island.

452. MLLE DODU (second version) *(fig. 351)*
Pen and wash; 174 x 174 mm.; signed under model's shoulder "E. Manet."
Coll.: Grenville L. Winthrop; Fogg Art Museum, Harvard University, Cambridge, Mass. (bequest of Grenville L. Winthrop).

453. LA CONVALESCENTE *(fig. 13)*
Sanguine; 113 x 129 mm.; stamp E.M.
Bibl.: Hanson, under no. 135.
Exh.: London, 1932, no. 971; Orangerie, 1932, no. 109.
Coll.: R. Koechlin, Paris; Cab. des Dessins (RF 23 332) (bequest of R. Koechlin, 1931).
  The etching, Guérin, no. 65, is based on this drawing.
Text ref.: pp. 17, 41, 75.

454. TÊTE D'HOMME COUCHÉ *(fig. 352)*
Lead; 208 x 270 mm.
Coll.: Cab. des Dessins (RF 30 531).

455. AMAZONE À CHEVAL
Watercolor; 210 x 270 mm.; signed lower right "E. Manet."
Bibl.: Tabarant, 1931, no. 65; Tabarant, 1947, p. 277.
Coll.: Vollard, Paris; Brooklyn Museum, New York.

456. VENISE
Watercolor; 200 x 305 mm.; signed and dated lower right "E.M. 75."
Coll.: Gallery M. Guyot, Paris (present location unknown).

457. NYMPHES *(fig. 349)*
Wood engraving; 43 x 98 mm.; date, 1876.

Catalogued by Guérin, no. 93. (Our text gives our reasons for inclusion of this and the next engraving in this catalogue.) Illustration for S. Mallarmé, *L'Après-midi d'un faune* (Paris: Derenne, 1876).

Text ref.: pp. 20, 21, 77.

458. FAUNE (*fig. 14*)

Wood engraving; 70 x 124 mm.; date, 1876.

Catalogued by Guérin, no. 93. Illustration for S. Mallarmé, *L'Après-midi d'un faune* (Paris: Derenne, 1876).

Text ref.: pp. 20, 21, 28, 77.

459. LA BELLE POLONAISE (*fig. 338*)

Wash; lower right, initial "M"; date, 1876.

Bibl.: Waldmann, 1910, p. 30 (ill.); Tabarant, 1931, no. 67.

Sale: 1884, no. 151.

Coll.: Aristide, Paris, 1884 (present location unknown).

Related to the painting *La Serveuse de bocks* (Jamot, no. 336, fig. 155).

Text ref.: pp. 78, 79.

460. LA BELLE POLONAISE

Wash; stamp E.M.; date, 1876.

Bibl.: Tabarant, 1931, no. 68.

Sale: 1884, no. 152.

Coll.: T. Duret, Paris, 1884 (present location unknown).

Related to the autographic wash, Guérin, no. 83.

461. TÊTE DE FEMME (*fig. 55*)

Lead and quill pen; 288 x 213 mm.; stamp E.M.

Coll.: Cab. des Estampes (Dc 300d-res. no. 16).

The model appears to be that of the autographic drawing *La Belle polonaise*, Guérin, no. 83.

Text ref.: p. 79.

462. M. ARNAUD À CHEVAL (*fig. 353*)

Lead; 297 x 263 mm.

Coll.: Cab. des Dessins (RF 30 522).

Related to the painting *M. Arnaud à cheval* (Jamot, no. 266).

463. VASE DE JARDIN

Wash; 330 x 240 mm.; date, 1876.

Bibl.: Tabarant, 1931, no. 66; Tabarant, 1947, p. 292.

Sale: 1884, no. 160.

Coll.: Aristide, Paris, 1884 (present location unknown).

464. INTÉRIEUR DE CAFÉ (*fig. 354*)

Lead; 111 x 173 mm.; stamp E.M.

Coll.: Cab. des Dessins (RF 30 404).

465. COUPLE AU CAFÉ (*fig. 355*)

Lead; 142 x 187 mm.; stamp E.M.

Coll.: Cab. des Dessins (RF 30 403).

466. FAURE DANS LE RÔLE D'HAMLET (*fig. 337*)

Pen and wash; 265 x 175 mm.; date, 1877.

Bibl.: *Marées Gesellschaft* portfolio (Munich, 1922), pl. XI; Glaser, no. 11; Tabarant, 1931, no. 69; Tabarant, 1947, p. 300.

Coll.: A. Beurdeley, Paris; Dr. Hans R. Hahnloser, Berne.

Related to the painting (Jamot, no. 277, fig. 186).

467. CHAT ASSIS (*fig. 357*)

Lead; 107 x 115 mm.; stamp E.M.

Coll.: Cab. des Dessins (RF 30 382).

468. CHAT ASSIS (*fig. 358*)

Lead; 81 x 117 mm.; stamp E.M.

Coll.: Cab. des Dessins (RF 30 383).

469. CHAT ASSIS (*fig. 359*)

Lead; 94 x 40 mm.; stamp E.M.

Coll.: Cab. des Dessins (RF 30 384).

470. CHAT ASSIS (*fig. 356*)
Lead; 95 x 65 mm.; stamp E.M.
Coll.: Cab. des Dessins (RF 30 385).

471. CHAT COUCHÉ
Lead; 87 x 115 mm.
Coll.: Cab. des Dessins (RF 30 386).

472. CHAT COUCHÉ
Lead; 89 x 115 mm.; stamp E.M.
Coll.: Cab. des Dessins (RF 30 387).

473. CHAT ASSIS
Lead; 100 x 115 mm.
Coll.: Cab. des Dessins (RF 30 388).

474. CHAT SE LÈCHANT (*fig. 360*)
Lead; 162 x 117 mm.
Coll.: Cab. des Dessins (RF 30 390).

475. CHAT (*fig. 362*)
Lead; 126 x 100 mm.; stamp E.M.
Coll.: Cab. des Dessins (RF 30 394).

476. CHAT ASSIS (*fig. 363*)
Lead; 85 x 115 mm.; stamp E.M.
Coll.: Cab. des Dessins (RF 30 395).

477. DEUX CHATS
Lead; 100 x 114 mm.
Coll.: Cab. des Dessins (RF 30 392).

478. CHAT ASSIS ET TÊTES DE CHAT (*fig. 361*)
Lead; 81 x 113 mm.; stamp E.M.
Coll.: Cab. des Dessins (RF 30 393).

479. CHAT ASSIS ET TÊTES DE CHAT (*fig. 56*)
Lead; 90 x 114 mm.; stamp E.M.
Coll.: Cab. des Dessins (RF 30 389).
Text ref.: pp. 2, 81.

480. CHAT COUCHÉ ET GUÊTRES DE FEMME
Lead; 90 x 114 mm.
Coll.: Cab. des Dessins (RF 30 391).

481. UNE VICTORIA (*fig. 365*)
Lead and wash; 112 x 83 mm.; signed lower
left "E.M."; date, *ca.* 1877.
Exh.: Orangerie, 1932, no. 114 (2).
Coll.: Cab. des Estampes (Dc 300d-res. no 12).
Related to the painting *La Rue Mosnier aux
drapeaux* (Jamot, no. 289, fig. 323).
Text ref.: pp. 33, 35.

482. FIACRE (*fig. 367*)
Lead; 168 x 170 mm.; date, *ca.* 1877.
Bibl.: Waldmann, 1910, p. 195 (ill.).
Coll.: Cab. des Dessins (RF 30 350).
Text ref.: pp. 33, 35, 78.

483. AU PARADIS (*fig. 370*)
Autographic wash; 244 x 339 mm.; date, 1878.
Catalogued by Guérin, no. 82. Illustration
for "Croquis parisiens" series in *Revue de
la Semaine* (see Guérin, under no. 82).
Text ref.: p. 15.

484. TROIS SPECTATEURS (*fig. 369*)
Autographic wash; 70 x 100 mm.; stamp E.M.
Bibl.: Tabarant, 1931, no. 75 ("Au Café-con-
cert"); Rewald, p. 5 (ill.).
Sale: 1884, no. 138.
Coll.: Bernstein, Paris, 1884 (present location
unknown).
Text ref.: p. 78.

485. GROUPE DE SPECTATEURS (*fig. 371*)
Litho crayon; 173 x 271 mm.; signed lower
right "E. Manet."
Bibl.: Agnes Mongan, *Great Drawings of All
Time* (New York, 1962), under no. 795;
Hanson, no. 175.
Coll.: F. Koenigs, Amsterdam; D. Daniels, New
York.
Related to the autographic drawing *Quatre
spectateurs*, Cat. No. 486.

129

486. QUATRE SPECTATEURS (*fig. 368*)
Autographic wash; 520 x 800 mm.; stamp E.M.
Bibl.: Tabarant, 1931, no. 75 ("Au Café-con-
cert").
Sale: 1884, no. 138.
Coll.: Bernstein, Paris, 1884 (present location
unknown).
Text ref.: p. 78.

487. AUDIENCE ET CHEF D'ORCHESTRE
(*fig. 27*)
Lead; 205 x 135 mm.; stamp E.M.; date, *ca.*
1878.
Bibl.: Rey, p. 35 (ill.); Mathey, 1963, fig. 75.
Coll.: E. Rouart, Paris.
  Related to Cat. No. 488.
Text ref.: pp. 38, 39, 40, 78, 79.

488. AUDIENCE ET CHEF D'ORCHESTRE
(*fig. 28*)
Wash; 205 x 135 mm.; stamp E. M.; date, *ca.*
1878.
Bibl.: Rey, p. 44 (ill.); Mathey, 1961, fig. 123.
Exh.: Orangerie, 1932, no. 110.
Coll.: E. Rouart, Paris.
Text ref.: pp. 38, 39, 42, 79.

489. CHEF D'ORCHESTRE (*fig. 376*)
Wash; 213 x 135 mm.; stamp E.M.
Bibl.: Rey, p. 44 (ill.); Mathey, 1961, fig. 122.
Exh.: Orangerie, 1932, no. 111.
Coll.: E. Rouart, Paris.
Text ref.: pp. 78, 79.

490. AUDIENCE ET ORCHESTRE (*fig. 372*)
Black crayon; 130 x 165 mm.; stamp E.M.
Coll.: Cab. des Dessins (RF 30 526).

491. AUDIENCE AU CAFÉ-CONCERT (*fig. 378*)
Lead; 164 x 235 mm.
Coll.: Cab. des Dessins (RF 30 525).

492. AUDIENCE ET ORCHESTRE (*fig. 373*)
Lead and wash; 216 x 280 mm.; stamp E.M.
Coll.: Cab. des Dessins (RF 30 523).
  Related to Cat. No. 490.

493. CHANTEUR ET MUSICIENS (*fig. 374*)
Lead; 185 x 294 mm.; stamp E.M.
Bibl.: Mathey, 1961, fig. 26.
Coll.: Cab. des Dessins (RF 30 402).

494. MUSICIENS À L'ORCHESTRE (*fig. 375*)
Black crayon; 177 x 270 mm.; stamp E.M.
Coll.: Cab. des Dessins (RF 30 524).

495. AU CAFÉ
Wash and gouache; 235 x 195 mm. (255 x 195
mm. in Tabarant, 1947).
Bibl.: Tabarant, 1931, no. 70; Tabarant, 1947,
p. 327.
Exh.: 1884, no. 167.
Coll.: L. de Fourcaud, Paris, 1917 (present lo-
cation unknown).

496. BUSTE D'HOMME AU CAFÉ
Lead; 290 x 212 mm.
Coll.: Cab. des Dessins (RF 30 306).

497. SCÈNE DE RUE
Black crayon; 290 x 212 mm.
Coll.: Cab. des Dessins (RF 30 307).

498. CHANTEUSE DE CAFÉ-CONCERT
(*fig. 377*)
Black crayon and wash; 128 x 83 mm.
Bibl.: Rey, p. 47 (ill.).
Coll.: E. Rouart, Paris.
Text ref.: pp. 5, 34.

499. FEMME ÉCRIVANT AU CAFÉ (*fig. 54*)
Lead; 82 x 104 mm.; stamp E.M.; date, *ca.* 1878.
Coll.: Cab. des Dessins (RF 30 467).
Text ref.: p. 78.

500. HOMME ACCOUDÉ, AU CAFÉ (*fig. 381*)
Lead and wash; 185 x 147 mm.; stamp E.M.
Coll.: Cab. des Dessins (RF 30 532).
  Related to the painting *Le Bouchon* (Jamot,
no. 292, fig. 383).

501. LE BOUCHON (LE CABARET EN PLEIN
  AIR) (*fig. 379*)
Lead and wash; stamp E.M.
Bibl.: Waldmann, 1923, p. 177 (ill.); Mathey,
  1963, fig. 63.
(Location unknown.)
  Related to the painting (Jamot, no. 292, fig.
  383).
Text ref.: pp. 78, 79.

501a. LE BOUCHON (LE CABARET EN PLEIN
  AIR)
Lead; 140 x 92 mm.
Bibl.: May possibly be the drawing described
  in Tabarant, 1947, p. 331; Hanson, no. 173.
Coll.: C. A. Slatkin, New York.
  The subject is in all essentials the same as that
  of the wash drawing listed above (see Cat.
  No. 501).

502. LA RUE MOSNIER AU BEC-DE-GAZ
  (*fig. 24*)
Lead and wash; 278 x 441 mm.; signed lower
  right "E.M."; date, 1878.
Bibl.: Richardson, fig. 62; Mathey, 1961, fig.
  121; Hanson, no. 142.
Coll.: J. Doucet, Paris; The Art Institute of
  Chicago (given in memory of Tiffany
  Blake).
Text ref.: pp. 33, 34, 78.

503. LA RUE MOSNIER (*fig. 380*)
Lead and wash; 190 x 360 mm.
Bibl.: Tabarant, 1947, pp. 325, 326; Richard-
  son, fig. 61; Pataky, no. 43 (ill.).
Coll.: P. von Majovszky, Budapest; Budapest
  Museum of Art.
Text ref.: pp. 78, 79.

504. FIACRE ET BEC-DE-GAZ (*fig. 364*)
Lead; 146 x 103 mm.; date, 1878.
Coll.: Cab. des Dessins (RF 30 455).
  Related to the painting *La Rue Mosnier aux
  drapeaux* (Jamot, no. 289, fig. 323).
Text ref.: p. 33.

505. L'HOMME AUX BÉQUILLES
Wash; 273 x 196 mm.; date, 1878.
Bibl.: Bazire, p. 81 (ill.); M-N, 1926, II, fig.
  231; Mathey, 1963, fig. 70; Hanson, no.
  143.
Exh.: Wildenstein, 1948, no. 51.
Coll.: Metropolitan Museum of Art, New York
  (Harris Brisbane Dick Fund purchase,
  1948).
  Related to the painting *La Rue Mosnier aux
  drapeaux* (Jamot, no. 289, fig. 323).
Text ref.: p. 33.

506. FIACRE (*fig. 366*)
Lead; 120 x 96 mm.
Coll.: Cab. des Dessins (RF 30 456).

507. TÊTE DE FEMME DE PROFIL (*fig. 394*)
Lead and sepia wash; 85 x 103 mm.
Coll.: Cab. des Dessins (RF 30 468).

508. TÊTE DE FEMME DE PROFIL
Watercolor; 105 x 100 mm.; date, 1878.
Coll.: Private collection, Milwaukee, Wis.
  Related to the painting *Sur le Banc* (Jamot,
  no. 361, fig. 219).

509. GUSTAVE COURBET (*fig. 392*)
Pen and wash; 168 x 238 mm.; signed lower
  left "E.M."
Bibl.: Barbara Holleman, "Portrait de Courbet," *Les Amis de Gustave Courbet*, Bulletin no. 28 (Paris-Ornans, 1961), pp. 1–11.
Coll.: J. E. Blanche, Paris, 1884 (present location unknown).
  A number of fakes of this drawing are extant
  on the market or in private collections.
  Two of these are reproduced by Rey, p. 19,
  and by Matthiesen, in the catalogue of the
  Matthiesen exhibition of Manet's works,
  Berlin, 1928, pl. XLV. I am much indebted
  to Mrs. Holleman for the above information relating to the provenance of the original drawing, and to its visual source, a
  photograph of Courbet by E. Carjat, probably taken around 1868–1870.
Text ref.: p. 29.

1879–1883

510. TÊTE DE FEMME AU COL DE DENTELLE (*fig. 383*)

Lead and pen; 170 x 115 mm. (mat size).
Coll.: Durand-Ruel, Paris.
    Related to the pastel of Mlle Marie Colombier (Rewald, no. 6; Jamot, no. 419).
Text ref.: p. 36.

511. TÊTE DE FEMME AU COL DE DENTELLE (*fig. 385*)

Pen.
Bibl.: Duret, 1902, p. 165 (ill.).
(Location unknown.)
Text ref.: p. 36.

512. TÊTE DE FEMME AU COL DE DENTELLE (*fig. 384*)

Pen.
Bibl.: Rewald, p. 13 (ill.).
(Location unknown.)
Text ref.: p. 36.

513. TÊTE DE FEMME AU COL DE DENTELLE (*fig. 382*)

Pen.
Bibl.: Rey, p. 26 ("Mlle Jullette Dadu") (ill.).
Coll.: M. Guérin, Paris, 1932 (present location unknown).
Text ref.: pp. 36, 82.

514. MARIE COLOMBIER

Pen; 530 x 340 mm.
Bibl.: Rey, *Manet*, 1938, fig. 93.
(Location unknown.)

515. LA CAPELINE

Lead.
Bibl.: Rey, p. 22 (ill.).
Coll.: M. Guérin, Paris, 1932 (present location unknown).

516. FEMME ACCOUDÉE

Bibl.: Bazire, p. 110 (ill.).
(Location unknown.)

517. AU THÉÂTRE (*fig. 390*)

Crayon, quill pen, and wash; 150 x 215 mm.; stamp E.M.
Bibl.: Tabarant, 1931, no. 73 ("Au Café-concert").
Sales: 1884, no. 141 ("Au Théâtre, le Paradis"); Degas collection, Georges Petit Gallery, Paris, March 26–27, 1918, no. 218.
Coll.: E. Chabrier, Paris, 1896 (present location unknown).

518. FEMME ASSISE SUR UN BANC (*fig. 389*)

Lead; 182 x 117 mm.
Coll.: Cab. des Dessins (RF 30 469).

519. PAON (*fig. 386*)

Lead; 156 x 90 mm.
Coll.: Cab. des Dessins (RF 30 564).

520. INTÉRIEUR DE CAFÉ (*fig. 391*)

Lead and wash; 141 x 186 mm.; stamp E.M.; date, *ca.* 1880.
Coll.: Cab. des Dessins (RF 30 527).

521. SALAMANDRE ET ABEILLE (*fig. 401*)

Lead and watercolor; 95 x 143 mm.; stamp E.M.
Coll.: Cab. des Dessins (RF 30 562).

522. GUEULE DE LOUP (letter)

Watercolor; 200 x 129 mm.
Coll.: Cab. des Dessins (RF 11 178).

523. ROSE (letter)

Watercolor; 200 x 125 mm.
Coll.: Cab. des Dessins (RF 11 181).
Text ref.: p. 83.

524. DEUX LISERONS (letter) (*fig. 388*)

Watercolor; 200 x 127 mm.
Coll.: Cab. des Dessins (RF 11 172).
Text ref.: p. 36.

525. LISERON ROSE (letter) (*fig. 387*)
Watercolor; 201 x 124 mm.
Coll.: Cab. des Dessins (RF 11 170).
Text ref.: p. 36.

526. MARGUERITE ET ABEILLE (letter)
Watercolor.
Coll.: Cab. des Dessins.
Text ref.: p. 83.

527. MARGUERITE
Watercolor.
Bibl.: Tabarant, 1931, no. 94.
Sale: 1884, no. 126.
Coll.: Trager, 1884 (present location unknown).

528. FLEURS ROSES (letter)
Watercolor; 201 x 124 mm.
Coll.: Cab. des Dessins (RF 11 177).

529. ÉGLANTINES (*fig. 395*)
Watercolor; 194 x 121 mm.
Bibl.: Hanson, no. 190.
Coll.: Mr. and Mrs. Alex M. Lewyt, New York.

530. PERVENCHES (*fig. 396*)
Watercolor; 193 x 120 mm.
Bibl.: Hanson, no. 189.
Coll.: Mr. and Mrs. Alex M. Lewyt, New York.

531. BRANCHE D'IRIS
Watercolor; 355 x 249 mm.; stamp E.M.
Bibl.: Tabarant, 1931, no. 84; Martin, pl. 25; Rey, *Manet*, 1962, p. 49 (ill.).
Coll.: C. Ormond, Wiltshire, England.

532. FLEURS (letter-head)
Watercolor; stamp E.M.
Bibl.: Tabarant, 1931, no. 90d; Tabarant, 1947, p. 393.
Sale: 1884, no. 127.
Coll.: Durand-Ruel, Paris, 1884 (present location unknown).

533. FLEURS DIVERSES
Watercolor; stamp E.M.
Bibl.: Tabarant, 1931, no. 135.
Coll.: Samson, 1884 (present location unknown).

534. FEUILLE
Lead and watercolor; 120 x 80 mm.
Bibl.: Tabarant, 1931, no. 96.
Sale: Pellerin, 1926, no. 40.
Coll.: Bucher, Paris, 1926 (present location unknown).

535. FEUILLE ET COLIMAÇON (letter)
(*fig. 397*)
Watercolor; 146 x 107 mm.
Bibl.: Hanson, no. 187.
Coll.: Mr. and Mrs. Alex M. Lewyt, New York.

536. TROIS PRUNES (letter) (*fig. 398*)
Watercolor; 139 x 120 mm.
Bibl.: Hanson, no. 186.
Coll.: Mr. and Mrs. Alex M. Lewyt, New York.

537. NOIX
Watercolor; stamp E.M.
Bibl.: Tabarant, 1931, no. 90a; Tabarant, 1947, p. 393.
Sale: 1884, no. 127.
Coll.: Durand-Ruel, Paris, 1884 (present location unknown).

538. FRAISE
Watercolor; stamp E.M.
Bibl.: Tabarant, 1931, no. 90b; Tabarant, 1947, p. 393.
Sale: 1884, no. 127.
Coll.: Cheramy, Paris, 1906 (present location unknown).

539. PÊCHE (letter)
Watercolor; 201 x 128 mm.
Coll.: Cab. des Dessins (RF 11 171).

540. PÊCHE
Watercolor; stamp E.M.
Bibl.: Tabarant, 1931, no. 90c; Tabarant, 1947,
    p. 393.
Sale: 1884, no. 127.
Coll.: Durand-Ruel, Paris, 1884 (present loca-
    tion unknown).

541. PRUNE (letter)
Watercolor.
Bibl.: Facsimile reproduction in J. Guiffrey,
    Edouard Manet: Letters with Aquarelles
    (New York: Pantheon Books, 1944).
(Location unknown.)

542. MIRABELLE (letter) (*fig. 400*)
Watercolor; 201 x 124 mm.
Bibl.: Rey, *Manet*, 1938, p. 19 (ill.).
Coll.: Cab. des Dessins (RF 11 180).
Text ref.: pp. 37, 83.

543. DEUX PRUNES (letter)
Watercolor; 170 x 125 mm.
Bibl.: Tabarant, 1931, no. 97; Tabarant, 1947,
    p. 393.
Exh.: Bernheim-Jeune Gallery, Paris, April
    1928.
Coll.: M. Faure, Paris (present location un-
    known).

544. DEUX POMMES
Watercolor; signed lower right "E.M."
Bibl.: Tabarant, 1931, no. 101.
(Location unknown.)

545. PRUNE (letter)
Watercolor; 202 x 126 mm.
Bibl.: Hoetink, no. 181 (dated *ca.* 1880); Han-
    son, no. 185.
Coll.: Museum Boymans-van Beuningen, Rot-
    terdam (Inv. no. FII 73).

545a. CINQ PRUNES
Watercolor; 224 x 160 mm.
Bibl.: Hoetink, no. 180.
Coll.: Museum Boymans-van Beuningen, Rot-
    terdam (Inv. no. FII 72).

546. UNE CHÂTAIGNE (letter)
Watercolor.
Bibl.: Tabarant, 1947, p. 394.
Exh.: Orangerie, 1932, no. 116.
Coll.: Mme B. Monet, Paris, 1947 (present lo-
    cation unknown).

547. PHILIPPINE (*fig. 399*)
Watercolor; 200 x 124 mm.
Coll.: Cab. des Dessins (RF 11 185).
Text ref.: pp. 37, 83.

548. AMANDES
Watercolor; stamp E.M.
Bibl.: Tabarant, 1931, no. 92.
Sale: 1884, no. 136.
Coll.: M. de Lostalot, Paris, 1884 (present lo-
    cation unknown).

549. COLIMAÇON (*fig. 25*)
Lead; 132 x 117 mm.; stamp E.M.
Coll.: Cab. des Dessins (RF 30 448).
Text ref.: pp. 37, 39, 40, 81.

550. COLIMAÇONS (*figs. 402, 403*)
Lead.
Bibl.: Rey, p. 28 (ill.).
Coll.: E. Rouart, Paris.
Text ref.: p. 39.

551. COLIMAÇONS ET TOUFFE D'HERBE
    (*fig. 404*)
Watercolor; 197 x 125 mm.
Coll.: Robert Allerton, Chicago; The Art In-
    stitute of Chicago (gift of Robert Aller-
    ton).
Text ref.: pp. 39, 81.

552. CHAT DE DOS (letter) (*fig. 57*)
Watercolor; 155 x 99 mm.
Bibl.: Rey, *Manet*, 1938, p. 20 (ill.).
Coll.: Cab. des Dessins (RF 11 176).
  Related to Cat. No. 479.
Text ref.: pp. 2, 37, 81.

553. CHAT COUCHÉ DE PROFIL (letter)
  (*fig. 405*)
Watercolor; 180 x 113 mm.
Bibl.: Rey, *Manet*, 1938, p. 21 (ill.).
Coll.: Cab. des Dessins (RF 11 179).
  Related to Cat. No. 478. On the verso, *Poire
  et branche*, watercolor (fig. 406).
Text ref.: pp. 36, 37.

554. CHAT ET SON OMBRE
Watercolor.
Bibl.: Tabarant, 1947, no. 651 (ill.), p. 393.
Coll.: N. Makeev, Paris, before 1947 (present
  location unknown).

555. CHAT DANS LES FLEURS
Watercolor; stamp E.M.
Bibl.: Tabarant, 1931, no. 91.
Sale: 1884, no. 127.
Coll.: Durand-Ruel, Paris, 1884 (present loca-
  tion unknown).

556. ARROSOIR (*fig. 58*)
Lead and wash; 203 x 128 mm.; stamp E.M.
Coll.: Cab. des Dessins (RF 30 500).
  Related to Cat. No. 457.
Text ref.: p. 83.

557. ARROSOIR (letter)
Watercolor.
Coll.: Cab. des Dessins.

558. FRUIT, TÊTE, HIRONDELLE, CREVETTE
  (letter) (*fig. 407*)
Watercolor.
Bibl.: M-N, 1926, II, 72–73, figs. 281, 282.
(Location unknown.)

On another page of this letter, addressed to
Henri Guérard, are three heads of women,
two of which represent Mme Auguste
Manet and Mme Edouard Manet (Mathey,
1963, fig. 57).
Text ref.: pp. 37, 38.

559. CITRON, HUÎTRE ET CREVETTES (letter)
  (*fig. 408*)
Watercolor; 200 x 120 mm.; upper right, in
  Manet's hand, "Excusez cela c'est du chic
  E.M."
Bibl.: Tabarant, 1931, no. 102; Martin, pl. 24.
Exh.: Matthiesen, 1928, no. 64; Orangerie,
  1932, no. 119.
Coll.: Bernheim-Jeune, Paris; Jos. Hessel, Paris,
  before 1947 (present location unknown).
Text ref.: 37, 38.

560. ANIMAUX: CHAUVE-SOURIS, COQ,
  ÉCREVISSE, ETC. (letter)
Watercolor.
Bibl.: Tabarant, 1931, no. 103.
(Location unknown.)

561. CLOCHE À MELON ET GRENOUILLE
Lead and watercolor; 110 x 100 mm.
Bibl.: Tabarant, 1931, no. 95.
Sale: Pellerin, 1926, no. 37.
Coll.: Godefroy, Paris, 1926 (present location
  unknown).

562. CLAUDE MONET (*fig. 393*)
Watercolor; 950 x 900 mm.; signed lower right
  "E. Manet."
Bibl.: Duret, 1902, p. 129 (ill.); Waldmann,
  1910, p. 166 (ill.).
(Location unknown.)
Text ref.: p. 29.

563. MLLE MARGUERITE
Lead; 185 x 120 mm.
Bibl.: Rey, p. 17 ("Mme Guillemet") (ill.).
Coll.: E. Rouart, Paris.

On the verso is a lead pencil sketch of another figure in a similar pose, but which appears to be related to the pastel *Jeune femme au chapeau à bords rabattus* (Jamot, no. 535, fig. 263). The profile is very similar; the position of the hands is different.

Text ref.: p. 81.

564. MLLE MARGUERITE
Watercolor; 200 x 120 mm.; signed lower right "E.M."
Bibl.: Tabarant, 1931, no. 82 ("Tête de jeune fille").
Exh.: Matthiesen, 1928, no. 63; Orangerie, 1932, no. 120.
Coll.: Bernheim-Jeune, Paris; Jos. Hessel, Paris, 1932 (present location unknown).
Text ref.: p. 81.

565. MLLE MARGUERITE
Pen; 125 x 95 mm.
Bibl.: Duret, 1902, p. 179 (ill.).
Coll.: C. E. Slatkin, New York.

566. JEUNE FILLE DEVANT LA MER
(MLLE MARGUERITE)
Watercolor; 180 x 130 mm.
Bibl.: Duret, 1919, pl. 35; Tabarant, 1931, no. 81; Tabarant, 1947, p. 192; Mathey, 1963, fig. 69.
Sale: Eugène Blot collection, Paris, June 2, 1933, no. 27.
Coll.: E. Blot, Paris, 1933 (present location unknown).

567. MLLE MARGUERITE
Medium (?); 125 x 100 mm.
Bibl.: Bazire, p. 75 (ill.); Tabarant, 1947, p. 392.
(Location unknown).
This drawing was, in our opinion, clumsily imitated by an unknown hand in the drawing illustrated in Mathey, 1963, fig. 65. Related to Cat. No. 566.

568. DEUX TÊTES DE FEMMES (letter)
(fig. 410)
Watercolor; 180 x 112 mm.
Bibl.: Rey, *Manet*, 1938, p. 22 (ill.).
Coll.: Cab. des Dessins (RF 11 182).
The following passages from the text of this letter, referring to the model for the two heads, to whom the letter is addressed, throw much light on Manet's views and procedures concerning the need for the model's presence, and his occasional use of a photograph as a source of thumbnail portrait sketches such as these: "Ce qu'on fait de chic ne vaut rien. Si au moins j'avais le modèle devant moi. . . . Envoyez donc votre photographie que je puisse vous avoir plus surement si je fais un croquis de vous."
On the verso: *Chat et hirondelle.*
Text ref.: p. 38.

569. TÊTE DE FEMME (letter) (fig. 409)
Watercolor.
Bibl.: Rey, *Manet*, 1938, p. 23 (ill.).
Coll.: Cab. des Dessins.
Text ref.: pp. 37, 82.

570. EVA GONZALES ET HENRI GUÉRARD
(letter)
Watercolor.
Bibl.: Tabarant, 1931, no. 104.
(Location unknown.)

571. TÊTE DE FEMME ET TÊTE D'HOMME
(letter) (fig. 411)
Wash and watercolor; 202 x 123 mm.
Bibl.: Tabarant, 1931, no. 85.
Coll.: J. Blot, Paris, 1931; The Art Institute of Chicago (gift of Mrs. Gilbert W. Chapman).
Tabarant identifies the portraits as those of M. and Mme Guillemet.

572. FEMME EN ROBE BLEUE (ISABELLE
  LEMONNIER) (*fig. 413*)
Watercolor; 201 x 124 mm.
Bibl: J. Guiffrey, *Lettres illustrées d'Edouard
  Manet* (Paris: M. Legarrec, 1929), pl. 2;
  Rey, *Manet*, 1962, p. 61 (ill.).
Coll.: Cab. des Dessins (RF 11 173).
Text ref.: pp. 37, 81, 82, 83.

573. FEMME EN COSTUME DE BAIN
  (*fig. 412*)
Watercolor; 200 x 100 mm.; signed lower
  right "E.M."
Bibl.: Tabarant, 1931, no. 80.
Exh. Matthiesen, 1928, no. 66; Orangerie, 1932,
  no. 118.
Coll.: Jos. Hessel, Paris, 1931 (present location
  unknown).
Text ref.: pp. 37, 82.

574. FEMME EN COSTUME DE VOYAGE
  (*fig. 414*)
Watercolor; 200 x 120 mm.; signed lower right
  "E.M."
Bibl.: Tabarant, 1931, no. 78.
Exh.: Matthiesen, 1928, no. 65; Orangerie, 1932,
  no. 117.
Coll.: Jos. Hessel, Paris, 1932 (present location
  unknown).
Text ref.: p. 37.

575. FEMME EN COSTUME DE VOYAGE
  (letter)
Watercolor.
Bibl.: Tabarant, 1931, mentioned under no. 78;
  illustrated (on p. 14) in the catalogue of
  the Matthiesen exhibition (1928).
Coll.: Private collection, Berlin, 1928 (present
  location unknown).

576. FEMME EN COSTUME DE VOYAGE
Watercolor; 200 x 120 mm.; signed lower left
  "E.M."
Bibl.: Tabarant, 1931, no. 79; reproduced on

the cover of the journal, *The Arts* (Nov.
  1925).
Coll.: Jos. Hessel, Paris; Et. Bignou, Paris;
  Kraushaar, New York.

577. ISABELLE PLONGEANT (*fig. 4*)
Watercolor; 200 x 123 mm.
Bibl.: Tabarant, 1931, no. 86; Rey, *Manet*, 1962,
  p. 75 (ill.).
Coll.: Cab. des Dessins (RF 11 175).
Text ref.: pp. 5, 82.

578. JEUNE FILLE LISANT (*fig. 421*)
Wash; 170 x 110 mm.
Bibl.: Tabarant, 1947, p. 392.
Sale: Pellerin, 1926, no. 48.
(Location unknown).

579. MME ÉDOUARD MANET EN BUSTE
  (*fig. 422*)
Wash; 168 x 127 mm.
Bibl.: Waldmann, 1910, p. 42 (ill.).
Exh.: "Drawings from the Collection of Curtis
  O. Baer," Fogg Art Museum, Harvard
  University, Cambridge, Mass., Jan.–Feb.
  1958, no. 48.
Coll.: Curtis O. Baer, New York.
  Related to the painting *Portrait de Madame
  Manet à Bellevue* (Jamot, no. 397, fig. 57).
Text ref.: p. 37.

580. TÊTE DE FEMME (*fig. 418*)
Wash; stamp E.M.
Bibl.: Tabarant, 1931, no. 77 (first sheet of two
  sheets juxtaposed).
Sale: 1884, no. 139.
Coll.: Gauthier-Lathuille, Paris; Pinakothek,
  Munich.
Text ref.: p. 37.

581. TÊTES DE FEMMES (MME MANET MÈRE
  ET MME ÉDOUARD MANET)
Wash; stamp E.M.
Bibl.: Tabarant, 1931, no. 77 (second sheet of

two sheets juxtaposed); Rey, p. 16 (ill.).
Sale: 1884, no. 139.
Coll.: Gauthier-Lathuille, Paris; Pinakothek,
Munich.

582. CHAPEAUX DE FEMMES
Wash; signed lower right "E.M."
Bibl.: Waldmann, 1923, p. 25 (ill.).
(Location unknown.)

583. TÊTE ET BAS DE ROBE (letter)
(figs. 415, 417)
Watercolor; 200 x 124 mm.
Coll.: Cab. des Dessins (RF 11 186).
Text ref.: pp. 36, 82.

584. PIEDS DE FEMME (fig. 416)
Lead and wash; 88 x 73 mm.
Coll.: Cab. des Dessins (RF 30 492).
   Verso: Poire et branche (pear tree branch
   with fruit).

585. JAMBES DE FEMME SOUS UNE TABLE
(fig. 26)
Lead and watercolor; 185 x 120 mm.
Coll.: Cab. des Dessins (RF 30 521).
Text ref.: pp. 36, 37, 82.

586. DRAPEAUX (letter) (fig. 419)
Watercolor; 180 x 112 mm.; inscribed with the
   words "Vive l'amnistie!"
Coll.: Cab. des Dessins (RF 11 183).
Text ref.: p. 36.

587. LAMPIONS (letter) (fig. 420)
Watercolor; 179 x 112 mm.
Coll.: Cab. des Dessins (RF 11 174).
Text ref.: pp. 36, 41.

588. PRINTEMPS (fig. 423)
Pen and wash; 312 x 212 mm.
Coll.: Fogg Art Museum, Harvard University,
   Cambridge, Mass.

Drawn on the back of a photograph of the
   painting Le Printemps (Jamot, no. 470,
   fig. 190) (see figs. 424 and 425).
Text ref.: pp. 11, 14, 41, 83.

589. PERTUISET, LE CHASSEUR DE LIONS
(fig. 428)
Pen and light wash; 245 x 295 mm.; signed be-
   low the tree "E. Manet," with the men-
   tion "Pertuiset le chasseur de lions."
Bibl.: Tabarant, 1947, p. 403.
Exh.: Matthiesen, 1928, no. 67.
Coll.: Private collection, Berlin, 1928 (present
   location unknown).
   Related to the painting (Jamot, no. 454, fig.
   281) (see fig. 427).
Text ref.: p. 83.

590. PERTUISET (fig. 426)
Pen; signed lower right "E. Manet."
Bibl.: M-N, 1926, II, 94 (ill.).
   Drawing illustrating Tireurs de pistolet by
   the Baron de Vaux (Paris, 1883).

591. ANNABEL LEE DEBOUT (fig. 429)
Black crayon and wash; 462 x 292 mm.; an-
   notated lower right "Édouard Manet,
   Étude pour Jeanne."
Bibl.: Tabarant, 1947, pp. 417–418; Hoetink,
   no. 176, dated ca. 1879–1881; Hanson, un-
   der no. 136.
Coll.: Museum Boymans-van Beuningen, Rot-
   terdam (Inv. no. FII 20).
Text ref.: p. 24.

592. ANNABEL LEE DEBOUT
Wash; 311 x 232 mm.
Bibl.: Glaser, fig. 8; Tabarant, 1931, no. 110
   ("Femme au bord de la mer"); Hanson,
   no. 136.
Sale: 1884, no. 150 ("Au bord de la mer").
Coll.: E. Raynal, Paris; Mr. and Mrs. Alex L.
   Hillman, New York.
   Related to the painting Jeune femme dans un
   jardin (Jamot, no. 321, fig. 89).

593. ANNABEL LEE ÉTENDUE SUR LA GRÈVE
   (*fig. 430*)
Wash; 445 x 550 mm.; stamp E.M.
Bibl.: Tabarant, 1931, no. 112.
Sale: 1884, no. 143.
Coll.: Bernstein, Paris; Pellerin, Paris, 1884
   (present location unknown).
Text ref.: p. 24.

594. LA CITÉ EN LA MER
Watercolor; 425 x 265 mm.
Bibl.: M-N, 1926, II, fig. 307; Tabarant, 1947,
   p. 419.
Coll.: N. Makeev, Paris (present location un-
   known).
   This drawing is an interpretation of Edgar
   Allan Poe's poem *The City by the Sea*, and
   was intended as an illustration for Mal-
   larmé's translation.

595. LA CITÉ EN LA MER (*fig. 431*)
Wash; 473 x 405 mm.
Coll.: H. P. Kraus, New York; Col. R. Gimbel,
   New Haven, Conn.
   Reproduced in *Les Poèmes d'Edgar Poe*,
   translated by S. Mallarmé (Paris: Vanier,
   1889), facing p. 101.
   This is a slightly more elaborate version
   of the preceding drawing. It may well, for
   this reason, be a first draft which was
   further simplified in the second version
   (Cat. No. 594) in view of its eventual
   reproduction.
Text ref.: p. 24.

596. LA DORMEUSE (*fig. 16*)
Lead; 93 x 141 mm.; stamp E.M.
Bibl.: Rey, p. 22 ("La Convalescente") (ill.).
Coll.: Cab. des Estampes (Dc 300d-res. no. 3).
Text ref.: pp. 24, 25, 81.

597. LA DORMEUSE (*fig. 17*)
Wash; 95 x 143 mm.; stamp E.M.; signed center
   left "E.M."

Bibl.: Meier-Graefe, fig. 102; Tabarant, 1931,
   no. 113.
Exh.: Orangerie, 1932, no. 114 (5).
Sale: 1884, no. 142.
Coll.: Cab. des Estampes.
Text ref.: pp. 24, 25, 81.

598. BAR AUX FOLIES-BERGÈRE
Watercolor; 230 x 200 mm.
Bibl.: Tabarant, 1947, p. 423; *Apollo* (June
   1962), p. 297, fig. 4 (dimensions given:
   222 x 247 mm.).
Sale: Hôtel Drouot, Paris, April 1, 1914.
Col.: A. Proust, Paris (present location un-
   known).

599. MME JULES GUILLEMET EN CHAPEAU
Black chalk; 314 x 219 mm.
Bibl.: Richardson, fig. 74.
Coll.: Hermitage, Leningrad.

600. MME JULES GUILLEMET
Pencil and wash; 168 x 127 mm.
Exh.: "Drawings from the Collection of Curtis
   O. Baer," Fogg Art Museum, Harvard
   University, Cambridge, Mass., Jan.–Feb.
   1958, no. 49.
Coll.: Curtis O. Baer, New York.
   Related to the pastel (Jamot, no. 430, fig.
   223).

601. MME JULES GUILLEMET EN ROBE BLEUE
Watercolor; 125 x 205 mm.
Bibl.: Glaser, p. 429, no. 676; Tabarant, 1931,
   no. 108; Tabarant, 1947, no. 676; Martin,
   pl. 8.
Coll.: H. Cassirer, Berlin 1922 (present location unknown).

602. UN CAFÉ PLACE DU THÉÂTRE FRANÇAIS
Lead and wash; 135 x 167 mm.
Bibl.: Meier-Graefe, fig. 109; Tabarant, 1947,
   no. 678, p. 432; Martin, pl. 31.
Coll.: A. Pellerin, Paris; Knoedler and Co.,
   Paris; Hanley, Bradford, Pa.

ILLUSTRATIONS

FIGURE 59 *(see Cat. No. 2)*.

FIGURE 60 *(Cat. No. 2)*.

FIGURE 62 *(see Cat. No. 3)*.

FIGURE 61 *(Cat. No. 3)*.

FIGURE 64 *(see Cat. No. 4).*

FIGURE 65 *(Cat. No. 4).*

FIGURE 63 *(Cat. No. 5).*

FIGURE 66 *(Cat. No. 8)*.

FIGURE 67 *(see Cat. Nos. 7,8)*.

FIGURE 69 (*see Cat. No. 9*).

FIGURE 68 (*Cat. No. 9*).

FIGURE 70 *(Cat. No. 11)*.

FIGURE 71 *(see Cat. No. 11)*.

FIGURE 73 *(see Cat. No. 12)*.

FIGURE 72 *(Cat. No. 12)*.

FIGURE 74 *(Cat. No. 15)*.

FIGURE 75 *(see Cat. No. 15)*.

FIGURE 76 (Cat. No. 14).

FIGURE 77 *(Cat. No. 16)*.

FIGURE 78 *(see Cat. No. 16)*.

FIGURE 79 (*Cat. No. 18*).

FIGURE 80 (*Cat. No. 19*).

FIGURE 81 (*see Cat. Nos. 18, 19*).

FIGURE 83 *(see Cat. No. 17)*.

FIGURE 82 *(Cat. No. 17)*.

FIGURE 84 *(Cat. No. 21)*.

FIGURE 85 *(see Cat. No. 21)*.

FIGURE 87 (see Cat. Nos. 22, 23).

FIGURE 86 (Cat. No. 22).

FIGURE 88 (Cat. No. 23).

FIGURE 90 *(see Cat. No. 24)*.

FIGURE 89 *(Cat. No. 24)*.

FIGURE 92 *(see Cat. No. 29)*.

FIGURE 91 *(Cat. No. 29)*.

FIGURE 95 *(Cat. No. 25)*.

FIGURE 94 *(see Cat. No. 26)*.

FIGURE 93 *(Cat. No. 26)*.

FIGURE 96 *(Cat. No. 27)*.

FIGURE 97 *(Cat. No. 28)*.

FIGURE 98 *(Cat. No. 30)*.

FIGURE 100 *(see Cat. No. 31)*.

FIGURE 99 *(Cat. No. 31)*.

FIGURE 102 *(see Cat. No. 32)*.

FIGURE 101 *(Cat. No. 32)*.

FIGURE 106 *(see Cat. No. 33).*   FIGURE 103 *(Cat. No. 33).*

FIGURE 104 *(Cat. No. 36).*

FIGURE 105 *(Cat. No. 39)*.

FIGURE 107 *(Cat. No. 37)*.

FIGURE 108 *(Cat. No. 41)*.

FIGURE 109 *(see Cat. Nos. 40, 41)*.

FIGURE 110 *(Cat. No. 40)*.

FIGURE 112 *(see Cat. No. 42)*.

FIGURE 111 *(Cat. No. 42)*.

FIGURE 113 *(Cat. No. 43).*

FIGURE 115 *(see Cat. Nos. 43, 44).*

FIGURE 114 *(Cat. No. 44).*

FIGURE 116 *(Cat. No. 46)*.

FIGURE 117 *(see Cat. No. 45)*.

FIGURE 118 *(Cat. No. 45)*.

FIGURE 119 *(Cat. No. 47)*.

FIGURE 121 *(Cat. No. 48)*.

FIGURE 120 *(see Cat. Nos. 47, 48)*.

FIGURE 122 *(Cat. No. 50)*.

FIGURE 123
(see Cat. No. 50).

FIGURE 124 *(Cat. No. 49)*.

FIGURE 125
(see Cat. No. 49).

FIGURE 127 *(see* Cat. No. 51*)*.

FIGURE 126 *(Cat. No. 51)*.

FIGURE 128 *(Cat. No. 53)*.

FIGURE 129 *(see Cat. No. 53)*.

FIGURE 131 *(Cat. No. 56)*.

FIGURE 130 *(Cat. No. 54)*.

FIGURE 132 *(Cat. No. 57)*.

FIGURE 133 *(Cat. No. 58)*.

FIGURE 134 *(see Cat. Nos. 55-58)*.

FIGURE 135 *(Cat. No. 61)*.

FIGURE 136 *(Cat. No. 126)*.

FIGURE 137 *(Cat. No. 59)*.

FIGURE 138 *(see Cat. No. 59)*.

FIGURE 139 *(Cat. No. 64)*.

FIGURE 140 *(Cat. No. 67)*.

FIGURE 141 *(Cat. No. 62)*.

FIGURE 142 *(Cat. No. 63)*.

FIGURE 143 *(Cat. No. 73)*.

FIGURE 144 *(Cat. No. 74)*.

FIGURE 145 *(Cat. No. 70)*.

FIGURE 146 (*Cat. No. 72*).

FIGURE 147 (*Cat. No. 71*).

FIGURE 148 (*Cat. No. 81*).

FIGURE 149 *(Cat. No. 82)*.

FIGURE 150 *(Cat. No. 84)*.

FIGURE 151 *(Cat. No. 96)*.

FIGURE 152 *(Cat. No. 86)*.

FIGURE 153 *(Cat. No. 97)*.

FIGURE 154 *(Cat. No. 93)*.

FIGURE 155 (*Cat. No. 91*). FIGURE 156 (*Cat. No. 95*).

FIGURE 157 (*Cat. No. 99*).

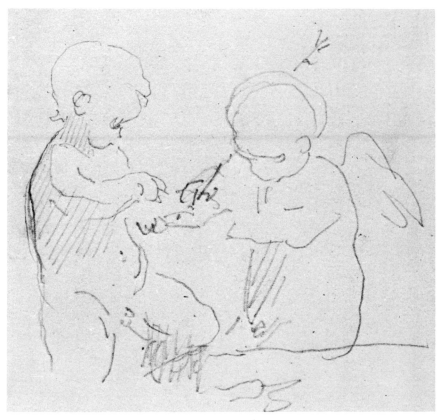

FIGURE 158 (Cat. No. 104).

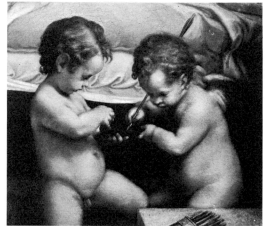

FIGURE 159 (see Cat. No. 104).

FIGURE 160 (Cat. No. 87).

FIGURE 161 (see Cat. No. 87).

FIGURE 162 (*Cat. No. 90*).

FIGURE 164 (*see Cat. No. 102*).

FIGURE 163 (*Cat. No. 101*).

FIGURE 165 (*Cat. No. 102*).

FIGURE 166 *(Cat. No. 111)*.

FIGURE 167 *(Cat. No. 113)*.

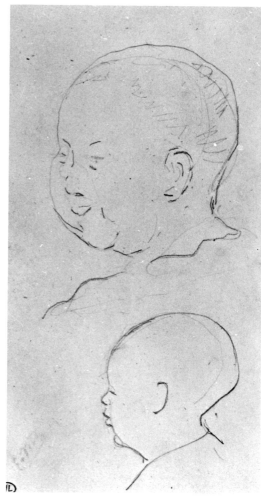

FIGURE 168 *(Cat. No. 106)*.

FIGURE 169 *(Cat. No. 100)*.

FIGURE 170 *(see Cat. No. 100)*.

FIGURE 171 *(Cat. No. 165)*.

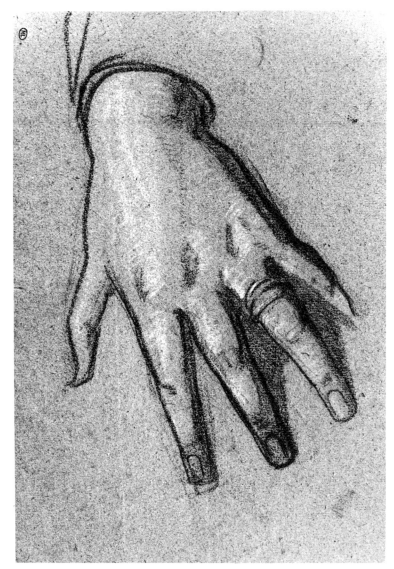

FIGURE 172 *(Cat. No. 105)*.

FIGURE 173 *(Cat. No. 128)*.

FIGURE 174 *(Cat. No. 109)*.

FIGURE 175 *(Cat. No. 116)*.

FIGURE 176 *(Cat. No. 118)*.

FIGURE 177 *(Cat. No. 125)*.

FIGURE 178 *(Cat. No. 115)*.

FIGURE 179 *(Cat. No. 117)*.

FIGURE 180 *(Cat. No. 120)*.

FIGURE 181 *(Cat. No. 124)*.

FIGURE 182 *(Cat. No. 127)*.

FIGURE 183 *(see Cat. No. 127)*.

FIGURE 184 *(Cat. No. 130)*.

FIGURE 185 *(Cat. No. 131)*.

FIGURE 186 (*Cat. No. 135*).　　　　FIGURE 187 (*Cat. No. 136*).

FIGURE 189 *(Cat. No. 134)*.

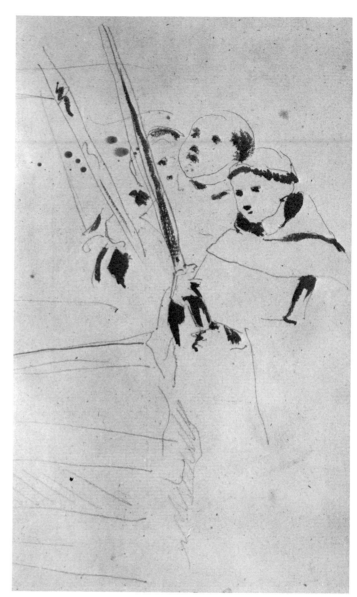

FIGURE 190 *(Cat. No. 133)*.

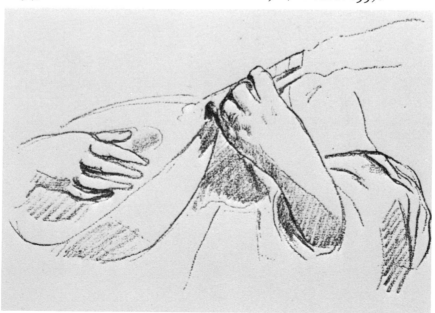

FIGURE 188 *(Cat. No. 137)*.

FIGURE 191 *(Cat. No. 140)*.

FIGURE 192 *(Cat. No. 141)*.

FIGURE 194 *(Cat. No. 152)*.

FIGURE 193 *(Cat. No. 143)*.

FIGURE 195 *(Cat. No. 153)*.

FIGURE 196 *(Cat. No. 149)*.

FIGURE 197 *(Cat. No. 151)*.

FIGURE 198 *(see Cat. No. 151)*.

FIGURE 199 *(Cat. No. 146)*.

FIGURE 200 *(Cat. No. 148)*.

FIGURE 201 *(Cat. No. 147)*.

FIGURE 202 *(see Cat. No. 161)*.

FIGURE 203 *(Cat. No. 161).*

FIGURE 204 *(see Cat. No. 161)*.

FIGURE 205 *(Cat. No. 160)*.

FIGURE 206 *(Cat. No. 157)*.

FIGURE 207 *(Cat. No. 159)*.

FIGURE 208 *(see Cat. No. 166)*.

FIGURE 209 *(Cat. No. 166)*.

FIGURE 210 (*Cat. No. 170*).

FIGURE 211 (*Cat. No. 172*).

FIGURE 212 *(Cat. No. 175)*.

FIGURE 213 *(Cat. No. 180)*.

FIGURE 214 (*Cat. No. 178*).

FIGURE 215 *(see Cat. No. 178)*.

FIGURE 216 (*Cat. No. 179*).

FIGURE 217 *(see Cat. Nos. 178, 179).*

FIGURE 218 *(Cat. No. 185)*.

FIGURE 221 *(see Cat. Nos. 185, 186).*

FIGURE 219 *(Cat. No. 182).*

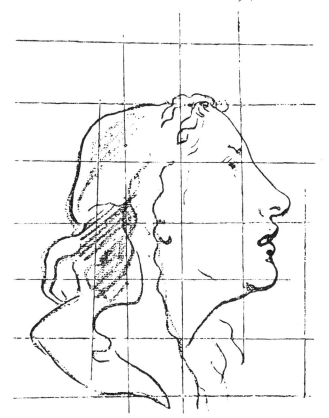

FIGURE 220 *(Cat. No. 183).*

FIGURE 222 *(Cat. No. 193)*.

FIGURE 223 *(Cat. No. 192)*.

FIGURE 224 *(Cat. No. 194)*.

FIGURE 225 *(Cat. No. 195)*.

FIGURE 226 (see Cat. No. 196).

FIGURE 227 (see Cat. No. 196).

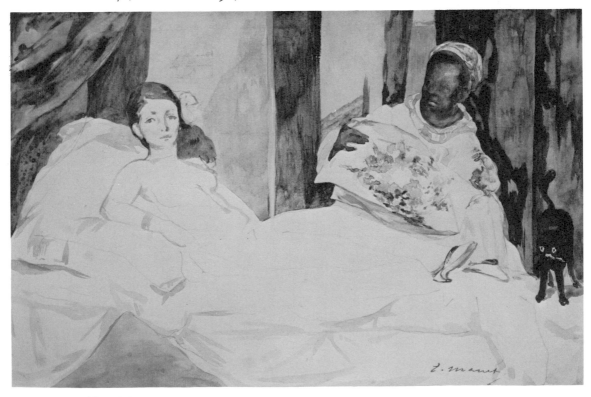

FIGURE 228 (Cat. No. 196).

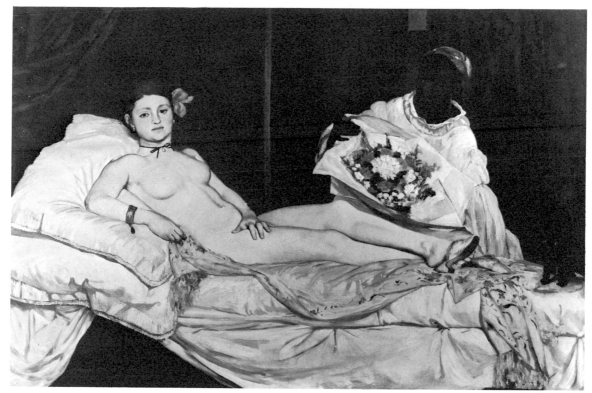

FIGURE 229 *(see Cat. No. 196)*.

FIGURE 230 *(Cat. No. 197)*.

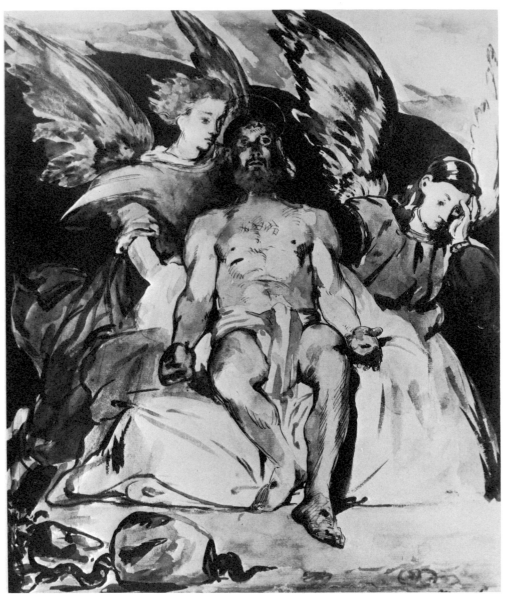

FIGURE 231 *(Cat. No. 198)*.

FIGURE 233 *(Cat. No. 203)*.

FIGURE 232 *(Cat. No. 208)*.

FIGURE 234 *(Cat. No. 207)*.

FIGURE 236 *(see Cat. No. 205)*.

FIGURE 237 *(see Cat. No. 203)*.

FIGURE 235 (*Cat. No. 205*).

FIGURE 238 (*Cat. No. 218*).

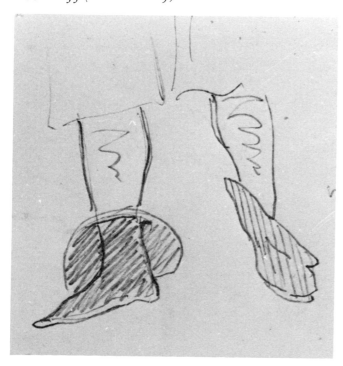

FIGURE 239 (*Cat. No. 221*).

FIGURE 240 (*Cat. No. 223*).

FIGURE 241 *(Cat. No. 229)*.

FIGURE 243 *(Cat. No. 225)*.

FIGURE 242 *(Cat. No. 231)*.

FIGURE 244 *(Cat. No. 224).*

FIGURE 245 *(Cat. No. 226).*

FIGURE 246 *(Cat. No. 216).*

FIGURE 247 *(Cat. No. 232)*.

FIGURE 248 (*Cat. No. 235*).

FIGURE 249 (*Cat. No. 236*).

FIGURE 250 (*Cat. No. 238*).

FIGURE 251 (*Cat. No. 250*).

FIGURE 252 (*Cat. No. 246*).

FIGURE 254 *(see Cat. No. 240)*.

FIGURE 253 *(Cat. No. 269)*.

FIGURE 255 *(Cat. No. 253)*.

FIGURE 256 *(Cat. No. 249)*.

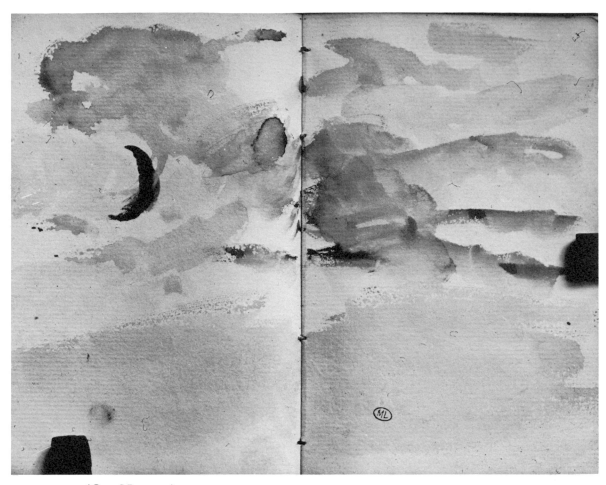

FIGURE 257 (*Cat. No. 270*).

FIGURE 258 (*Cat. No. 259*).

FIGURE 259 (*Cat. No. 257*).

FIGURE 260 *(Cat. No. 282)*.

FIGURE 261 *(Cat. No. 284)*.

FIGURE 262 *(Cat. No. 283)*.

FIGURE 263 *(Cat. No. 276)*.

FIGURE 264 *(Cat. No. 289)*.

FIGURE 265 *(Cat. No. 292)*.

FIGURE 266 *(Cat. No. 291)*.

FIGURE 267 *(Cat. No. 293)*.

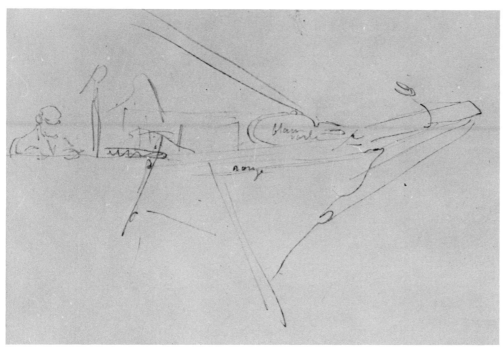

FIGURE 268 *(Cat. No. 301)*.

FIGURE 269 *(Cat. No. 300)*.

FIGURE 270 *(Cat. No. 302)*.

FIGURE 271 *(Cat. No. 299)*.

FIGURE 272 *(Cat. No. 303)*.

FIGURE 273 *(Cat. No. 311)*.

FIGURE 274 *(Cat. No. 308)*.

FIGURE 275 *(Cat. No. 315)*.

FIGURE 276 *(Cat. No. 312)*.

FIGURE 277 *(Cat. No. 306)*.

FIGURE 278 (*Cat. No. 326*).

FIGURE 279 (*Cat. No. 327*).

FIGURE 282 (*Cat. No. 333*).

FIGURE 283 (*Cat. No. 338*).

FIGURE 280 (*Cat. No. 319*).

FIGURE 281 (*Cat. No. 324*).

FIGURE 284 *(Cat. No. 337)*.

FIGURE 285 *(Cat. No. 343)*.

FIGURE 286 *(Cat. No. 334)*.

FIGURE 287 *(Cat. No. 342)*.

FIGURE 288 (Cat. No. 341).

FIGURE 289 (Cat. No. 346).

FIGURE 290 (Cat. No. 349)

FIGURE 291 (Cat. No. 347).

FIGURE 292 (Cat. No. 361).

FIGURE 293 *(Cat. No. 356)*.

FIGURE 294 *(Cat. No. 358)*.

FIGURE 295 *(Cat. No. 368)*.

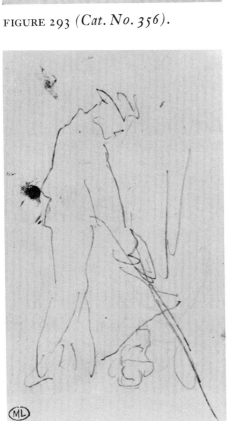

FIGURE 296 *(Cat. No. 367)*.

FIGURE 297 *(Cat. No. 353)*.

FIGURE 298 *(Cat. No. 352)*.

FIGURE 299 *(Cat. No. 388)*.

FIGURE 302 *(Cat. No. 392)*.

FIGURE 300 *(Cat. No. 389)*.

FIGURE 303 *(Cat. No. 393)*.

FIGURE 301 *(Cat. No. 390)*.

FIGURE 304 *(Cat. No. 434)*.

FIGURE 305 *(Cat. No. 381)*.

FIGURE 308 *(Cat. No. 380)*.

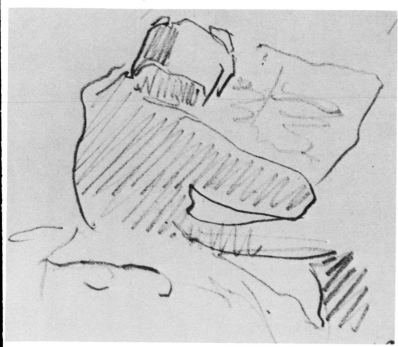

FIGURE 306 *(Cat. No. 382)*.

FIGURE 307 *(Cat. No. 384)*.

FIGURE 309 *(Cat. No. 377)*. FIGURE 310 *(Cat. No. 378)*.

FIGURE 311 *(Cat. No. 371)*. FIGURE 312 *(Cat. No. 374)*.

FIGURE 313 *(Cat. No. 373)*.

FIGURE 315 *(Cat. No. 376)*.

FIGURE 314 *(Cat. No. 375)*.

FIGURE 316 *(Cat. No. 396)*.

FIGURE 317 *(Cat. No. 399)*.

FIGURE 318 *(Cat. No. 397)*.

FIGURE 319 *(Cat. No. 407)*.

FIGURE 320 *(Cat. No. 404)*.

FIGURE 321 *(Cat. No. 402)*.

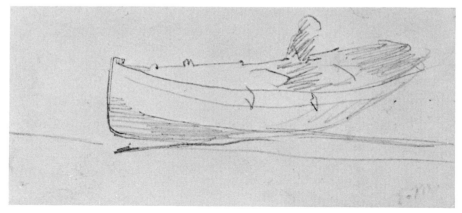

FIGURE 322 *(Cat. No. 403)*.

FIGURE 323 *(Cat. No. 417)*.

FIGURE 324 *(Cat. No. 405)*.

FIGURE 326

FIGURE 325 *(Cat. No. 406)*.

FIGURE 327 *(Cat. No. 411)*.

FIGURE 328 *(Cat. No. 408)*.

FIGURE 329 *(Cat. No. 413)*.

FIGURE 330 *(Cat. No. 412)*.

FIGURE 331 *(Cat. No. 414)*.

FIGURE 332 *(Cat. No. 418)*.

FIGURE 333 *(Cat. No. 419)*.

FIGURE 334 *(Cat. No. 421)*.

FIGURE 335 *(Cat. No. 422)*.

FIGURE 336 *(see Cat. No. 422)*.

FIGURE 337 *(Cat. No. 466)*.

FIGURE 338 (*Cat. No. 459*).

FIGURE 339 (*Cat. No. 420*).

FIGURE 340 (*Cat. No. 440*).

FIGURE 341 *(Cat. No. 437)*.

FIGURE 342 *(Cat. No. 441)*.

FIGURE 343 *(Cat. No. 445)*.

FIGURE 344 (*Cat. No. 443*).

FIGURE 345 *(Cat. No. 444)*.

FIGURE 346 *(Cat. No. 448)*.

FIGURE 347 *(Cat. No. 449)*.

FIGURE 348 *(Cat. No. 447)*.

FIGURE 349 *(Cat. No. 457)*.

FIGURE 350 *(Cat. No. 451)*.

FIGURE 351 *(Cat. No. 452)*.

FIGURE 352 *(Cat. No. 454)*.

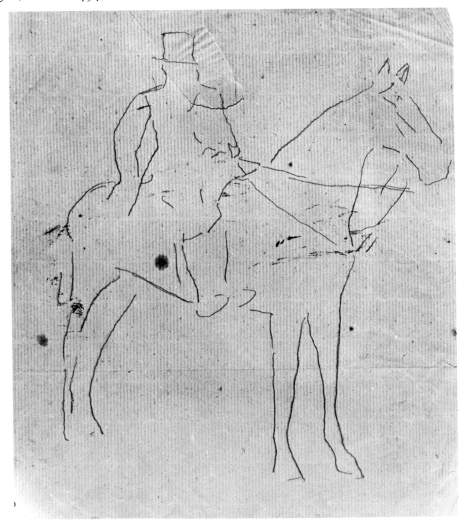

FIGURE 353 *(Cat. No. 462)*.

FIGURE 354 *(Cat. No. 464)*.

FIGURE 355 *(Cat. No. 465)*.

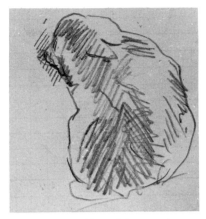

FIGURE 356 *(Cat. No. 470)*.   FIGURE 357 *(Cat. No. 467)*.

FIGURE 358 *(Cat. No. 468)*.   FIGURE 359 *(Cat. No. 469)*.   FIGURE 360 *(Cat. No. 474)*.

FIGURE 361 *(Cat. No. 478)*.

FIGURE 362 *(Cat. No. 475)*.

FIGURE 363 *(Cat. No. 476)*.

FIGURE 364 (*Cat. No. 504*).

FIGURE 365 (*Cat. No. 481*).

FIGURE 366 (*Cat. No. 506*).

FIGURE 367 (*Cat. No. 482*).

FIGURE 368 (*Cat. No. 486*).

FIGURE 369 (*Cat. No. 484*).

FIGURE 370 (*Cat. No. 483*).

FIGURE 371 *(Cat. No. 485)*.

FIGURE 372 *(Cat. No. 490)*.

FIGURE 373 *(Cat. No. 492)*.

FIGURE 374 *(Cat. No. 493)*.

FIGURE 375 *(Cat. No. 494)*.

FIGURE 376 (*Cat. No. 489*).   FIGURE 377 (*Cat. No. 498*).

FIGURE 378 (*Cat. No. 491*).

FIGURE 379 (*Cat. No. 501*).

FIGURE 380 (*Cat. No. 503*).

FIGURE 381 *(Cat. No. 500)*.

FIGURE 382 *(Cat. No. 513).*

FIGURE 383 *(Cat. No. 510).*

FIGURE 384 *(Cat. No. 512).*

FIGURE 385 *(Cat. No. 511).*

FIGURE 386 (*Cat. No. 519*).

FIGURE 387 (*Cat. No. 525*).

FIGURE 388 (*Cat. No. 524*).

FIGURE 389 (*Cat. No. 518*).

FIGURE 390 (*Cat. No. 517*).

FIGURE 392 (*Cat. No. 509*).

FIGURE 393 (*Cat. No. 562*).

FIGURE 391 (*Cat. No. 520*).

FIGURE 394 (*Cat. No. 507*).

FIGURE 395 *(Cat. No. 529)*.

FIGURE 397 *(Cat. No. 535)*.

FIGURE 398 *(Cat. No. 536)*.

FIGURE 396 *(Cat. No. 530)*.

FIGURE 399 (*Cat. No. 547*).

FIGURE 400 (*Cat. No. 542*).

FIGURE 401 (*Cat. No. 521*).

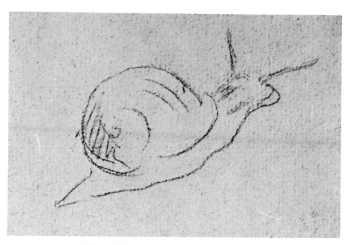

FIGURE 402 *(Cat. No. 550)*.

FIGURE 403 *(Cat. No. 550)*.

FIGURE 404 *(Cat. No. 551)*.

FIGURE 405 (*Cat. No. 553*).

FIGURE 406 (*Cat. No. 553*).

FIGURE 407 (*Cat. No. 558*).

FIGURE 408 (*Cat. No. 559*).

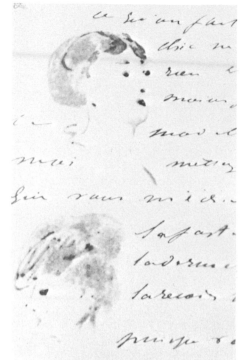

FIGURE 409 (*Cat. No. 569*).

FIGURE 410 (*Cat. No. 568*).

FIGURE 411 (*Cat. No. 571*).

FIGURE 412 (*Cat. No. 573*).

FIGURE 413 (*Cat. No. 572*).

FIGURE 414 (*Cat. No. 574*).

FIGURE 415 *(Cat. No. 583)*.

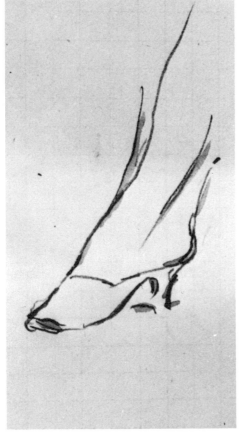

FIGURE 416 *(Cat. No. 584)*.

FIGURE 417 *(Cat. No. 583)*.

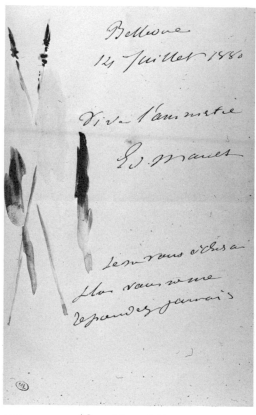

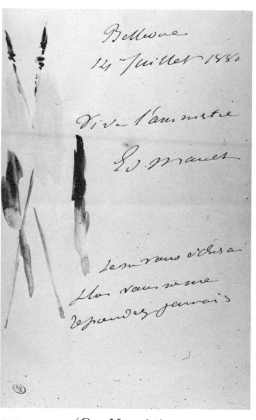

FIGURE 418 *(Cat. No. 580)*.

FIGURE 419 *(Cat. No. 586)*.

FIGURE 420 *(Cat. No. 587)*.

FIGURE 422 *(Cat. No. 579)*.

FIGURE 421 *(Cat. No. 578)*.

FIGURE 423 *(Cat. No. 588)*.

FIGURE 424 (see Cat. No. 588).

FIGURE 425 (see Cat. No. 588).

FIGURE 426 (Cat. No. 590).

FIGURE 427 *(see Cat. No. 589)*.

FIGURE 428 *(Cat. No. 589)*.

FIGURE 429 (*Cat. No. 591*).

INDEX

Unless otherwise indicated, the works listed in the index are by Edouard Manet. Works in watercolor, wash, sanguine, ink, pencil, crayon, charcoal, and combinations of these media are all referred to in the index as drawings. Items from the Catalogue are indexed only if reference is made to them in the text. Numbers in roman type refer to pages of the text; numbers in italics, to the Catalogue numbers (not the page numbers); and numbers preceded by *fig(s)*. refer to illustrations.